THE LION
WHO NEVER ROARED

THE LION
WHO NEVER ROARED
JACK LESLIE
The Star Robbed of England Glory

Matt Tiller

Foreword by
Viv Anderson MBE

First published by Pitch Publishing, 2023
Reprinted 2023
2

Pitch Publishing
9 Donnington Park,
85 Birdham Road,
Chichester,
West Sussex,
PO20 7AJ
www.pitchpublishing.co.uk
info@pitchpublishing.co.uk

ISBN 978 1 80150 431 7

Typesetting and origination by Pitch Publishing
Printed and bound in Great Britain by TJ Books, Padstow

Contents

Acknowledgements

THE NUMBER of people who deserve thanks for their help is almost as big as Jack Leslie's goal tally. This would have been impossible without all their support and patience, but top of the table are his granddaughters, Lesley, Lyn and Gill, who embraced the campaign and shared their lives and memories with me. Talking to them and looking at their albums of photographs, cuttings and the medals that survive brought Jack's personality and achievements to life in a way nothing else could. Credit is also due to the many extended family members.

In the play-off spots are Greg Foxsmith, who gets another mention in the introduction, so I'll move on to my wife Lucy Haley and son Aubrey. They sneak past Greg on penalties to win promotion. This endeavour has been a labour of love that would have been impossible without theirs. The practical and emotional support has been immense. Appreciation is due to my siblings, Erica (thanks for putting me up on campaign and research trips!) and Luke, my parents, Vivienne and Sgt Maj. John Douglas Tiller, and wider family and in-laws (cheers Dave Haley!). I'm indebted.

Richard Amofa is a brilliant young football journalist whose writing on Jack for The Athletic blew me away. He has joined me on this journey as a contributor and consultant. His insight and editorial input have been crucial. Bill Hern, co-author of the excellent *Football's Black Pioneers*, kindly shared his research with me and has been an encouraging voice of reason with a sharp critical eye. John Eales' comments, suggestions and fact-checking helped me greatly. His compilation of Jack's statistics is a fantastic resource on the Jack Leslie Campaign website.

Everyone involved in the Jack Leslie Campaign has done something amazing. Sculptor Andy Edwards' dedication to his work and desire to tell the story through it has been rock solid. He did one hell of a job. Tony Fitz-Gerald first told me the story and was the first to join our committee, who are all fine human beings. They are Rob Bullen, Jamie Burton, James Curno, Neandra Etienne, John Griffiths, Amanda Jacks, Lee Jameson, Hayley Kemp, Richard Leppard, John Lloyd, Iffy Onuora, Patrick Strode, Jon Treharne and George Connett (the great-grandson of Jack's sister Letty).

The football clubs Jack is associated with all stepped up. Plymouth Argyle chairman, Simon Hallett, along with the management, staff and supporters have been incredible. Nods to Andrew Parkinson, Trevor East, Dan Cole, Christian Kent, Zac Newton and David Ray. West Ham United was a massive part of Jack's life and I particularly appreciate Tom Degun and Carlton Cole's support. Tim Crane produces the *West Ham Years* newsletter, and his tribute to Jack with reminiscences of players and staff was a great, and moving, resource. I salute Rob O'Brien and all at Barking FC, formerly Barking Town, where a teenage Jack began his football career. A great club with a great history.

The game is nothing without the fans. Huge shout-out to 97-year-old Charlie Trevethan for his support, friendship and memories. Also, to Mark Stephens, who in 2020 introduced me to his dad, Bill. As very young lads in the early 1930s, Charlie and Bill saw Jack Leslie play. Their memories may be somewhat hazy but the warmth of feeling towards their Argyle hero has shone through the decades and is as clear as day. Bill sadly passed away a few months after I spoke to him but, as I write, Charlie is still with us. I hope to have a coffee with a nip of something stronger with him again soon.

The player who's always mentioned alongside Jack Leslie and should never be forgotten is Argyle's all-time leading goalscorer, Sammy Black. Sammy's daughter, Gloria Spilsbury, and granddaughter, Tracy Charlick, kindly shared memories and memorabilia with me. It was fantastic to talk to Pete Lake, the great-nephew of one of Jack's best mates and fellow Argyle great, Fred Titmuss.

The words of Viv Anderson MBE, who spoke about Jack at the start of the campaign, are an inspiration. I can't thank him enough for his contribution to this book with his moving foreword. Similarly, Ronnie Mauge, who followed in Jack's footsteps from London to Plymouth. His promotion-winning goal at Wembley for Argyle in 1996 is etched in the memory and I thank him for all his passion, help and support. Also, massive thanks to Sir Trevor Brooking and Clyde Best, who knew and loved Jack.

The Football Association (FA) comes in for plenty of criticism in this book but FA chair and FIFA vice-president, Debbie Hewitt, has made a fundamental difference. The awarding of a posthumous honorary cap for Jack has had a genuine positive impact on the family. Thanks also to James MacDougall and other FA staff who have helped the campaign and, by association, this book. Jack did play for the Essex County FA several times. Thanks to Phil Sammons and Brendan Walshe for sharing material and enthusiasm.

In terms of research, many people have assisted greatly. Dr Alex Jackson and Peter Holme at the National Football Museum Archives. The University of Plymouth, especially Deborah Morris, Dr Kathryn Napier Gray, Lee Whittock and the interns who have contributed research and editorial comments; Andrew Swabey, Callum Forwood and Cerys Godlington. Martin Johnes of Swansea University kindly shared his research. The staff at the British Library have been tremendous, notably Karen Waddell. Appreciation to archivist Stacey Anderson at The Box in Plymouth, who unearthed some amazing images of Jack.

Greens on Screen deserves its own headline. This website created and updated by Steve Dean for 25 years is just brilliant. Without it, grappling with Argyle's fixtures, results and league positions would have been a pulsating headache. GoS saved me masses of time. All its contributors have made a difference, but I must mention Roger Walters, who sent me some very useful information. Plymouth Argyle Heritage Archive has just taken over the website now Steve has retired, and it too has been invaluable. Matt Ellacott, Bob Wright and others have created a fantastic and growing resource. Thanks also to Andy Jago, who sent his research in the early days of the campaign, and Ian Deacon, grandson of Leslie Deacon, who played alongside Jack in the 1920s. And David Jack, namesake and grandson of the England and Argyle legend and great-grandson of Jack Leslie's

Plymouth manager, Bob Jack. David unearthed an incredible letter written by a childhood friend of our Jack. Another wonderful and enlightening letter came from Hazel Cadmore, the daughter of one of Jack's friends in East Ham of the 1940s and 50s.

Other writers on black history and football pioneers, Stephen Bourne, Phil Vasili and David Gleave, have helped along the way.

Several journalists have covered the story, but a few have gone out of their way to help, particularly Matt Barlow of the *Daily Mail*, but also Michael John-Jennings at *The Times*, Sam Blackledge at ITV, Jonathan Oakes at Sky Sports and Chris Errington, *Plymouth Live*'s Argyle correspondent, who follows in the footsteps of those who wrote about Jack a century ago.

I couldn't fail to mention one man to whom I wish I could send a copy of this book, Gordon Sparks. Sparksy is one of the few people who never played for the club yet earned the right to be called a Plymouth Argyle legend. His passionate, evocative commentaries were loved by many who, like me, had left the city for work and could rarely make it to home matches. Like Jack, he was genuinely talented enough to be heard nationally. I was privileged to work with Sparksy in my first job as a journalist at Plymouth Sound Radio in the heady days of Neil Warnock at Argyle's helm. Gordon passed away in 2022. Too soon.

I owe a huge debt of gratitude to the Society of Authors. Without its grant assistance there's no way I could have completed, and probably wouldn't have started, this. Thanks to Hugh Barker for helping me get this book picked up, to my editor Ivan Butler for expertly knocking it into shape and to Jane Camillin at Pitch Publishing for taking it on and making it happen. This has been a privilege and I can't thank them enough.

Thanks to all my friends who have offered words of kindness and encouragement, particularly Andy Wilson, Alan McArthur, Nigel Rundle, Kavus Torabi, Peggy Melmoth, Isabel Forrester, Mark Foxsmith, Carl East, Michael Spicer, Jane Common, and Army football legend, Pete Ball.

Finally, I tip my hat to everyone who has supported the Jack Leslie Campaign. Please do visit jackleslie.co.uk, where you'll find even more information about Jack and the statue.

Author's Note

ONE OF my boyhood dreams was to write history books. This was positively realistic compared to another fantasy – to pull on that green jersey and play for the mighty Plymouth Argyle. It's still taken several decades to get there but the connection with my football club makes it all the sweeter.

The responsibility of telling Jack Leslie's story is, like Argyle, massive. A huge privilege but not as daunting as leading your team out in an FA Cup tie against Arsenal at Highbury. Jack and his players lost valiantly and controversially that day in 1932 with the referee making several debatable (dodgy?) decisions. Oh, the injustice. Reflecting on Jack's qualities, I don't think facing the Gunners daunted him at all. Here was a man who regretted being too young to fight in the trenches and put in gruelling shifts riveting metal in the East London docklands through both the First World War and the Blitz of the Second. He hit the crossbar and scored Argyle's second in that Arsenal match. On the pitch, Jack Leslie feared nobody.

I hope that football lovers and Plymouth Argyle fans will enjoy this book because I want to shout about Jack Leslie's skill, determination and bravery from the rooftops. And, in part, this is a celebration of his fantastic career. But his place in the history of the sport is important not only for his achievements but also for what he represented. Jack was the only black professional in the Football League when he was selected for England and for much of his career. So, this must come into the story because it's a crucial part of it. If only the colour of his skin and heritage were irrelevant to his football career and life, but they weren't. They had an impact on him, attracted comment and abuse and affected decisions. The tales of derring-do on icy pitches or impossible mud baths, wonder strikes, diving headers and promotion-winning glory are all fantastic to research and write. But learning about Jack's family and the significant black community in Britain before the *Empire Windrush* arrived at Tilbury has been enlightening and fascinating. I hope you embrace that too.

There are a few footnotes where I think it's useful to know the source. Most of the quotes are newspapers referred to in the text, so I've only noted the few where that's not clear.

Jack was a very common name in the early 1900s. Everyone seemed to be called Jack. And the Plymouth Argyle manager in Jack's time was Bob Jack. If I refer to Jack, then it's always Jack Leslie. I hope it doesn't get too jacking confusing. Another historical inconvenience is that Plymouth became a city in October 1928, so I've stuck to the timeline and described it as a town until that date.

There are a few notes of caution. I remember Adrian Chiles having to follow an interview with Jack's granddaughter, Lyn, on his 5Live show with an apology when she quoted her granddad talking about what other players and fans would shout at him. Lyn herself suffered abuse as a schoolgirl, so it feels harsh to get a reprimand when the context is clear. There are times when I share quotes from articles written in the 1920s and 30s that contain this type of language. I believe it's important to see this as it was written and try to give as much context as possible. Any quotes are exactly as written in the publication, so if inverted commas are used around a word, then that's how they originally appeared.

I guess this bit is a caveat to make sure you know what you're getting into. Hopefully, an enjoyable biography of an outstanding sportsman but also a book that delves into themes that shouldn't but can be divisive. Whether or not you consider yourself fully woke, anti-woke or medium-woke (woke agnostic, maybe?), I hope to simply convey how things were for Jack Leslie through his life and particularly as a professional footballer in the 1920s and 30s. Wish me luck.

Foreword

THE FIRST time I heard the name Jack Leslie was when a BBC journalist contacted me in 2020, and I was shocked, but was I surprised? Sadly, not. Many of the stories of those black footballers who came before me are yet to be told and I was more than happy to support the campaign to honour Jack with a statue. I had already been involved in the Arthur Wharton Foundation celebrating the remarkable first black professional, who died in 1930, while Jack was still playing.

What happened to Jack Leslie is a crying shame, but he broke the mould in his time just as people say I did in 1978. I didn't realise it at the time, but taxi drivers still tell me they remember my debut, so I imagine it would have been similar for Jack. The significance of what he achieved and the impact of the injustice that happened to him probably came later in life.

It's incredible to read Jack's story and how his selection to play for his country was swept under the carpet. I think he was the same ilk as me in wanting to dismiss whatever abuse he got and get on with forging a career. To achieve what he did for Plymouth Argyle and become a local hero, he must have been some player. Jack would have been getting all kinds of stick, just like I did, so I can relate to what he went through, but I was lucky to have the likes of Laurie Cunningham and Cyrille Regis around me, whereas Jack was on his own. Having Brian Clough as a manager helped me and I remember walking out on to an away ground once and saying to him, 'I don't think I can play today.' Mr Clough's reply stuck with me: 'You are here because you've got the ability, you wouldn't be otherwise. You are playing.' I got through those tough times, and I hope Jack had the same kind of support. He certainly went out and gave it his all, just as I did.

Jack's life story is inspiring and important; it's part of our history and culture. I consider my parents, Myrtle and Audley, as heroes and pioneers of the Windrush Generation. Jack was the son of an immigrant who journeyed here too, and his experiences offer the same kind of insight into an earlier period. What they went through to help future generations is worth reflecting on and sharing.

When I read about children racially abusing sport stars on social media today, it makes me very sad and shows that we must keep talking about it. The characters who have gone through so much to move society forward should never have been forgotten. I was proud to meet Jack Leslie's granddaughters at Wembley to join the FA in awarding them his posthumous honorary cap 98 years after he was selected. Recognition such as this is part of the process in moving forward, but it can't stop there. I tell the FA, there are so many brilliant black ex-players who have been there and got the T-shirt. Very few are in management or senior positions within the game and that has to change. If you've got the qualifications, if you're good enough, you should be given the opportunity. I've no doubt Jack would agree.

I hope you enjoy reading about Jack Leslie. Learning about his talent and commitment, I think we would have been great team-mates. I'd have had my work cut out facing him, mind.

Viv Anderson MBE

Chapter One

Introduction

DID THE name Jack Leslie mean anything to you before the summer of 2020? I'm guessing not. In fact, unless you're a Plymouth Argyle fan of a certain age (quite old, sorry), I would put money on it. Jack would approve. He was a betting man who had a flutter on the horses and regular card games with family and friends, including his teammates on those long old pokes to Burnley, Bury and Buenos Aires. That last one isn't a fantasy football typo. Jack Leslie's Plymouth Argyle really did travel to 'The Argentine' to showcase their skills nearly a century ago.

But for those who weren't aware of this huge character in Britain's national sport between the wars, then don't worry, you join a crowd of heads hanging in shame. And that crowd includes my thick skull. It was only in 2019 that this shining light of the beautiful game truly entered my consciousness. Yet, in the 1920s and 30s when he plied his sporting trade, John Francis Leslie – the official name recorded on Jack's birth certificate – *was* nationally famous.

Jack was a feared playmaker and goalscorer from his inside-left position, what became the famous No. 10 shirt during his career. He was Plymouth's Pelé, the footballer Jack loved above all others as he watched international football long after his own playing career was over.

And, while Jack's background was very different to those early, upper-class footballing pioneers of the late 19th century such as Lord Arthur Kinnaird, he was known as a gentleman of the game. Aggressive and tough on the pitch, for sure. But Jack played fair … if only the sport he loved played fair with him.

Because Jack Leslie should be known as the first black footballer to represent England. In 1925 that honour was denied him due to the colour of his skin. I say that with absolute confidence. As soon as I began to research this story, I discovered this was no footballing myth. And as I've undertaken more research, a tower of truth has built on those foundations of confidence. A truth as weighty as the bronze statue that now stands outside the ground where Jack Leslie plied his trade a century ago. Home Park. It's in the middle of Central Park and it's where Plymouth Argyle play when they're at home. It's also where Jack Leslie was given the incredible news by his club manager that he had been picked for England in October 1925. The structure has changed, and the quality of the pitch has improved, but history and truth remain.

More than half a century would pass before a young right-back who played for his hometown club got the call. Viv Anderson took that England cap back to Nottingham with dignity and humility. A fitting reflection of how Jack bore the weight of his rejection, at least publicly.

But how did that decision in 1925 affect Jack Leslie at the time and through the rest of his life? This is a crucial question, but I'm mindful that I have no qualifications to talk about how someone directly affected by racism might feel. Many of us have experienced rejection and disappointment. The proposal for this book was turned down many times before finding a home, but the reasons weren't due to the colour of my skin, and I can't know what it's like to be judged negatively day in, day out because of it. When considering this, I defer to others, including Jack's family and black footballers who themselves experienced abuse and adversity in their careers. I'm indebted to football journalist, Richard Amofa, whose perspective on the text and analysis of Jack's treatment putting it in today's context has proved invaluable.

This book will dig deep into that shameful incident and show how it is one part of a narrative, the story of how the significant black population of Britain in the early 20th century was treated. What must it have been like for Jack growing up as the son of a Jamaican immigrant and a white English woman in Canning Town, one of the poorest areas of East London, at that time? I think it's important to have a sense of Jack's community, the struggles they endured and what living conditions must have been like. Much has been spoken about the Windrush Generation's impact on British society, and rightly so. Books, features and television documentaries have covered racism in football from the 1960s and 70s to the present day. Again, rightly so, and I recommend Emy Onuora's excellent *Pitch Black* as a thoroughly researched and brilliantly written work on that subject. There's less discussion about racism in the early 1900s, which in many ways was more open and shocking than that fuelled by the far right in the mid-20th century. Jack Leslie never had to back-heel a banana or receive a deluge of horrific tweets after missing a penalty, but he did face abuse and discrimination. Racism did exist.

Jack Leslie was a different kind of pioneer to the likes of West Bromwich Albion's 'Three Degrees', Viv Anderson and West Ham United's Bermudian striker Clyde Best, who remembers Jack well from his time in the boot room at the club. And those inter-war decades were a very different time. An exciting period, no doubt, as football emerged from the darkness of the First World War when the professional game was suspended. It roared into action with huge crowds flocking to what fans already considered the national sport. Wembley was built and the first FA Cup Final held there in 1923 was a scene of controversy and near disaster as dangerous number of fans turned up to see the match. The 1924 final was, sensibly, an all-ticket affair. Imagine being a part of this explosion of hunger for a game that could elevate young men from any background to legend status. What a time for Jack Leslie as a young player. His talent allowed him to become a hero, but when he began his football journey, he didn't know that his background was the only thing that would hold him back from the ultimate footballing accolade.

This was also a time when the UK was grappling with itself, its empire and how it treated its people at home and abroad. Nothing shone a brighter light on this than the two world wars that almost bookend Jack Leslie's career. As any young hopeful, Jack would have had issues to deal with and negotiate to make it in the game. He obviously handled those well, but the England selection shows there were some things out of his control. That decision must be seen in the context of how other people of colour were treated in this country at the time. It was complicated. The British approach to recruitment in the First World War was varied and often racist, but not exclusively so. Meanwhile, the treatment of black American GIs by the white British population during the Second World War was often positive, but not exclusively so. It's a minefield. Let's try to get through it and hopefully learn something along the way.

Figures such as Jack *are* relevant today. The fact that you're reading this is proof of that. It's heart-breaking that he was neither celebrated in his own lifetime, nor the injustice recognised and somehow made good. Jack himself would probably be wondering what the fuss was about. In the 60s, he returned to his old stomping ground of Home Park. Jack, along with his striking partner and fellow club legend, Sammy Black, were welcomed with open arms and a standing ovation. He was blown away that anyone remembered him, let alone a crowd of thousands. When he relived that moment with his family, Jack would choke up.

Jack Leslie played 400 times for Plymouth Argyle across 14 seasons, scored 137 goals and captained the club in the early 1930s. A standing ovation well earned.

Sadly, as the supporters who saw him lace up his boots and dominate the Home Park turf dwindled in number, the memories of Jack and his team-mates were lost in the mists of time. Like any club, Plymouth Argyle has had its ups and downs, but there are treasured highlights. The FA Cup semi-final in 1984 was massive for a Third Division club, even more so than now, and players such as Tommy Tynan and Kevin Hodges are remembered by my friends and me with the same fondness as Jack and Sammy in the 60s.

It seemed that until recently Jack and his team-mates had almost been forgotten, even though they earned the right to be remembered for their significant footballing achievements (in Plymouth terms!) alone. Argyle's highest-ever league finish is fourth in the Second Division, something they've achieved twice, the first time being in 1932 when Jack was captain and top scorer with 21 goals. And there's the exploits on the South American tour of 1924, which the Green Army really should dine out on a lot more.

Aside from the feeling of sadness that Jack wasn't celebrated more in his later years, there's also the sense of an opportunity lost. One Argyle legend of the modern era is Ronnie Mauge, creator of one of my greatest memories as a fan and that of thousands of others. Ronnie scored the only goal in Plymouth's victory against Darlington in the 1996 Third Division play-off final. He's the only Argyle player to have scored at Wembley to date and has happy memories of the club and city. That feeling is, of course, mutual. But although Plymouth has a fascinating, diverse history, the Argyle squad in the 90s was a multicultural melting pot compared to the city's population. Ronnie says these trailblazers, their struggles and achievements matter:

> I'm from East London and moved to Plymouth as a young player and, like Jack Leslie, I found it a fantastic city with great people. So, when I heard about Jack, I felt this was an important story, part of Plymouth history and black history. He should be spoken about in the same breath as Viv Anderson, Cyrille Regis, Laurie Cunningham and Brendon Batson. I also thought about what it would have meant to me had I known Jack's story when I signed for Argyle. As a young black man moving to the West Country miles from home, do you know what? It would have empowered me. We look into the past to correct the future and that's what stories like Jack Leslie's can do. I am proud of the fans, the people of Plymouth and the club for what they have done now.

Had Jack plied his sporting trade this century he would have built a very comfortable life for himself and his family. He might even have become a wealthy man living in Sandbanks alongside Harry Redknapp, whose boots Jack shined at West Ham in the 60s. 'Turns out, we should have been shining his boots,' said Harry on hearing of his former colleague's story. Jack was never one to boast or bemoan the denial of his place in the England team, but that crowning glory should have been his.

How so, when he was a Third and then Second Division player? I believe a Premier League club would have swooped for Jack and sent his career into orbit; all the reports suggest he was that good and that other clubs did want to sign him. He won plaudits in many national newspapers including the *Daily Mirror, The Times* and the *Daily Mail*. Yet, the talent that made him a legend of the game was all but forgotten after his playing years, and on his death certificate Jack's trade is listed as boilermaker. That may have reflected most of his working years but certainly not his true calling.

Plymouth can count itself lucky to have had a manager who possessed the foresight to sign Jack from Barking Town in 1921. Bob Jack, himself a legendary player for Argyle before taking the reins, not only spotted this talent but also showed faith. It took a few seasons for Jack to establish himself, but once he did, Bob wouldn't let him free from his grasp. The rest is history. Or, rather, a footnote in history until 2020.

When I first heard the tale of Jack Leslie and the England selection during a drunken chat with a fellow Plymouth Argyle fan, Tony Fitz-Gerald (cheers, Tony!) I listened with interest and knew I had to find out more but didn't truly believe it. It seemed incredible – a Pilgrim called up to play for England?! It must be an apocryphal tale; a nugget of truth that with each retelling became inflated to the size of a Saxon hoard. The difference with the Jack Leslie story is that it never attained such status and faded through generations.

Some people question it, their queries full of anger, disbelief and a caps lock key they just can't seem to type without. They wonder how it could possibly have been racism without some cast-iron statement to that effect by the FA, as if that were likely to be recorded. That shows a misunderstanding of how to examine the historical evidence and a failure to accept that racist societal attitudes existed in the early 20th century when we know they did. How can it be a surprise to anyone? Jack's rejection isn't the only story of its kind.

I dedicate a big chunk of the book to the England call-up, of course, where the story is told in as much detail as possible, but here are some of these key questions answered briefly.

Was Jack Leslie selected for the England team? Yes. His name was printed in several newspapers on Tuesday 6 October 1925 and in the days to follow. This came after the FA's International Selection Committee met on Monday, 5 October to discuss the England vs Ireland match to be played on Saturday, 24 October. Jack was listed as one of 13 players to travel to Belfast for the match.

Was he good enough? Without a doubt. He was noted as being of international class in the national press at the time of his selection and subsequently described as the best inside-left in the country on many occasions.

Even as a Third Division player? While it was rare for players at Jack's level to be selected, it wasn't unheard of and was more common in the 1920s and 30s. In fact, one member of that October 1925 England team played in the same division for Charlton Athletic who finished second from bottom, while Plymouth were runners-up … as usual. And, as we'll discover, international selectors were very aware of Argyle and some of the talent passing through their ranks despite the team's league position.

If Jack was so good, why wasn't he playing at a higher level? Plymouth Argyle were very highly regarded in the 1920s and the team developed and attracted top talent. The maximum wage for a professional footballer was fixed so he wouldn't have been earning more elsewhere. In fact, Argyle's incredible record while narrowly missing out on promotion meant Jack was paid more in bonuses than if he had been at another club. Managers and directors had virtually all the power in the transfer of players at the time. Many big clubs wanted to sign Jack and there were times when he wanted a move, but Bob Jack point-blank refused.

Was his rejection down to the colour of his skin? There's no footballing reason for the deselection. The evident controversy that followed in the press at the time can be set alongside Jack's personal testimony, and his unimpeachable character confirms it. I believe Jack Leslie.

Surely the FA must have known he was black? Some, but not necessarily all the 14-strong selection committee must have known. There was either a disagreement within the committee or external pressure was applied. This doesn't negate the argument. Instead, it makes it all the *more intriguing and suggests that some spoke up for Jack while others were against him.*

How dare I accuse FA officials of being racist? *The simple answer is … I'm not. It was a shameful, racist decision to deselect Jack Leslie and effectively close the door on his chance of playing for England. But I don't want to accuse individual FA selectors, at least some of whom must have actively promoted the idea of Jack being picked. They knew he was black, knew he was English and knew he was good enough.*

There's an assumption by some that the Jack Leslie story was concocted in response to the Black Lives Matter protests of 2020 that took place in the wake of the killing of George Floyd and the subsequent toppling of the Edward Colston statue in Bristol. A cursory search can find references from 1925 through to the present day.

The fact is, while Jack's story has been told several times over the years, it never gained the momentum of 2020. It was reported in the most oblique way in 1925 after the deselection itself, with one newspaper questioning the FA after the Press Association assured them Jack had been selected. The FA denied it even though the team had been printed up and down the country. And one Plymouth reporter said he was banned from revealing the truth behind the story, while alluding to it on the same page. It was, without doubt, public knowledge that Jack had been named in the England team. What would have become a media and social media storm today was, in 1925, quickly dismissed. It was next day's chip paper and, for Jack, nothing but eyes awkwardly turning away and a dream shattered.

While there were no protests as there might be today, it's clear from the Argyle archives that fans felt Jack had been treated badly. It's referenced in the match programme when he visited in 1965. It's more than 50 years after the event when the tale resurfaces in the national consciousness. Jack was interviewed by Brian James of the *Daily Mail* not long after Viv Anderson's ground-breaking selection in 1978. Jack tells his story in a matter-of-fact way, and I quote this interview throughout the book. He didn't seem to be a man who wanted to make an issue of his treatment, and his granddaughters say he never sought opportunities to discuss it. They knew it was a painful memory he carried for the rest of his life, and it clearly runs deep in the family.

A similar recounting occurred a few years later in journalist Brian Woolnough's 1983 book, *Black Magic*. The title and much of the language is, let's just say, of its time. Despite this, it would have been a progressive piece in that era of open hostility to black players from the terraces when racist England fans refused to accept that they could and should pull on that treasured shirt. Woolnough focuses on stars who emerged in the 70s and 80s, such as Viv Anderson, Cyrille Regis and John Barnes, but in his introduction lends a few paragraphs to Jack, describing him as 'the most successful of the early coloured players'. He continues: 'Leslie will always be convinced that he should have become the first coloured player to be selected for England ... Leslie, however, was never selected for the team.'

Much of the writing repeats that he was never selected, simply believing the original FA denial rather than digging any deeper. That's true from 1978 to the present day. In 2004, BBC South West produced a report for their local current affairs show *Inside Out*, which goes into a little more depth about Jack as a player and his feelings about what happened, but not into the detail. They interviewed Jack's daughter, Evelyn, who sadly passed away in 2022 aged 94. Eve, as her parents always called her, carried the story and remained righteously angry on her father's behalf until the end. So, tiny sparks continued to be generated but they failed to light the touchpaper and fizzled out, forgotten once again until the events of 2020. That summer of anger and protest didn't invent the story, but rather shone a light on it and on the effort to create a lasting memorial, a statue of Jack Leslie.

That effort is the Jack Leslie Campaign, which originated in 2019 after further pub-based discussions with Greg Foxsmith, a lifelong suffering friend and chair of Argyle's London supporters' branch. Greg is a solicitor advocate with a fierce campaigning drive. Although I've thankfully never needed his services in court, I was aware of his reputation, and his advocacy skills were such that, after three and a half pints of Tribute (okay, it may have been a different ale, but I do like Tribute and it's a key Argyle sponsor), I agreed we should go for it and raise funds to build a statue of Jack. Unlike many a half-cut resolution, I don't regret it. Without him, neither the monument nor this book would have happened.

One of my main aims in this book is to paint a picture of Jack Leslie as a player and a person, telling his life story in as much detail as I've been able to find and can fit in. The campaign has been a hell of a thing and the greatest joy is the friendship we now have with Jack's family, especially his three granddaughters. Lesley, Lyn and Gill carry their grandfather's legacy with care, honesty and love.

Yet, despite their pride and love, or perhaps because of it, they didn't shy away from any stories that were less than flattering about their grandfather. He was a human being, not a saint. I'm not saying he wasn't a wonderful man; it's abundantly clear that he was. Everyone I've spoken to who knew Jack seemed to love him and he had good friends and a close family throughout his life. But I bet if his wife, Lavinia Leslie née Garland, were alive today (she would be 123, so that would be some going), then she would have plenty to add. Jack and Win, as Lavinia was known, had a long, happy and successful marriage. But Lesley, Lyn and Gill are Win's granddaughters too. Stories have been passed down the generations and have now been passed on to me. The integrity of these three doughty women in handling their legacy with such self-awareness is to be applauded.

Jack Leslie is almost a household name now. And, not only that, but his story is also being more widely told in a bid to spread the important message of inclusivity. His family tell me that he would have been proud to know that his story is being used to educate people against the evils of racism. It's certainly helped to educate us.

Although this legacy is vitally important, I don't believe Jack saw himself as a pioneer and we must be careful how we approach and handle it. He knew he stood out among his peers, and he knew it had an impact. When this gifted man was rejected by his country for no other reason than the colour of his skin, there were no Black Lives Matter protests, no footballers taking the knee and no statues of slave traders toppled from their plinths. Jack saw and experienced adversity and he lived to see the terrace racism of the 80s and the attitude of some fans to black England players when they did push through and win selection.

It's difficult, nay impossible for us to know or explain Jack's experience. People old enough to have seen Jack play will tell you his race wasn't something they particularly thought about or commented on. They're sincere in the statements, of course, and on a personal level Jack says he felt welcomed by the people of Plymouth. But there had been race riots targeting black communities in 1919, the contributions of people of colour to Britain's war efforts were roundly ignored and statements made in the press and national publications are startlingly overt in their racism. It would be wrong to think it wasn't an issue in the days before Windrush. Jack's experience is proof enough.

There's one thing Jack's granddaughters have told me that's at once shocking, but then when you stop to think about it, your heart sinks too. It's something their nan, Win, said to them. In fact, it was more vehement than that. She impressed it upon them, almost as an order. Their grandmother, Jack's wife, told them they should never marry a black man. This was a woman who loved her husband deeply and had seen his parents have a strong, mixed marriage too. But she also lived through Jack's treatment, faced a barrage of abuse herself for being in a mixed marriage and saw their daughter, Eve, face discrimination. Lyn says, 'I went out with a black doctor once and nan did her nut.' Lesley remembers this was all down to what their grandmother had gone through, 'She didn't want the same problems for us. And wherever you go, you are going to find bigoted people who don't look at the person but look at the colour of their skin.' Abuse did affect them, particularly when they were at school, and Gill, the youngest of the three sisters, remembers being called shocking names because of her heritage. How deep the wounds run.

Those people who don't seem to like the attention on black history and stories of historical injustice in Britain miss the irony that's staring them in the face. They tell us with incredulity that history is being rewritten in an anti-patriotic way or that the focus on black history is a pendulum swing too far. Will major figures such as Henry VIII or Queen Elizabeth (First and Second) be swept under the carpet of political correctness? I don't think so. Even as Winston Churchill's views on race and actions across British colonies receive critical attention, his status as the leader who saw the nation through the Second World War is hardly under threat. Without protest and discussion, current issues of inequality and injustice are left unaddressed, just like the treatment of Jack Leslie almost a century ago. History evolves as new information comes to light and new momentum drives research into new areas. This isn't rewriting or changing history. History is a product of its own time, and it's time to tell Jack's story.

Actually, it's not time, it's late. We're late in telling these stories. But at least they're being told. It's never *too* late.

Chapter Two

Go! Guts! Goals!

THE 'THREE Gs' of this chapter title was Jack Leslie's motto. For someone who was considered one of the most intelligent footballers in the country, it sounds rather direct, simplistic almost. But his genius on the pitch was instinctive. And it's a fitting title in looking at what kind of man Jack was because they're his words. It's a real insight into his positive, determined attitude on the pitch and in many ways reflected his life off it. To make a living as a professional player gave Jack a huge sense of pride because achieving that goal is no easy task. It isn't now, and it wasn't in the 1920s. You need resilience and courage. Jack Leslie had those qualities, for sure. And if you're an attacker, gutsy or not, you have to get goals. If you don't, you're dropped.

Jack Leslie's quality is summed up in Plymouth Argyle's Diamond Jubilee book, *All About Argyle 1903–1963*. In his history of the club up to that year, W.S. Tonkin asked, 'What about the best-ever individual player? From a galaxy of Home Park stars over the years, the choice is not easy; but few would dispute the claims of David Jack, Neil Dougall, or Jack Leslie for this distinction.' Of those three, only one was never awarded an international cap.

Peter Hall, who worked at the club for decades, watched Jack in 1933 when Argyle beat Manchester United 4-0 on the opening day of the season. Peter passed away in 2021 but spoke to the BBC in 2004: 'I always remember that Jack Leslie played a huge part in that win – it was a real treat to see him play. He was everywhere, his passing was first class, and his shooting power was enormous.' And 97-year-old Charlie Trevethan, who must be Plymouth's oldest living fan, was at that match too: 'Jack was the ultimate football player and, as the papers say, the best inside-left in England and with Sammy Black, the best side players on the left flank. They could show the players today how to play football and how to score goals.'

However, it's also important to know that Jack Leslie was not perfect. He was a humble, fair, charismatic man, without doubt, but he was also a man of his time and there are aspects of his life that are surprising. Here's a man who suffered a great injustice due to the colour of his skin, yet Jack's granddaughter, Lesley, remembers one of his favourite television programmes was '*The Black and White Minstrel Show*, believe it or not! I think it was the music more than anything else.' And, while Jack was no George Best and had a long, happy marriage, it's fair to say his head was turned just a little as a young, successful and popular professional footballer. There were no champagne fountains, he was more of a brown ale kind of guy. But Jack was earning more than double the wage of a boilermaker, the work he would otherwise be doing at the docks, up to his elbows in grease. Let's not be too hard on him.

I'm looking directly into Jack's eyes. It's a moving photograph given to me by his granddaughters on the day the statue was unveiled and it came with a personal poetic message on the reverse of the frame. A treasured gift that I'm taking time to consider more deeply as I nervously attempt to write a portrait of this man whose life was nothing short of remarkable. He's 77 years old and sitting in his final place of work. It's a small, dark room at the old Boleyn Ground, and behind him hang the West Ham United players' boots that he looked after with precision, care and love. Many of the footballers whose footwear he cleaned and repaired will never need their names rekindled in the public's imagination. After all, Martin Peters, Geoff Hurst and Bobby Moore were World Cup winners. Alongside them, legends such as Sir Trevor Brooking, Harry Redknapp, Clyde Best and many other players and staff remember Jack well and with love. And within those eyes looking back at me there's pride, determination, warmth and the sparkle that kept Jack firmly in the minds of friends, family and colleagues. He was someone who stuck in your memory. But there's also a sincere and almost painful sense of the burden of unjust disappointment that Jack carried through his life. Taking just a few moments to engage with this portrait, it's hard not to choke.

This photograph was taken in 1978, the year Viv Anderson became the first black player to win a full England cap. This was huge news. Black players were becoming more commonplace in the Football League in the 1960s and 70s, but they faced a barrage of abuse and there was a section of England fans who couldn't bear the thought of any in the national side. West Ham United was pioneering in its diverse recruitment policy. The club fielded three black players – Clyde Best, Ade Coker and Clive Charles – six years before West Bromwich Albion. Despite this, emerging from the Boleyn Ground tunnel for an opposition player of colour was as intimidating as any other stadium. Jack saw what was happening before him and, I'm sure, reflected on his own treatment.

Jack never seemed openly bitter about what happened to him at any stage of his life and applauded Anderson sincerely on the accolade. Yet the circus that surrounded the Nottingham Forest full-back's achievement surely reignited, and even heightened, the feeling of rejection, of a deserved opportunity denied, that Jack must have felt.

> Listen, that was different times. I won't lie and say it don't matter. It does. That Viv Anderson got a cap, and I'm glad. Not because he's coloured, but because he's good enough so he's entitled to it. I think I was entitled to it. Honestly, I'm not a boasting man. But I was good enough.

Those final words say so much, and that's exactly what I'm seeing when I look up from my screen to the black-and-white photograph hanging above it. From the age of 24 when the England call came, Jack Leslie knew he had what it took to play for his country. He was a skilled, physical sportsman, a leader on the pitch who was humble and gentle off it. There's more to Jack than this thumbnail sketch but it's certainly true that he wasn't a boasting man. In fact, many of the West Ham United players who chatted to Jack almost every week of their lives didn't know he had a professional career, let alone that he had been picked for England.

Sir Trevor Brooking, who became part of that club's set-up in 1966, talks about his old colleague with a beaming smile and has been only too happy to help the campaign. He even turned up as a surprise guest at one of our online events during the pandemic, which Jack's granddaughters absolutely loved. They remember their granddad telling them he liked Brooking, and the feeling was definitely mutual:

> Jack joined in 1967 and was fantastic for the next 15 years. He was our boot man so if we needed anything doing, he would sort it out. He was very affable, very chatty, and never ever mentioned anything about his own career which is a credit to his modesty. He was a lovely fella and it's great that there is now a statue in his memory.

* * *

So, what was Jack Leslie like as a player? He began as an outside-left, what we would call a left-winger, but found his home in the playmaker role at inside-left. Physical, aggressive, tireless and brave … absolutely. But skilful, versatile and creative too, a reader of the game who always looked to push his team forward. Match reports of hard-won battles – tough draws and heavy defeats as well as great victories – create a portrait of a footballer who was always trying to make things happen, no matter the situation. It's no surprise, then, that he became club captain, excepting perhaps for the fact that it was very rare for people of colour to be given positions of authority. Jack had worked hard over many seasons and had not only proved himself, but also shown that he was a team player. He was popular with his fellow professionals, the club bigwigs and, of course, the fans. Bob Jack said this of Jack after Argyle's promotion success in 1930: 'On his best form he can be ranked as the best inside-left in the country.' The gaffer may have been a little biased but the same was said in local and national papers throughout Jack Leslie's career. Writers often wondered why he was being overlooked for England, forgetting all about the rejection of 1925 and how it had been swept under the carpet.

There are countless reports of Jack's skill. His footwork was often 'dazzling' and 'a pleasure to watch', while precision passes threading team-mates through on goal are frequently mentioned. He was the kind of player every team needs, someone who can break up play, work an opening and unlock the opponents' defence. And he could score both beautiful and straightforward goals. Jack often broke through to go one on one with the keeper or shot from distance, striking or skimming crossbars and often, thankfully, hitting the target. Jack Leslie was a player you wanted to see pull the trigger. His hefty tally and the heart of a lion gave Plymouth Argyle one hell of a player.

Tactics and formations were very different in the 1920s and 30s, although the sport was evolving, and it seems that Jack was one of those footballers who broke the mould. The players set up in a 2-3-5 formation with the emphasis on getting the ball forward as quickly as possible. Teams always lined up in that formation on paper in the English Football League throughout the inter-war years.[1] The reality could be a bit more flexible, of course, but attempting to do things differently did, at times, lead to criticism where Jack was concerned. One column by the key local writer on all things Argyle for the *Football Herald*, 'Pilgrim', suggested in February 1930 that Jack should stop tracking back, saying, 'Five forwards are better than four, especially when the fifth might be one of Jack Leslie's build and aggression.' He does mitigate his statement: 'I do not and never have minimised the value of Leslie's work as a forager and picker up of short clearances.'

It was commonplace for writers to have pen names at a time when sports journalism was blossoming. 'Pilgrim' was a massive Jack Leslie fan and, having read a great deal of his work now, I've got a soft spot for him too. He's the scribe banned from telling the truth behind the England decision but who clearly wanted to reveal it. His name was Henry Patrick Twyford, known as Pat, and he served in the First World War before joining the *Western Morning News* and then writing for the *Football Herald* too. When writing for *The Snooze* (our affectionate name for the genteel *Morning News*), Twyford used the moniker 'Tamar'. So, whenever I mention 'Pilgrim' or 'Tamar', it's our Pat. He usually backed Jack, and the player's energetic, ground-covering work won over our local wordsmith. In December 1930, commenting on a tight 3-2 home victory against Wolverhampton Wanderers, which Jack missed through injury, 'Pilgrim' bemoans:

> How Leslie was missed … I see some comment has been made of the fact that there appears to be a big gap between the forwards and the halves. Is not the whole solution of this to be found in the absence of Leslie? Leslie is the one man who forms the distinct alliance between the two departments.

Jack Leslie was clearly part of the movement away from the rigid 2-3-5 into more of a 2-3-2-3 (the W formation becoming the W-M), with inside-forwards the most important players on the pitch. This meant that wingers, along with the centre-forward, were positioned further upfield. Jack and his partner on the left wing, Sammy Black, were famed for their combination play and goalscoring and this development in tactics perhaps explains why Sammy tops Argyle's all-time scoring charts while Jack is fourth, although injury curtailing Jack's career also meant he played fewer matches. Jack said he and Sammy never talked tactics, but they clearly knew instinctively how to carve open their opponents' defences, and the inside-left obviously saw the benefit of playing deeper to spot and exploit those gaps. I suspect Jack Leslie frequently found 'pockets of space' nearly a century before that phrase entered the pundits' handbook.

Talking of clichés, 'he's got an engine on him' is the type of thing Wright, Shearer and co. would surely use of Jack today. They might also suggest that engine would run more efficiently if he gave up the Player's cigarettes. A fug of smoke in the dressing room wasn't uncommon back then as half-time tabs accompanied a steaming cup of tea before the restart. Jack Leslie was a heavy smoker throughout his life but his fitness as a footballer, physical work as a boilermaker and working into his retirement at West Ham must have helped him live to the ripe old age of 87.

The commentary of 'Pilgrim' on Jack's positioning may have been contradictory but he does constantly praise how he covered the ground and often saved his team from disaster. This was picked up in the nationals too. Reporting a 3-1 win at Charlton in April 1931, the *Daily Mail*'s headline was 'TEN PLYMOUTH MEN WIN. LESLIE THE HERO' and described the impact Jack had when they went a man down: 'Leslie went to centre-half, and it was the play of this man that saved the day. He was everywhere, covering both backs, shutting the middle path, and keeping McKay the Charlton danger man, under strict control. Few men have played so well as Leslie in this game.' Even if his approach occasionally failed, it's clear that Jack Leslie was the kind of player a crowd love. They knew he would give his all and most of the time it worked. Sometimes it didn't. That's football.

As for his bravery, the astonishing diving header that was Jack Leslie's final goal for Argyle says it all. This gargantuan effort against Fulham in December 1935 came after a terrible eye injury had kept him out for 15 months. 'His goal was a splendid example of determination. He actually threw himself at the ball when it came across low from Vidler.' In the end, that injury finished his career. There's also a fantastic report in *The People* from 1931 with the headline 'PLYMOUTH CAPTAIN SCORES BY A FACE!' It details Jack's unusual technique with glee:

> There was a good deal of speculation as to how Jack Leslie, the Plymouth captain, managed to deflect the very fine corner from Black for an equalising goal against Preston last week-end. The truth was that he turned it past Hughes with the side of his face. It was a bit of a sting, but the result was worth it, for it inspired Argyle to get the winning goal three minutes later.

Foot, shin, thigh, forehead, face ... if you're a goalscorer then you get it over the line any way you can. They all count.

Not only would Jack lift the crowd when going forward with clever, determined and courageous play, but also, when the chips were down, he put his body on the line at the back. Incredibly, given how dangerous the game was, substitutes weren't allowed until 1965. So, for nearly 80 years of competition in the English Football League, if a player was injured, they had to hobble on until the final whistle or hobble off and the team would continue with ten men. In Jack Leslie's time, it would usually fall on him to drop back to midfield as centre-half. And when he did, Jack won plaudits. In December 1930, Argyle welcomed Tottenham Hotspur, already famous for twice winning the FA Cup.

In the first half the Pilgrims' keeper Harry Cann had to retire after a brave stop was followed by a boot gashing his head open. Fred Titmuss – a good friend of Jack's – drew the short straw and went in goal, while Jack withdrew to centre-half and was, 'a tower of strength with his splendid kicking'. Argyle won 2-0, and when Cann trotted back on to the pitch with his head wound fully bandaged, the crowd went wild.

Playing Spurs must have had that effect on Argyle, or maybe the North Londoners were to the 30s what Wimbledon's crazy gang were to the 80s and 90s. It was a Good Friday match at White Hart Lane in 1933 and Plymouth's centre-half Harry Bland was off with concussion within a minute. Back steps Jack to fill that void in the middle of the park once again. According to 'Pilgrim': 'When they retired undefeated at the end and the 45,000 spectators rose to give them an ovation I have never before witnessed on any away ground – well, it just told its own tale.'

The match clearly stayed with Jack, as he shared his memory of it with Leslie Yates, writing for the *Sunday Independent*, a Plymouth paper, in 1972:

> I must have had a good match that day in what was a hard fought draw for our disorganised team. Anyway, a Tottenham player – I can't remember who – said to me 'Here, listen' as we walked off. Everybody in the stands seemed to be clapping and it grew louder as we approached the players' tunnel. I wondered what it was all about until the Spurs player said, 'They're giving YOU an ovation.' I can tell you it was a wonderful feeling to hear applause like that on an away ground.

A goalless draw can sometimes feel like a glorious win.

Incredibly, the return home fixture at Home Park was on the Easter Monday and again Argyle were effectively reduced to ten men when their right-winger was injured, although he stayed on the pitch. Again, Jack dropped deep and Argyle fought valiantly for a draw. In Jack Leslie's time as a player, Plymouth Argyle never lost against Tottenham Hotspur.

There are so many standout features of Jack's play but more than anything it's his intelligence that comes to the fore. Superlatives abound and, in this compared to other descriptions, his skin colour is more frequently mentioned. He's 'a coloured genius' said the *Daily Mail* in its report of the massive FA Cup tie against Arsenal in 1932. Later the same year the *Manchester Guardian* said of Plymouth's 3-1 win against United, 'The Argyle owed much to Leslie, a coloured player, who is the captain of the side and the "brains" of the attack.' *The People* said in 1931, 'The dark-skinned Leslie is still the life and soul of the attack,' and the next year it described his 'generalship' and called him 'that coloured opportunist'. It wasn't unusual for sports writers to pick up on athletes of colour, but I do wonder whether the prevalent racial stereotypes were at play here. They're positive about his play and it's somehow worthy of comment that a black player can command the game in such a way. It's not dissimilar to the way in which footballer and First World War hero Walter Tull was described. Their talent was surprising to white commentators who had a fixed view of the attributes and, in their minds, limitations of other races.

These are the challenges that Jack and black footballers throughout the ages have faced. Bernard Joy was a 'gentleman' amateur who played for the Casuals and Corinthians. He also signed as an amateur with several league clubs, including Fulham and Arsenal. Joy went on to become a famous football reporter from the 50s to the 70s. In 1975 he wrote how he couldn't see a black English footballer 'overcoming the temperamental and physical obstacles' that he believed stood in the way of them winning an international cap.[2] He lists these as temperament, English conditions, physical contact and barracking. Joy may not have been aware of Jack's selection in 1925 and he may not have seen him play, but he would have been aware of Jack Leslie. Joy was playing from 1931 when Jack was at his peak, attracting rave reviews nationwide.

It's clear that these preconceptions are utter nonsense, but it's exactly these attitudes that Jack came up against. He was strong and talented enough to let his football do the talking but that wasn't enough for his country. Bernard Joy played for England once in 1936, the last amateur to do so. What an irony that 50 years after Jack's selection for a match Joy probably read about as a teenager, this player turned pundit wrote off black English players' international hopes.

The final thing to say about Jack as a player is that he was, by all accounts, incredibly popular within the dressing room as well as with the fans. Long-time servant, Argyle captain and regular international for Wales, Moses Russell, treated the *Sports Budget* periodical to a club tour in 1928, introducing his team-mates: 'Ah! You all know who that merry fellow is. Yes, you're right, it's Jack Leslie, the happiest chap in the whole camp. Born where? Africa? Not on your life. "Darkie's" a real Londoner.' Moses clearly hadn't been on a diversity and inclusion course. Jack was often described in such terms. Sometimes he says it *was* shouted in an abusive way at him, but it was also often how he was described in the press and by his peers. It's impossible to know exactly how he felt about such descriptions.

Was this language of the time that had no impact, or even used endearingly among friends? Or perhaps it hurt, but Jack had to show that it didn't affect him for fear that he couldn't take the 'banter'. Jack was genuinely well liked, but it's also clear that he was seen as different and had to cope with that on the pitch and in the dressing room.

We've seen how aggressive and powerful Jack was on the pitch and one story his granddaughters tell is in some ways surprising, but if you think about it, it fits his character entirely. Sammy Black, the mercurial goalscoring left-winger, with whom Jack shared a special relationship on the pitch, was often targeted with the kind of crunching tackles that would get a straight red these days. 'Pilgrim' wrote, no doubt with a sigh, in September 1925 of 'Black's Usual Fate … being fouled when opponents found him too clever for them.' Now, Sammy would have often been the shortest player on the pitch at 5ft 6 (and a half!) and had a reputation. A defender would want to intimidate him in a bid to cancel him out, but if an opposition player started getting in his friend's face, Jack would react. Lesley says, 'He wouldn't have it, he wouldn't have them pick on Sammy Black. He told me that he would go and say, "Watch it or you'll have me to contend with!"'

Jack's granddaughters admired him for his sense of right and wrong. He hated injustice. So, his looking out for Sammy Black makes sense and shows why he was a great choice as captain. And the memories of those who saw him play confirm this. In 2020 I spoke to nonagenarian Argyle fan, Bill Stephens, who saw Jack play when he was just a boy in the early 1930s. Bill sadly passed away later that year, but it was a privilege to have the chance to hear him talk about Jack:

> I remember my father saying he was at a game and Jack wasn't playing, but he was just standing there watching. He thought it was a good chance to go and speak to him, so he went up to him to tell him what a great player he was. He was a real gent, he played the game the right way, he didn't cheat, and he didn't foul.

I promised this book wouldn't be a hagiography, yet through this entire chapter I've been praising Jack to the hilt. Naturally, there's the odd match where Jack didn't play at his best and he joined Argyle as a very young, promising player, having performed well at amateur club Barking Town for two seasons. He wasn't the finished article by any means, and it took time for Jack to establish himself in the first team at Plymouth. But from the very start he showed leadership qualities and formed strong bonds with team-mates. There's one photograph of Jack, still a teenager, as part of the Essex County team and there's a real sense of affection between the players. In one, Baden Herod – who alongside Jack was presented a cap by a French official for playing six or more times for their county – is sitting behind Jack with his arms round his shoulders. In another, Jack has his arms around his team-mate at Barking, Essex and Argyle, Alf Rowe. You get a real feeling of a man who cared for those around him, wanting to get the best out of them for the team and themselves.

Jack was a player who took responsibility throughout his career. In the fourth round of the Essex Senior Cup in 1920, he won a penalty after being fouled in the box. He was just 18, yet, with many more senior players in the team, was given the responsibility in a crucial cup tie and took the opportunity with 'a deadly shot', according to the *Chelmsford Chronicle*. Jack never took penalties for Argyle. Maybe that's because he missed two in a match later that season. Jack Leslie was a great player but there isn't a footballer out there who hasn't missed a chance, not even Pelé.

* * *

His attitude and approach to football say a lot about Jack Leslie's personality. He had charisma on and off the pitch. This was a charming and funny man with a twinkle in his eye that family and friends often mention. Jack had a mischievous side, liked to have a pint with mates and made friends easily throughout his life. Two incredible letters show this clearly. The first was written in the mid-1980s by a long-lost school friend, E.J. Griffiths, who had moved to Australia. He spotted his old mate in an article by sportswriter David Jack (grandson of Argyle manager, Bob). E.J. had lost touch with Jack, but still had clear and fond memories of him, their close friendship and how they played football and cards together at the weekends. And in the second, wonderful recent letter, Hazel Cadmore, now 98, wrote to Jack's granddaughters after seeing news of the statue on TV. She realised this was the man who used to share pints after work with her father in the 1940s and 50s. Hazel says he stood out among other men: 'I don't remember the names of my father's other friends, but I remembered Jack Leslie with the sparkling, kind eyes.' His wedding photos show how strong his relationships were with his team-mates too. Among Jack and Win's guests were not only current players at Argyle but also old comrades from his first amateur team, Barking. What an impact Jack had on the lives of so many people.

And, while he was serious on the pitch, the players also enjoyed themselves and Jack clearly liked to have a good time. There's certainly a sense that he felt at home in the dressing room, as evidenced by some of the memories from West Ham players and staff, even though he wasn't a boisterous young footballer but an elderly man caring for boots in the background. Rob Jenkins, the club physio at the time, remembers how they would have a cup of tea and 'sometimes we'd drink something a little bit stronger!' He goes on to recall young players looking for advice:

> They asked Jack if it was okay to have a drink the night before a game and he replied that a couple of beers was fine to settle the nerves and to get some sleep. Inevitably, they asked him if it was alright to have a 'bit of the other' the night before a game. Jack didn't think that was acceptable at all. 'Anyway, you can always make up for it afterwards,' he said, which made us all laugh![3]

Jack was philosophical too. In 1933 he penned an article that pops up in the *Halifax Daily Courier and Guardian*, but that I suspect was syndicated and appeared in more than one local paper as Halifax is a fair distance from Plymouth.

The fact he was given this platform is an indication of Jack's reputation nationwide.

In *Football and Fickle Fortune* Jack reflects on how luck plays a part in success and failure. With Plymouth Argyle missing out on promotion by a whisker as runners-up in Third Division South six times in a row in the 1920s, he knew it. 'Then our fortune changed,' reflected Jack on finally going up in 1930. 'I think you'll agree with me that we deserved it.' What's particularly remarkable about his piece is that he talks about Manchester City player Fred Tilson, who 'must be regarded as one of the unluckiest players in the game. I understand he missed a schoolboy international cap, a full international cap, and the chance of a Cup medal – all through injury.' Incredible to think of Jack empathising with a fellow player's misfortune in missing out on the honour he was so cruelly denied. He ends thus: 'It's great to be a footballer when your luck's in, but ...' Jack would know that more than any other player.

There's so much to love and admire about what Jack Leslie achieved and silently confronted. And we haven't even touched on the abuse he received from the terraces and how his wife, Win, was treated because she had married a man of colour. It's also fascinating to think about what Jack was like as a young husband and father and how tough it must have been for his wife when he was travelling around the country, and occasionally the world, plying his trade. I can tell you with certainty that it wasn't easy. And, although he was a working-class, left-wing, union man, his talent meant he mingled with upper-class sportsmen, dignitaries and officials. In Plymouth he even became a Freemason, a discovery that came as a surprise. Maybe that's how he got away with the occasional minor traffic offence as he was, according to his granddaughters, 'an absolutely terrible driver'. Jack Leslie, a man not to be trusted behind the wheel of a vehicle, was someone you could trust with your life on the football pitch.

As a grandfather he was playful and engaging with Lesley, Lyn and Gill. He would make up his own characters to put smiles on their faces and, no doubt, give his only child, Eve, a break from childcare. They speak with great affection of Jack, their granddad:

> He obviously had a charisma, and he had this lovely voice, he was a tenor singer, and it held you, you were just mesmerised by him. All our friends wanted to come round and would ask him to tell them stories. He made up characters and always left his funny tales on a cliff-hanger.

The three of them grew up with Jack and Win in the same house as their parents and remained tight-knit. Jack cherished his family and this shines through brightly whenever I speak to Lesley, Lyn and Gill.

I hope this gives you a sense of the man who's looking down on me before we embark upon his journey. What I can see is a life well lived and a person of substance. He embodied so much more than his motto. His goalscoring days were decades in the past, but he still had go and he still had guts. Jack Leslie surely deserved a fourth G … Glory.

Chapter Three

Young Jack

AT THE age of just 12, John Francis Leslie boarded a ship to escape the country of his birth, Jamaica. Born on 17 December 1863 in Hope Bay, his island childhood was not a happy one and drove him to seek adventure at sea and, eventually, a new home in England. It was there that John met Annie Regler, a seamstress from Islington in London. They married, settled in the city and had two daughters and a son named after him ... John Francis Leslie. We know him better as Jack.

It's important to consider Jack's family background because his heritage is so fundamental to his life. Both his parents' stories are fascinating too. It must have been quite a thing for his dad to both come to that decision to leave and act upon it at such a young age. He was a seaman who travelled the world before he settled in England, and the story of his departure is passed down through the family. It's said that he was treated so badly by his own family that he just had to leave. Slavery had been abolished, but its legacy was raw. Plantation owners had been compensated for their financial loss, despite huge financial gains from this horrific, enforced labour, while the enslaved people had not. John Francis Senior must have borne the sharp end of the continued mistreatment of the black population. His brave choice was perhaps reflected in his son when he left home to pursue his career in Plymouth. A shorter journey, but still a great adventure for a young Jack Leslie.

John's decision to head east doesn't sound like much of a choice. It was something he had to do and wasn't uncommon. The stories of black immigrants to the UK from the Caribbean in the late 19th and early 20th centuries that are on record tell many a similar tale. One was the temperance campaigner, Celestine Edwards, who fled Dominica aged about 12, just like John. Celestine also became a seaman before settling in Britain in the 1870s. He even visited Plymouth on a lecture tour in 1893.[4]

There's quite a tale to unpack in Jack's dad's journey. He was, his great granddaughters relate, once taken to the top of a hill as a young child and told that one day all the land he could see would be his. Jamaica was, of course, an island of sugar and coffee plantations that belonged to former slave owners. Jack's granddaughter Lesley says they've been told their great-grandfather was one of twins, but he had a rough time:

> The other twin was white and great-grand-dad was black and obviously the white one was treated far better than the black one and he just couldn't put up with it. I think he must have been treated really badly and so he became a mariner, he actually ran away. That is the story we've been told coming through our mum.

Lesley's younger sister, Lyn, goes on to tell another family fable that follows their great-granddad's daring childhood getaway:

> It was in later years when a ship that he was on was coming to port. His sister arrived in a Rolls-Royce with all furs on and said, 'Come back home, it's different now,' but he refused to go home.

The inference is that John was the son of one of the plantation owners and there were Jamaican plantations in the hands of Scottish landowners called Leslie. In 1834 the Powis Gateway in Aberdeen was built using compensation money given by the British government to slave owners after abolition. They're adorned with a bust of three black men, supposedly to commemorate the family's link with the granting of their freedom. The man who commissioned this piece of ancestral self-aggrandisement was one John Leslie of Powis.

The only record of our John Francis Leslie's family is on his marriage banns, noting his father as Edward Leslie, a painter, who was born in 1801. That would have meant he was in his 60s by the time John came along. Not impossible, but it seems unlikely. The notion that a slave owner could be in their family tree is something the granddaughters struggle to comprehend, says Lesley:

> I find it very difficult to come to terms with and to be honest I hadn't really given it an awful lot of thought until I saw Ainsley Harriott on *Who Do You Think You Are?* and he discovered that one of his family members was a slave owner and he was devastated. It was at that point I thought, 'Oh my God, it's possible that is our family history too.' And I remember watching *Roots* and it so affects you because you know that sometime your family has gone through that and it's heart-breaking. There is nothing you can do about it, but to come to the realisation that running through my blood is possibly the blood of a slave owner ... it is difficult to get your head round.

John Francis Leslie Senior wanted to sever ties with his Jamaican past entirely. Whatever abuse he suffered and whatever the explanation, it ended there. In England he found love and happiness in a strong family. Jack Leslie's back story gives just a glimpse of what his father, like many others who arrived in this country decades before the *Windrush*, had to cope with. What courage and resilience to take such a risk and seek a new life. It paid off. The struggles weren't over, but the outlook was now far brighter for the Leslie family.

Jack Leslie's dad bore the burden of his family history and troubles as a child with strength and lightness. Transferring to the rough streets of East London was clearly not a problem for this well-travelled young man and he was able to pass this resolve on to his son. Jack's childhood was by no means easy, but it was probably a breeze compared to his father's early years. With his mother Annie, who must have been equally strong given how mixed marriages were looked upon by many, Jack was given the solid foundation and family support his dad never had.

Jack loved his father, and Lesley says they were similar characters:

> I know my granddad thought the world of him and mum loved him. She said what a lovely, kind man he was, very much like granddad, I think. They had a similar kindness and gentleness about them, very generous and giving people considering what they must have gone through.

John was a friendly soul who worked hard to provide for his family and establish himself in his community. He had sailed the world by the time he met Annie in London and they were married in the District Church of St Paul's, Bow Common on 22 August 1891. John continued to go to sea for the next few years, which explains the long gaps between the birth of their three children: Letitia, known as Letty, in 1892, Edith in 1897 and, finally, Jack in 1901. John and Annie first shared a home in Limehouse, which was, according to historian Fiona Rule, 'one of the most vice-ridden and poverty-stricken places in the metropolis'.[5] By the time Annie was pregnant with Jack they had moved further east to Canning Town, while John had hung up his sea boots and found work as a labourer.

Canning Town is where Jack spent his childhood and, if you'll forgive the seafaring metaphor, there were stormy waters to navigate. It would make sense for the family, with a third child on the way, to move further out and have more space. At the turn of the century, Canning Town was still part of Essex and it was where the poorest dock workers lived. This was not an upgrade on Limehouse. It lay outside the planning regulations laid down in the Metropolitan Buildings Act, and when the area was developed around the middle of the 19th century there was no water supply or sewage system. No wonder, then, that this is where the lowly paid workers, many being immigrants, settled. Henry Morley wrote in 1857:

Many select such a dwelling place because they are already debased below the point of enmity to filth; poorer labourers live there, because they cannot afford to go farther, and there become debased. The Dock Company is surely, to a very great extent, answerable for the condition of the town they are creating.[6]

Hopefully, it wasn't quite so bad by the turn of the century, and the 1890 Housing Act brought improvements, but the original slums weren't cleared until the 1930s. Canning Town was, like other homes of dockyard workers in Cardiff and Liverpool, where many black seamen from overseas settled. There had been black residents here long before John came with his family, but it was around this time and through Jack Leslie's childhood that this district became a distinctly multicultural community with many mixed marriages like John and Annie's. For much of the white population, John and other black immigrants were a novelty and Lesley recalls being told how he rubbed along with people in the area:

He'd walk along the street and all the children used to gather around him and he used to hand out pennies, it wouldn't have been a lot, might even have been farthings, just small coins to the kids. The children weren't being nasty just, you know, thinking this is a strange person here. But he was always very kind.

Lyn continues that it was similar when their mum, Eve, who was born in 1927, was a child and wanted to be with her grandfather: 'All the kids wanted to hold his hand, so she had to fight her way through!' The fact that John was giving cash away suggests they weren't on the breadline. John and Annie were both working and if John was mostly treated well by the white people of Canning Town, then hopefully it was similar for Jack when he was a child.

What we see in these years is a mix of views and attitudes towards the black community. It's important to convey that context to understand what it might have been like for Jack Leslie as a child and how the prevailing attitudes also led to his treatment by the FA in 1925. The memories of Joseph Cozier, who himself ran away from his home of British Guiana at the age of 14, have been passed down, and his son Christopher says, 'Dad was respected in the community. Everyone called him "Mr Cozier". All the coloured men were respected and addressed as Mr. White and black people respected each other.' [7]

So, there was certainly a community that was integrating and showed understanding as they got to know each other. But there's no doubt that Jack and his family would have also faced abuse as there are many reports of mistreatment, and incidents of pubs, cafes and property owners turning away black people. There was an innate fear of the unknown that was – can you believe this? – stoked by the press. The *Daily Mirror* was, on the one hand, intensely racist towards the black American boxer Jack Johnson in 1910, being suspicious of his 'fantastic adornments as gold front teeth to match his waistcoat buttons ... We fear him. In time (it is not impossible) he may come over to England and be entertained at the Guildhall and tell us how to govern our Empire.' While a year later the same paper reported on the Congress of All Races, an event designed to promote understanding. The paper talked frankly of the suspicions the white population have of black people, 'We fear more than an occasional congress will be needed ... Familiarity may breed contempt, but it removes that curious longing to punch the foreigner's head.' They were certainly right that more work would need to be done.

The Leslie family may have been treated by some as such, but they were no foreigners. Annie was a Londoner and John made it his home. By the time Jack came along in 1901, the family had settled in Clifton Road, Canning Town, alongside Annie's widowed mother Catherine who was 73 but still working as a trouser finisher. John and Annie stayed in the area for the rest of their lives. They were proper East Enders, a happy family with parents who supported their offspring's aspirations. So, when tragedy struck it must have hit hard. By 1907 the family had moved to nearby Gerald Road, and we know this from a death certificate. In September of that year Edith was suddenly taken from them.

Child mortality was much higher a century ago, but that would in no way lessen the shock and grief when Edith passed away at just ten years of age. Annie was there, at home, and it was a sudden, shocking tragedy that would have left the family in pieces. The cause of death was 'Valvular Disease of the Heart, Syncope'. Syncope is the technical term for fainting or passing out – usually such a minor incident. But it can also, very rarely, be the symptom of a heart condition and prove fatal. Several footballers have been struck down by this shocking affliction in recent years. So, it seems that the death of John and Annie's middle child was totally unexpected. It's likely that Annie's mother Catherine would have been there, which must have been of some comfort to her. Letty was 15 and Jack had just turned six, so whether or not they saw the tragedy unfold they were old enough to understand this momentous event and for the grief to have an impact.

The memories of such kind, loving people that have been passed down are a testimony to the strength of the familial bonds that endure today. To cope with such a loss and maintain that outlook on life is quite something. It helped Jack when embarking on his own married life because, while it wasn't plain sailing, he had a long and successful relationship. John and Annie gave their son the tools to help him cope with the issues he would face in football. How else could Jack have managed to deal with them without any sign of bitterness? And that fortitude has been passed down the generations who have had more than their fair share of tragedy. It's awe-inspiring. The Leslies are made of strong stuff.

* * *

Jack's childhood obviously had its ups and downs, but that family foundation combined with the discovery of his sporting talent must have, on balance, made it a pretty good one. Despite the poor housing conditions and poverty in East London, there were many improvements in education and welfare at the time. Jack attended Hermit Road School, right next to Thames Ironworks FC's first ground. This was the club that would become West Ham United where Jack worked in his later years. It was a strong community school, but the surroundings were far from salubrious. The Hermit

Road recreation ground is now a pleasant green space with a fancy playpark, but in the mid-1890s was described as a 'barren waste' by the Irons' first manager.

Jack's granddaughters remember that he had violin lessons as a child, which suggests that the family had a little spare money. The young boy must have had some musical talent as he was also known for having an excellent singing voice – something that Plymouth Argyle fans would discover later at occasional concerts the players took part in. Jack sang at a local church and, according to his granddaughters, the choirmaster wanted him to train professionally. Young Jack wasn't interested, and he hated the violin. His mother made him practise but he would just play a few notes and then open his window a little and repeat the process until the gap was wide enough for him to scarper. Annie wasn't happy about that, but sport was his passion. He showed the talent and a mischievous streak to match at an early age.

In the most part, Jack's school days were a happy time, although there's no doubt he would have faced adversity, judgement and abuse. He didn't talk about the bad times because he didn't want to burden his family, but they would have willingly helped him carry that load. It's heartening to know that he built friendships at school that were so strong they were never forgotten. E.J. Griffiths and his brother were at Hermit Road with Jack, and his words are infused with affection as he recalls his talented mate: 'We were very close friends. Leslie was also a good cricketer and swimmer, he won the Gold Cup for Swimming at the London Schools Championships.' By the age of 14, when children left school, Jack was showing both sporting prowess and a drive to win. That talent and his warm personality drew people in. Jack also developed his love of playing cards as he and the Griffiths brothers would get together at their mate Billy's house every weekend.

School football was in its infancy when Jack was a lad. Exercise had been spartan physical drills until 1906 when cricket, hockey and football were introduced to the curriculum. Perfect timing for Jack Leslie. But it was outside the school gates where Jack truly began his journey towards professional football. That path was entwined with social movements of the time. The dockland areas of East London became a hotbed of union activity as workers fought for stable employment, pay and conditions. Jack's dad worked as a gas fitter's labourer for at least some of his son's childhood and in 1889 – the year of the great dock strike – men like him gained union recognition. This union became the General, Municipal and Boilermakers' Union, which Jack would join as a young boilermaker before his sporting career took off. Canning Town also saw efforts by socially conscious campaigners and organisations to improve the lot of the local population. The settlement movement was key to the development of many future sporting stars, including Jack.

The Mansfield House University Settlement was set up by a church minister on the Barking Road in Canning Town towards the end of the 19th century. It organised dancing, drama, debating and all manner of less alliterative activities. And it provided a new system of support for the community such as a benefit scheme that workers could subscribe to and then claim if sick. In 1892 one of the settlement residents founded a boys' club, first in a small hall, then a disused pub, and in 1900 the site was totally rebuilt as Fairbairn Hall. A donation from famous philanthropist J. Passmore Edwards made it happen, and Fairbairn House Boys' Club was born. It was all remarkably progressive stuff and, crucially for Jack, there were sports clubs. He swam, boxed and played cricket and football at a high standard and many of Jack's contemporaries would go on, like him, to achieve great success. Several would win international honours. Sadly, not Jack.

Jack was by all accounts a particularly good cricketer and was encouraged to pursue the game professionally, but football was his passion. The family has medals from 1917 when he played for Fairbairn House Under 16s and then later in the year, presumably after he turned 16 in August that year, for the Under 18s. And they had very good teams. In 1913 they won the Junior Federation Cup Final 8-4 against St Andrews from Westminster, despite Saints being 'the heavier team'. And in October 1918 it was noted how they dominated all events across the year. The senior and junior teams 'won the divisional championship for the Federation of London Working Boys' Clubs, and had therefore to play for the cups. In both finals the club was successful, the senior and junior teams winning their trophies for the sixth season in succession.'[8] The team names aren't listed but no doubt Jack would have played in most, if not all those competitions.

For Jack and a bunch of the best players, the Fairbairn team wasn't enough. In 1917 he and the Griffiths brothers formed their own team and entered the West Ham and District League. They had to rent a ground but the nearest they could secure was The Elms in Walthamstow, almost a two-hour trek from Canning Town. E.J. Griffiths, secretary of the team, wrote that they reached the cup final but were beaten 3-2 after playing extra time and being down to nine men. Tough match. At the end of the season a team of the best players from that league played none other than Fairbairn House at the biggest ground in East London, Upton Park, where Jack Leslie showed his football skills on a top club's pitch at the age of just 17. And he was honoured as the best player. Jack was making a name for himself, and Griffiths said he was surprised West Ham didn't snap him up after those performances.

Although Jack had new opportunities and life in Canning Town was much better than in the previous century, it wasn't a bed of roses. He received an education but, as was the norm, left school at 14. So, Jack Leslie put his schoolbooks under his bed, or possibly in the bin with his violin, and set out to learn a trade as the First World War was raging. His father impressed upon Jack the need to secure a decent job and not just rely on his football skills. That said, he didn't discourage his son; John was just being practical. And with that global conflict came the suspension of professional football so, in any event, the young Jack Leslie didn't know for sure whether he could turn his talent into cold hard cash.

Jack's teenage years were a time of great excitement, enjoyment and anticipation mixed with a fear of the future and actual fear. Towards the end of the war the Griffiths brothers, a little older than Jack, served in the Royal Navy. Jack and his family knew many young men who would leave these shores and some who would never return. But for them, the Great War began to have a real and deadly impact at home too. To say that football is more important than life and death is a great quote (or misquote), especially when knowingly delivered by a legend like Bill Shankly. But the population of Canning Town and the surrounding docklands faced mortal danger when German Zeppelin raids began in late 1915.

These were tumultuous times globally that affected Jack and his family directly, but he was getting on with the business of scoring goals and riveting iron. It's only later that he must have reflected on what he lived through. When interviewed by the *Daily Mail* in 1978, Jack was asked about this and said, 'One great sorrow was missing the Great War. I just come of age when it ended. I knew a lot who got killed. But I was upset I didn't get that chance to do a bit for me country.' It is incredible to read such patriotic words from someone rejected by his country in another sphere. But that wasn't unusual. There was great support for the war and a feeling that everyone should do their bit, and that included Jack's community in London's docklands. The Port of London Authority War Memorial lists 403 employees who lost their lives.

His father, John, was a gas fitter's labourer at Beckton Gas Works, and the 1921 census shows that Jack was also working there as a boilermaker's apprentice. Did he meet his love by the gas works wall? Almost certainly, as Win was from nearby Plaistow, and the dockland industries certainly made it a dirty old town. It was common for family members to find employment for their young men, and John helped his son get on the ladder at Beckton. It was 'the largest gas works in Europe', so there must have been plenty of opportunities.[9] The term boilermaker could mean literally making boilers or simply metalworking, and Jack is later described as a boilermaker, riveter and plater. Either way this was a skilled job and a step up for Jack from his father's occupation as a labourer. It was a good, honest trade that he could earn a living from if the football didn't work out. Even though it did, Jack would still need those skills to earn a wage once his glory days came to an end. There were no lucrative sponsorship deals or television punditry opportunities to avoid that. Where his football and metalworking skills entwined was in his ambidexterity. According to his granddaughters, Jack was in great demand because he could screw rivets effectively with his left and right hand, which was rare and highly desired. He was good with both feet and good with both hands.

In these apprenticeship years through the war Jack was working hard and playing football hard. Sport was a great distraction from the toll an horrific war was having on the country. And that pressure hit London's dockland areas heavier than most. The work there was a crucial part of the war effort, not only to unload supplies coming in by sea but for the multitude of manufacturing sites, including shipbuilding in places such as the famous Thames Ironworks and new, much-needed munitions factories. As a result, it was a clear and obvious enemy target. A raid on 13 June 1917 killed more than 40 people, including ten schoolchildren, and injured hundreds more.

The air strikes weren't the only danger. In January 1917 a fire broke out in a munitions factory in Silvertown causing an explosion that obliterated 900 houses, damaged around 70,000 more and killed 73 people. This enormous incident was subject to a virtual news blackout lest it affect morale, but Jack and his family knew about it. They would have heard the blast for starters. And the local council set up a relief office in Canning Town to help the victims, so local people rallied round. The response showed the fortitude of the population in an area that was one of the poorest in the country, but which made some of the biggest contributions. They would be called upon again and be even more greatly affected just two decades later.

Jack and Win's relationship points to a long courtship. The couple married in 1925, were very much in love and both from East London, so they would have met in the area. It's likely that happened at least a few years before the wedding and probably before his move to Plymouth. They would have shared tales of their wartime activities and family struggles. While Jack was riveting in the gas works, Win worked in a munitions factory. Conditions on the shop floor were awful and fraught with danger, as the Silvertown tragedy showed.

Win had a tougher upbringing than Jack. The family lived in accommodation that was far more cramped, and her father, William, is described as a 'lunatic' in the 1901 and 1911 censuses. What Jack's granddaughters remember being told is that William suffered a head injury that was so bad he had been left for dead before being treated and recovering. But it left him with severe mental health issues that affected his chances of employment, and he was often admitted to Goodmayes

Hospital, then known as an asylum. Despite this, and the fact that he was just 5ft 2in tall and, at 43, was two years above the upper age limit, he was able to sign up and go to France in 1915. It shows how desperate the country was. William served in the Army Service Corps for a year before being medically discharged. It's fair to say that this wasn't a job to which he was well suited. He sailed for Le Havre from Southampton on 24 September 1915 and a month later was punished for 'drunkenness on active service'. Oddly, his character was described as 'good' despite the boozing and having his pay docked for being absent from roll call in June 1916. Perhaps his superiors took pity on him. Looking back to the 1891 census, William is listed as deaf. The officials looking after those later records weren't exactly being alert to his disability. Jack and Win's granddaughters weren't aware of William's deafness, and this may have been as incorrect an assumption by the record keepers of 1891 as those who later called him a lunatic.

Whatever the true story of Jack's father-in-law's affliction, we can be sure that both Jack Leslie and his future wife would have been deeply affected by the First World War. It echoed through British society as service personnel returned home, many physically and mentally scarred by what they had seen and endured. And at home waves of grief had torn families apart. It may seem glib to mention such a thing alongside this, but the sport Jack had such a passion for had been dealt a huge blow too. The Football League and FA Cup had been suspended and players and clubs faced criticism for their perceived lack of commitment to the nation. The reality was that a great number of players enlisted and, of course, many were killed or suffered injuries that ended their playing careers.[10] Amid the joy of celebrations that greeted peace, 17-year-old Jack must have wondered what the future held. The cohesion that wartime can bring to society can be swiftly ripped apart by the sudden impact of peace. There was no clearer example of that than in Jack's home of Canning Town and the dockland areas of the UK.

* * *

The First World War created opportunities for immigrant workers as labour was desperately needed at home and abroad, so seamen flocked from Britain's colonies to its ports. Black men served in the trenches, at sea and in tough jobs that were crucial to the war effort. And they did so with the same intentions of serving 'King and Country' as their white compatriots, whether they had already made a life in the mother country or travelled from colonial territories. While their efforts filled a much-needed void, they weren't always welcomed.

There was a particular issue with local white men being angry with black men having relationships with white women. This led to violent attacks, and in 1917 several black sailors were attacked in Canning Town. The *Daily Express* (not them, surely!) wrote: 'In consequence of the infatuation of white girls for the Black men in the district some of the inhabitants are greatly incensed against Blacks.' Even before the worst outbreaks of violence that followed the armistice, black people like John Francis Leslie and many who had married white British women, were targeted. The women would often face abuse and violence, the flames of which were fanned by prejudicial pieces in the papers. What an irony that John's Jamaican heritage and back story, as passed through the family, hints at a possible relationship between white plantation owners, whose forefathers enslaved people, and local black women. This wasn't uncommon and was often non-consensual. While there was an integrated community and John was well liked, he wouldn't have escaped the ire of those with racist intent. This undercurrent would have been present throughout his life, and peace brought no dividend. A simmering threat of violence was about to boil over as the men who survived the trenches returned from the front. Some of those returning soldiers would come to play with and against Jack Leslie on the football pitch.

The year 1919 is known to have been one of 'race riots'. But that makes it sound as if ethnic minority groups were rioting. They weren't. They were the targets. In the ports of Cardiff, Liverpool, Edinburgh and in London's Canning Town, African, African-Caribbean, South Asian, Chinese and Middle Eastern workers, and their businesses and property, came under attack. By the end of the First World War there were around 20,000 black people in Britain.[11] Returning demobbed white men turned against black men, who they saw as taking their jobs and their women. Trade unions sided with the white British men, refusing to allow employment of black workers over whites. The irony is that many were members of the unions and had paid their dues. And a significant number of seamen who had come from Britain's overseas territories to aid its war effort wanted to return home but were unable because they couldn't find work on a ship to do so.[12] During this violence in 1919 and sporadic outbreaks in 1920 and 1921, five people were killed, many injured and at least 250 arrested.[13]

In this febrile atmosphere, violence erupted on the streets of East London in Stepney and spread to Canning Town, where Jack Leslie lived. An African-Caribbean sailor, Thomas Pell, was standing on his doorstep when a passer-by thumped him in the chest. The white man, James Grantham, claimed Pell had laughed at him. The sailor reacted and two other black seamen pulled their mate inside, trying to calm the situation, but things escalated. Grantham smashed the windows of Pell's home, crowds then joined in, and the three black sailors were forced to make a run for it. They were armed, which wasn't unusual as men carried knives and guns for their own protection. As Pell and his friends fled the mob, which included butchers armed with choppers, the trio fired warning shots over the attackers' heads. Incredibly, justice in a sense prevailed as the magistrate merely fined Thomas and friends for having revolvers without a licence, while Grantham got two months' hard labour for assault.[14]

Such attacks show how black people had to be on guard as violent men looked for an excuse to take their frustrations out on those they perceived to be doing them harm. Yet, they were mostly in the same boat, looking to earn a crust and survive. Jack Leslie was just turning 18 at the time of the riots and, while he would have known many a friendly face in Canning Town and the surrounding area, had to keep his wits about him. He was an apprentice, and his family was doing okay. That would have been resented by a returning soldier who found himself unemployed. Luckily, Jack had pace and there were times when he would have needed it on the streets as well as the sports grounds. Jack Leslie would show that speed and skill as he joined many other young hopefuls as they aimed for the top in their field ... football.

Chapter Four

Barking Mad

AS 1918 drew to a close, Jack Leslie and his family felt the mixture of relief and joy that swept the nation. That feeling hung over chats in the dressing rooms and gas works in Beckton. But it was tinged with grief for the friends they would never see again and guilt at having been too young to fight. Jack was just 17 when the war ended. Too young to serve but old enough to be fired up with a desire for adventure and patriotic fervour. He later talked of his regret that he was unable to 'do a bit for me country'. While it's well known that many boys younger than the lower age limit of 18 managed to sign up, the army cracked down on this after conscription was introduced in 1916. And Jack wasn't exactly having an easy time of it. Nothing compared to the trenches, but he toiled in a tough and vital reserved occupation as well as dodging the bombs that targeted his home and workplace.

It must have been a relief to his parents when the armistice was signed. They had already tragically lost one child, but Letty and Jack were doing well and set to make their way in life. And the timing gave this talented young sportsman the perfect opportunity to push on to great things. East London was, as it has been throughout football history, a hotbed of talent. Spectators were desperate to watch competitive matches again and, alongside the professionals at West Ham, there were many top amateur clubs that provided a pathway to the higher tiers. The next couple of years proved crucial for Jack as he took that path with one of those clubs, Barking Town, while also working alongside his dad at Beckton Gas Works as a boilermaker's apprentice. He made an immediate impact that would win him honours and send him on overseas adventures. It was the kind of start you would expect from someone who would soon be tipped for international success.

Throughout the war football remained as popular as ever but priorities had naturally shifted. The Football League was suspended at the end of the 1914/15 season as professional players and clubs were taking plenty of stick for supposedly not doing their bit.[15] Local football leagues, exhibition matches, and youth and women's football continued throughout the war years. Many spectators were soldiers at home on leave as well as the people working in crucial industries like Jack and his dad were. Who would want to deny them that entertainment and distraction? Jack spent much of his time outside work training and playing with Fairbairn House Boys' Club and then the team he set up with his mates in 1917. He also played cricket and bowls when summer came. Fairbairn House had the best youth teams in London and the South East and took part in local competitions. When the war ended, the Football League and FA, nationally and locally, prepared for the resumption of competitive football. The nation was hungry for it.

The crowds who turned out to watch the women's game is a testament to that desire. The famous Dick, Kerr Ladies FC pulled in 10,000 fans for a Christmas Day match in 1917, and the gate for their 1920 Boxing Day match against St Helen's Ladies was a staggering 46,000. Sadly, as is now well known, football's stuffy administrators bore down on this as harshly as they would on Jack. The FA Council expressed 'the strong opinion that the game of football is quite unsuitable for females and should not be encouraged'. In December 1921 clubs affiliated with the association were banned from hosting women's matches, which made fixtures far harder to organise. The issue was wrapped up in a depressing mix of misogyny and class bias with the FA raising questions around expense payments to female players and the distribution of money raised by these charity matches. They were wrangling the exact same matters in the men's game, but somehow the suits found a way to keep the men's game alive. Women, of course, did continue to play amid these constrained circumstances, but the FA ban wasn't lifted until 1971. The explosion in its popularity in recent years is a credit to the fortitude of those who kept going in the face of such adversity.

Professionalism had been around for decades, and even before the war a few players were labelled as 'mercenaries'. Most famous was the fabulous moustachioed Alf Common, who became Britain's first £1,000 footballer when Sunderland sold him to Middlesbrough in 1905. Jack would have been aware of the popularity of his chosen sport and the possibility of a career. After those difficult years when many players and officials had lost their lives, those involved in football were desperate to go again. Although we consider Canning Town as East London, back then it was just within the Essex border. By October 1919 there were 312 clubs and competitions registered with the Essex County FA, 43 more than the season before the war. The *Chelmsford Chronicle* worried that resources could be stretched: 'The boom in soccer has been greater than the supply of referees can cope with.' Just as the FA was furiously recruiting as many 'Knights of the Whistle' as they could, football clubs were recruiting players. This was the perfect opportunity for Jack.

As football clubs prepared for the resumption of league competition in August 1919, clubs were desperate for talent. Many former players were now either too old or were casualties of war, having either been killed in action, wounded, suffering the horrendous long-term effects of gas attacks or post-traumatic stress. It's remarkable seeing the resilient faces of many young men who had served then take their place on the pitch, many of Jack's future team-mates among them.

Jack Leslie was already a star of youth football in East London and Essex, so when Barking Town assembled its team in 1919 it was a coup to get him on board. Jack was one of the youngest among the ranks, many of whom would go on to forge successful professional careers. Barking were one of the leading amateur clubs in the area playing in the Premier Division of the London League against the likes of Charlton Athletic and Islington Town – did that mean divided loyalties for Jack's mum? The two divisions of the professional Football League were dominated by the north; out of 44 clubs only six were from the capital – Chelsea, Arsenal, Spurs, Fulham, West Ham United and … Clapton Orient. So, Jack would be competing at a level at least equivalent to League Two or the National League today. And the crowds were impressive, reaching several thousand for regular matches, while a cup tie against Spurs saw 7,800 throng to Barking's ground. A cup final between Barking and Leytonstone attracted nearly 15,000, and that's not far off Plymouth Argyle's gates today. Jack was about to play proper football on a big stage, a baptism of fire for an 18-year-old. He didn't falter. Jack Leslie's new club, Barking Town, opened on 30 August 1919 with a surprise 2-1 away victory against Catford Southend.

Clubs were keen to raise money for charity just as they had during the war and the London Charity Cup was described as a 'Peace Celebration' competition that aimed to bring in £1,000 for good causes. Barking took part and Jack would, no doubt, have been proud to play. It's a shame that black soldiers had been excluded from the victory parade that was part of the nation's Peace Day celebration that summer. I wonder whether Jack was aware that the authorities had dismissed the contribution of thousands of people of colour to the nation's war effort. It was this undercurrent that contributed to his treatment in 1925. Many communities held Peace Day parties, including Canning Town, but these took place just as rioting against black men and their families was flaring up. Given how well liked Jack and his family seem to have been and the fact that many local white people defended their neighbours against the racist attacks, I can only hope they were included in these events.

One thing that regularly crops up in relation to Jack's Barking years is his goalscoring record. Wikipedia claims he banged in 250 goals in his two seasons and that fact is oft repeated, although not by me, unless followed by this enormous caveat. In those two post-war seasons the club netted 336 goals, so our Wiki editor believes Jack scored nearly 75 per cent of his team's total. That seems highly dubious. He was playing outside-left, left-wing to you and me, and he hit the back of the net with far more frequency when he later moved to inside-left with Plymouth. Looking at what Barking match reports we have, Jack is very well regarded and scores frequently, but not as often as centre-forwards such as Frank Richardson. Frank left Barking for Plymouth alongside Jack and scored a hatful at Home Park. Perhaps the 250 figure includes goals Jack scored for Fairbairn House and his own amateur league team in 1917/18.

It's fair to say that their opening-day victory was a false start, as the first half of Barking Town's season was a mixed bag, but Jack Leslie stood out from the off. After a four-year hiatus, football clubs across the nation were cobbling together the best teams they could, and it was no surprise that it took a while for some to gel. Jack was playing in a team whose average age was 24, many of whom would turn professional, so it's even more remarkable that 18-year-old Jack was not only a first-team regular but also consistently recognised as a standout performer in match reports and league round-ups. And they were playing a lot of football. Barking competed in the London League, the South Essex League, several cup competitions, and charity matches. It's a testament to Jack's skill and determination in the rough and tumble of top-flight amateur football that he was an automatic pick.

In that first season it felt as if Barking Town were very much concentrating on the cups. They were doing okay in the London League but the less said about the South Essex League the better. A 6-1 home loss to Gnome Athletic put them second from bottom by Christmas. Things would pick up, but it was in the cup competitions that they shone. Keeping fit for so many different competitions must have been tough for Jack and his team-mates. No doubt, they were buoyed by the simple return of competitive football, and Jack was seeing his talent recognised. That must have been a huge boost, and the attention he received as a teenager led to some remarkable adventures and encounters in these formative years of his life.

Before regular competition even kicked off, there were exciting rumours in the column of 'Onlooker' in the *Westminster Gazette* of a London League representative team travelling to France for some charity exhibition matches. And one of the men behind this initiative was none other than Jules Rimet. He would soon be the third president of FIFA, go on to initiate the first World Cup in 1930 and give his name to the most famous trophy ever created. Jack would never play in a World Cup, in fact none of his peers would, since the FA refused to take part due to a dispute with FIFA. There was a definite feeling that England were better than foreign teams and didn't need to degrade themselves by playing matches to prove it. Rimet would, however, ensure that Jack's early career was gleaming.

Alongside his duties with the French FA, Jules Rimet was a vice-president of the London League, which had been invited to visit 'our gallant allies' that winter. Matches against a Paris League team were arranged for 1 and 2 November 1919. The first was for the Lord Dewar Trophy. Dewar was a whisky magnate, president of the London League, and the longest-staying guest at London's Savoy hotel from 1904–30. Would the thought of being selected for such an adventure even have crossed Jack Leslie's mind? This was only two months into his time at Barking Town. The local football community knew what a talented player he was, and that reputation preceded his signing for Barking. On Thursday, 30 October the team for the London League Paris Tour was revealed in the *Daily News*, and three Barking players made the 12-strong squad. They were George Hebden, a goalkeeper who had played in four schoolboy internationals, George Harris at centre-half and Jack Leslie on the left wing. What a wonderful surprise for Jack and Barking Town.

On the morning of Friday, 31 October, our intrepid footballers and officials set off from London Victoria at 8.45am. The whole escapade was 'excellently arranged' according to *The Globe*, and many papers delighted in giving us the precise itinerary. The party met at 8.15am, presumably to ensure they could get a cuppa and some decent table seats for the journey to Folkestone. There they would board a ferry to Boulogne, set to depart at 11.15, before finally arriving in Paris by 6.30pm. Plenty of time for a meal, a couple of pichets of bière or vin to settle the nerves and get a good night's sleep before the big match.

How proud must John and Annie Leslie have been as they waved farewell to their 18-year-old son on his first trip abroad? Just a year earlier, young men made the same journey to fight and die for 'King and Country'. Jack certainly felt as patriotic about that endeavour as any Englishman. And he had the courage and resilience of his immigrant father. Taking in the air on the train through Kent before boarding a ferry bound for France must have given Jack butterflies in his entire body. 'Onlooker' was confident and thought Jack was in a very good team that should win both matches. The gate receipts totalled around £1,000 across the two fixtures, a great boost for charity, and suggests that around 20,000 football fans greeted Jack in Paris that weekend. What a stage for an emerging player. Who knows whether the butterflies, the long journey or the bonhomie of a Parisian welcome affected them but, unfortunately, Jack's first overseas football tour didn't have a fairy-tale ending as the London team lost twice.

The first match for the Dewar Trophy took place at the Olympic Stadium in the French capital and was a close-run thing, but the Parisians won 4-3. The London team then played a friendly against the same opponents the following day at the home of Red Star FC, the club founded by Jules Rimet. The outcome was a less glorious 3-1 defeat. The party returned home the following day, leaving Paris at 10.15am and pulling into Charing Cross at 7.20pm. Jack was due at Beckton Gas Works the next morning, but he didn't care. As a future professional he would have reflected on moments that could have changed the matches, but this was a formative experience that stood Jack in great stead throughout his career and life. Working and socialising with different echelons of society was part and parcel of being a footballer. Without the sport, Jack would have been almost exclusively ensconced in his trade, locality and family. With it, he was crossing the Channel and hanging out with Lord Dewar and Jules Rimet.

It's fascinating to think of how Jack was treated by such people. He had earned the right to play at this level, but did he find himself having to act a certain way? Argyle legend Ronnie Mauge is now an ambassador for the club and says walking into a football club boardroom can still be uncomfortable:

We always have to act in a different way. We have to conform to the way we feel like they want us to behave. Going on those outings is very different to when you're playing. As an ambassador I am welcomed at Plymouth, but when I walk into other boardrooms at times they look at you as if you shouldn't even be there.

While Jack and his two Barking team-mates were off on their Paris jolly, the rest of the squad were having a tough time of it. Without three of their best players they struggled to hold a strong Custom House team to a 1-1 draw in the third qualifying round of the FA Amateur Cup. A replay the following week was dispiritingly described as a 'futile effort' by *The Sportsman*, and despite 25 minutes of extra time, still ended goalless. With no substitutes allowed it was a bruising encounter. On 12 November a second replay was to be like football's answer to *Gladiator*, as the same paper said it was a 'fight to the finish'. The match was held on neutral soil at West Ham's Upton Park, a ground Jack knew well. He had recovered from his Parisian travails and, according to *The Sportsman*, 'after some exceedingly clever passing, in which Leslie and Margetts excelled, the former placed a fine shot clean over the head of the Custom House goalkeeper'. Jack's goal was one of three Barking Town scored without reply. They were finally through to the fourth round.

Perhaps having to play the previous tie three times had an impact, as the fourth and final qualifying round didn't go to plan. Barking's excellent goalkeeper George Hebden picked up an injury, and despite the team's best efforts and a goal from Jack, they couldn't come back from a 4-3 deficit to Ordnance (Woolwich) at half-time, and the match ended 5-3.

Other cup competitions kicked off well. The London Senior Cup meant more qualifying rounds, although as a top amateur club, Barking Town were exempt until round three. At the end of November they beat Enfield 4-3 and then overcame Burberry (from New Malden, not the fashion house) 3-2 away. They were in the competition proper, but an absolute mud bath temporarily held them up. On 10 January 1920, 4,000 fans, the biggest crowd seen at Ilford in seven years, huddled in the pouring rain to watch the players slip and slide across the pitch. The first goal typified the sketchy conditions when an Ilford defender headed a cross into his own net. The second was a fine shot by Jack that 'glanced in at the far end of the net'. They were 2-0 up at half-time when the weather got even worse. Barking were ahead until the final seconds when Ilford managed to level the score at 2-2. They then played 15 minutes of extra time but even that seemed ridiculous to the fans as conditions were so atrocious. The referee probably couldn't tell the teams apart as they now looked like a Glastonbury mosh pit at dusk. By the final minutes spectators had no idea where the ball was and the tie went to a replay. Although Jack had scored, the *Eastern Counties Times* was on the fence in its analysis: 'Leslie did well though at times seemed a little disinterested.' Maybe he was dreaming of a hot bath. The papers agreed that the better team went through in the end. Jack nabbed the final goal of a 3-1 victory in the replay, watched by 4,209 supporters, a record home attendance. Barking Town were on the up.

After an inconsistent first half of the 1919/20 season the players were starting to gel and their form was winning plaudits. The *Westminster Gazette* hailed 'The Rise of Barking' in February 1920, and 'Onlooker' picked out their five cleverest players, calling them 'irresistible', having scored 24 goals in the last month while conceding just four. One of those five was, of course, Jack Leslie. The same stat was remarked upon in the *Daily Herald*, a national publication that would have particular significance in Jack's story yet to come.

This first season was a roller coaster for Jack, and with such a flurry of fixtures he hardly had time to catch his breath. By the spring of 1920, Barking Town had two significant cup runs underway and a solid start in Jack's first league season for a senior club. He had already been picked to represent his league, travelled to Paris, played in front of huge crowds on foreign soil and was being recognised by football writers for his talent. Jack was being talked about. What's remarkable is that there's no reference to his colour at this stage, only his talent. When we think about what was going on in the country at this time and the issues Jack faced later, this is surprising. There are far more frequent references to be found later in his career. Perhaps the fact that London was more multicultural even then made it less of an issue for commentary.

Jack's glittering first season was reaching its climax, and although any hopes of league success were long gone, cup glory still beckoned. Barking Town made the final of both the Essex and London Senior Cups and the West Ham Charity Cup. Football supporters really couldn't get enough competitive football on its return after the war, and neither could the players. Barking Town took on Grays Athletic in the Essex Cup on Easter Monday, 5 April 1920. 'Onlooker' thought Athletic were in cloud cuckoo land if they expected to win and predicted that Jack and his fellow front five's 'dashing forward play' would bring the cup to Barking. He rather smugly confirmed his prediction, although it was a close-run thing. In front of a record crowd of 10,000, Jack opened the scoring. Athletic equalised but Barking's centre-forward Fackrell hit the winner. It ended 2-1 to Barking and Jack lifted his first piece of silverware in a blue-and-white-hooped shirt.

As the days grew longer, fixtures came thick and fast, with frequent evening matches. You wonder whether the team had any kind of training. The *Chelmsford Chronicle* said most of the Barking players had a 'bit of a trot each evening. That's the way to keep the football leg and "wind" fit.' Tactical planning wasn't a feature of most football preparations in the 1920s, and with full-time work and regular matches there wasn't the time for more than a trot. In the last week of April, Jack Leslie played five times in six days. 'Onlooker' was sympathetic: 'Many amateur players would be very tired before Saturday's matches are reached.' Can you imagine such a run of fixtures today? Jack turned out for Barking Town on Monday, Tuesday and Wednesday evenings, then on the Thursday he had to squeeze in yet another match, possibly his biggest to date.

While the FA at a national level would be responsible for one of the most shameful decisions in the history of the game and one that would stay with Jack Leslie until he took his last breath, the regional officials played fair. In his first season of senior football, Jack Leslie was chosen to represent Essex against Norfolk on 29 April 1920. This was another great honour for young Jack, and after an intense week where Barking Town had failed to win a match, he bounced back with a goal. His club-mate Hills scored from the penalty spot, making it 2-0 and a winning start to Jack's county career. He would be a great servant to the Essex FA until he turned professional. Would those officials who selected him repeatedly on merit at this level believe he should be eligible for national as well as regional representation in the future? His skin colour was clearly no bar to his career at this stage.

On the other wing for Essex was outside-right Lt Frederick Nicholas of the famous amateur team, Corinthians. Fred was the grandfather of the cricketer and broadcaster Mark Nicholas and a phenomenal sportsman. He represented Great Britain in the 1920 Olympics, scored 28 times in 54 appearances for Corinthians and played first-class county cricket. It's great to think of a teenage Jack Leslie playing alongside well-to-do army officers, competing together on the same level, towards the same goal.

Just over a week after the county match Jack would have yet another 'biggest of his career to date'. There was certainly great anticipation of the London Senior Cup Final in the press, with several papers hyping up the fixture like some kind of 1920s version of a Sky Sports promo. The Barking Town match-up against rivals Leytonstone would take place at the prestigious venue of Upton Park where *The Globe* predicted 28,000 fans would attend, as West Ham neutrals would swell the crowd. It labelled Barking as favourites, but 'Onlooker' disagreed, as Jack's team had endured the tougher route to the final. He astutely observed that both sets of players would be absolutely knackered (not his exact words) by this stage of the season and it would essentially come down to who could hold it together. As it happened, the crowd was 15,000 but still a record for the competition, and 'Onlooker' was again proved right as Leytonstone got their revenge on Jack's team, winning 5-2.

There was just one last chance for Barking to end the season with bragging rights. They had lost the bigger final, but just a week later took on Leytonstone yet again in the West Ham Charity Cup Final. It wasn't played at the Hammers' ground, Leytonstone having home advantage, but it didn't help them. Barking lifted the trophy with Jack scoring in a 4-1 victory. A magnificent ending to the season for Jack and his Barking team. Mid-table obscurity had been the outcome in both the London and South Essex Leagues, but Barking Town had shone in the cups. The standard of play can't be stressed enough. This would have been a very tough few months for players, and by way of example, in the semi-final of the West Ham Charity Cup, Jack faced one Stan Earle of Clapton. Earle was a 23-year-old inside-right who would later sign for Arsenal before a successful 258-match spell at West Ham United. He was the player who would replace Jack in the England squad of October 1925 without explanation.

Jack wouldn't have a moment to bask in the glory of his achievements. There was no summer break in Ibiza with champagne and cocktails, it was back to the day job at Beckton Gas Works. But just think about the crowd sizes his team had been attracting week in, week out. Players in the lower leagues still achieve a level of celebrity status and Jack's performances got him noticed. Our friend 'Onlooker' rounded up a successful year of amateur football in the South East by picking out the star players across the competitions. Jack Leslie was in the mix as an exciting young forward who had been a joy to watch all season. As he walked to and from the gas works each day, no doubt football fans would stop, chat and hopefully buy him a few pints of brown ale. However, Jack's success may also have caused resentment from the same types who had attacked men of colour in the streets in 1919.

For Jack, the summer of 1920 was a time to reflect on his achievements and think about the future. As he celebrated his 19th birthday it would be dawning on him that the dream of becoming a professional footballer might become reality. With a trade to fall back on, he could push on to bigger things with the backing of his parents. George Hebden, Barking's fearless goalkeeper, was a year older than Jack and had been promptly picked up by Second Division Leicester City in May. Two other team-mates were signed by Barry, which helped them win the Welsh section of the Southern League the next season.

While Jack saw a few players move on he would wonder when his chance would come and who might make an offer for his services. Memories of his talent have been passed down through generations of fans, and Barking's current club president Dave Blewitt says, 'My late father Fred, who was born in 1906 and passed away in 1986, told me Jack was the greatest player he had ever seen play for Barking in his 60-plus years of watching the Blues.' Barking Town would have been keen to keep him for as long as they could to give them a chance of building on their cup success and making a bid to win the leagues.'

Looking forward to the new season, 'Onlooker' was excited by Barking's prospects. Despite losing three players they had a decent-sized squad with many future professionals in their ranks. Remarkably, more than 4,000 fans had turned out to watch the club's pre-season trial matches and it was noted that the selection committee would have a tough time choosing the starting XI for the opening fixture at Walthamstow's Gnome Athletic. So, no charismatic, power-wielding manager calling the shots here, just a group of club bigwigs picking the team, just like the committee that held Jack's England fate in their hands in 1925. The selectors seemed to have an easy choice in writing Jack Leslie's name on the team sheet at outside-left, and while a modern manager would baulk at this method of selection, it didn't hamper Barking Town's season. The Gnomes were no problem. Barking smashed them 4-1 and then 8-0 in the return fixture.

Having created a formidable team, Jack and his comrades decided this was a season to concentrate on the league *and* the cups. And, for Jack, it would mean a remarkable run of representative matches that again showed off his talent far and wide. It would also immerse him in a life far removed from that of the average boilermaker as he met and spent time with more senior officials at matches and fancy functions. This would be perfect preparation for turning pro and eventually becoming an international player.

Jack's first county match of this season came at the end of September when Essex faced Norfolk at Great Yarmouth. After a glittering start with Barking, Jack was joined by two club-mates, Alf Rowe and F. Fackrell, but they suffered a rare 5-1 defeat. It was, though, a one-off and Jack would play regularly and successfully for Essex throughout the season. While many other Barking players came in and out of the team, Jack was a permanent fixture, a testament to his talent and character as these representative teams were chosen by a similar brand of suited FA official as the international selectors, albeit at a lower tier.

Shortly into the season Barking Town faced their toughest test in Jack's time: a home tie against Tottenham Hotspur in the London Challenge Cup on 11 October 1920. Spurs were a First Division club and expected to win, of course, but pundits predicted a tough match. The top-tier team tried to persuade their amateur opponents to switch the match to White Hart Lane, given the expectation of a huge crowd, but Barking refused. They didn't want to give away home advantage and, according to 'Onlooker', 'the Hotspur officials are sending their full League team to meet the Barking men ... This will be a great struggle.' Also, Barking decided to charge a shilling to raise some money for ground improvements, and the home crowd of 7,800 helped bring in £300. With their full-strength team, Spurs won through 4-1, but Barking put up a gallant struggle, winning praise for their efforts in the *Daily Mirror* as well as the local press.

Although everything seemed rosy in terms of results for Barking and Jack's performances personally, the young winger was getting an insight into the politics of top-level football. In January 1921, *The Globe* reported on a dispute between the club and Jack's friend, James Dillimore. The inside-left was a future Millwall player who also lined up for Essex with Jack on several occasions. Dillimore hadn't played in almost six weeks, which would have been a huge blow for Barking and Jack, as the pair had forged a successful left-wing partnership, just as Jack would famously create with Sammy Black at Plymouth when he switched from outside-left to inside-left.

Although Barking were an amateur club, there were clearly issues to resolve to keep the squad happy. While players couldn't be paid, they could receive expenses, but this was often a fine line to tread with the FA. In the same article, *The Globe*'s commentator 'Referee' wrote: 'Gradually the troubles of the Barking club with the LFA and Essex FA are disappearing and there is every prospect of the team making a big fight for the Amateur, London, and Essex Cups this season.' Older, more strident types were now understanding their worth and making demands that sometimes clubs couldn't or wouldn't meet. Dillimore was quite a character, who stayed in touch with Jack and was a guest at his wedding in 1925. He might have even done a turn as he later became a street entertainer in Ilford, managing to tap dance despite the two broken legs that ended his football career. While Jack was a union man who would rail against injustice, he didn't speak out, or perhaps wasn't able to, when it came to his own situation. His youth and personality also combined with the knowledge that putting his head above the parapet as a man of colour wouldn't go down well.

One thing that's surprising is how rare it is to find mentions of Jack's colour at this early stage of his career. It's something often remarked upon in significant moments, especially when the England selection first happened. While there would have been very few players of colour at this level, writers living and working in or near East London would know their comparatively diverse community. It's not surprising then that possibly the first mention of it comes from a paper located a little further out, in Bromley, when Barking beat the local team 2-1 on 10 January 1921. 'Crusader' of the *Bromley Mercury* headed his commentary on Jack's efforts thus: 'Leslie – The Darkie', saying he was 'one of the more outstanding players'.

After their September defeat to Norfolk, Jack and Essex had a great run. They beat Suffolk 8-2 in October, featuring a hat-trick from the quick-stepping Dillimore, and Middlesex 2-0 in November, featuring two Leslie assists. In the latter match five Barking players took to the pitch, which shows how dominant they were locally. The post-match entertainment was hosted by Joseph Francis JP, six-time mayor of Southend. This was another exposure to a whole different culture. In the amateur teams there would be a combination of talented working-class men like Jack, many hoping to make it as professionals and escape the day job, with upper- and middle-class gentlemen who might consider themselves pure amateurs. A reflection of the mixing that took place in the trenches, but on a more level playing field. The officer class remained in charge of the game at board and administrative level, however.

Barking Town continued to progress well in league and cup competitions, but it was in playing for his county that Jack would have his greatest adventures. Eighteen months after his first trip across the

Channel, hanging out with Jules Rimet, another jaunt was planned for Easter. The Essex FA would be taking on their Normandy counterparts in the first-ever inter-county matches played abroad. 'Onlooker' reported that with a strong 14-man squad, including Jack Leslie and four of his Barking team-mates, the English team should win the two matches. Revenge for 1066 at last? We were now staunch allies, and much was made of these tours to play our friends across the Channel and similar return visits. There were to be no such matches against German or Austrian opposition for many years, and it was 1930 before England would play a friendly in Berlin.

The tour was another well-organised affair, the team leaving London Victoria at 8.20pm on Friday, 25 March and arriving in Normandy late that night. They were due back at the more civilised and precise time of 5.24pm on the Tuesday evening. W.H. Clark was in charge, with a business manager, E.A. Eden, who had also been on the previous tour with Jack. One official's sole responsibility was to look after the passports. I guess they didn't trust these young players not to forget or lose their paperwork. Probably sensible. Essex would play North Normandy at Le Havre on Sunday, 27 March and the full Normandy team in Rouen the following day. Naturally there was a 'Banquet of Honour' to follow, hosted by the mayor of Rouen.

The tour was another fantastic experience for Jack Leslie, still just 19, and this time more successful on the pitch. Essex beat North Normandy 2-0 and followed it up with a 4-2 victory over Normandy the next day. The party had a 'royal time' cementing the *Entente Cordiale* according to national newspaper the *Daily News*, and the banquet was a particularly memorable event for Jack. The Essex FA officials had asked the president of the Normandy FA to present their players with badges, but for three select players there was something special to top that. He would never have the chance to bear those famous three lions on his shirt, but Jack Leslie did bear the three swords of Essex on his shirt and on his head. Jack, Baden Herod and Barking team-mate Alf Rowe, who would also join Plymouth Argyle, were presented with a senior cap for playing six or more matches for their county. So Jack Leslie did get a cap.

The Essex FA has a cap dating from 1911; it's purple and adorned with that three-sword crest. This honour won by Jack is something the family weren't aware of until recently and can only wonder where it ended up. It's remarkable to think of Jack Leslie receiving his cap from a senior French FA official and at such a young age. Jack was a man with his feet on the ground, but he also enjoyed a beer or two, and that banquet was a night to enjoy after two victories and a joyous awards presentation.

The team spirit among that group seemed to be strong. They had clubbed together to gift their captain, F.C.J. Blake, a fancy silver cigarette case, and the team photos from Normandy are a wonder to behold, and revealing too. The camaraderie shines through these sepia-toned images from 1921. In one taken after the Easter Monday fixture, fellow cap-winner Baden Herod sits behind Jack, cradling him in the protective manner of an older brother. Jack could handle himself on the pitch but, having played with him often, perhaps Herod knew what Jack faced on and off the field of play. Baden Herod was not only blessed with a fantastic name, but also had a successful career with Charlton Athletic, Brentford and Spurs, who broke their transfer record in 1929 by paying £4,000 for him. At 15 he had enlisted to fight in the First World War, but was discharged when his age was discovered. He then joined up again when he turned 18. Herod was only a year older than Jack but in this photo Jack stands out as the baby of the team and there's something truly moving about it.

Another photo that dates from the same tour has a tale to tell. In it, Jack looks older but it must have been taken on Easter Sunday, the date of the previous match. Squinting in the Normandy sunlight accentuates a furrowed brow, and his hair is less tousled. The backdrop is a stone wall, and behind the players, who sit or crouch, stand the moustachioed bigwigs, some of whose facial hair is distinctly Gallic. It's another evocative picture, and if you look at Jack's hands resting on the shoulders of Alf Rowe, something remarkable catches your eye. On the ring finger of Jack's left hand is a wedding band, yet he didn't marry Win until 1925. They must have been courting by now. Soon he would be off to Plymouth and visits home would have been few and far between, excepting through the summer close season. Did Jack wear this ring at Win's behest to ward off any fanciful French admirers? Or had Jack himself decided it would be a sensible precaution? Given the couple had a successful marriage it's a lovely thought that they stayed true for several years before they wed.

Jack and his Barking team-mates' exertions on the pitch and celebrations off it for Essex in Normandy didn't affect Town's hopes of silverware. They ended as champions of the London League Premier Division and won the London Senior Cup, beating a club that's today as famed for its hipster fans quaffing expensive craft ale as its glorious history ... Dulwich Hamlet. Some 15,000 people watched that match at Millwall's ground in New Cross but there was one spectator that day who would change Jack Leslie's life: Mr Robert Jack, the manager and secretary of Plymouth Argyle Football Club. On a hot, sunny Saturday in the middle of May, the match ended 1-1 after 90 minutes. Extra time proved too much for the South Londoners and Barking Town dominated the additional minutes, scoring three times without response. Bob Jack was impressed.

Jack Leslie's last match in a Barking Town shirt came two weeks later on 28 May 1921. They had won through to the final of the West Ham Charity Cup for the second year in succession and would again face old rivals Leytonstone. The 6-1 thrashing Barking gave them looks good on paper, but have some sympathy for their opponents. Leytonstone lost their keeper early on after a collision and went down to nine men for a period when Jack's opposite number at right-back took a wound to the head. It was a different game back then.

With Jack Leslie's time at Barking Town coming to an end, it was an emotional close to the season, and the period 1919 to 1921 had seen two phenomenally successful campaigns for these talented young amateurs, who were forging reputations. Some of their contemporaries had already been picked up by Football League clubs and many would follow this summer. In just two seasons Jack had won four cups, one league championship, been selected to represent his league and county in matches abroad and even won a cap for being a constant in the Essex FA team.

Jack knew a professional career was on the cards. There are a few striking photographs of him with his Barking Town team-mates. One is wrongly transcribed as 1922/23, because Jack had already moved on by then and the trophies listed had been won by the club in 1919/20. What's more notable is that Jack is sat centre-stage, next to the club president. Here was a black teenager with the ball, a trophy and the world at his feet. Maybe the club president was trying to keep him close because he knew it would be a struggle to keep hold of him for much longer.

This period was also to a great extent the making of Jack Leslie as a man as well as a footballer. He was mixing with war heroes of all classes and officials from the higher echelons of society at home and abroad, while also working during the week in the tough environment of Beckton Gas Works. He was travelling, playing, banqueting and being honoured for his talent and success, while living with his family in one of the poorest areas of the country amid industrial unrest and attacks on members of his community. The fact that he went on to forge a successful, one-club professional career must be a testament to the stability his remarkable parents had given him and the comfort of his wife-to-be, Win. But as he kicked the ball for the last time in a Barking Town shirt and celebrated another cup win, Jack Leslie wasn't sure where the sport he loved would take him next.

Chapter Five

The Call of the Sea

EVEN WHEN recalling some of his most remarkable achievements in football, Jack Leslie was never guilty of an overstatement. I always hark back to the interview with the *Daily Mail* in 1978 because it's so rare, so rich and such an insight. In it you can feel the passion as his eyes widen and he finally allows himself to open up about his playing career. He never boasts about how many clubs wanted to sign him in that summer of 1921. Yet, the end of the 1920/21 football season must have been a period of excitement and hope as club bigwigs tapped him up, eager for his signature. Those tipping points when you're on the verge of success are monumental, particularly with the swirling emotions that course through a teenager. Within weeks of Jack's final appearance for Barking Town he would be able to call himself a professional footballer. But how on earth did Plymouth Argyle, a club more than 200 miles away from Canning Town, persuade him to join them?

Reports of Jack Leslie's talent and potential had spread across the capital and beyond. In that 1978 article Jack tells us that Chelsea, Spurs and nearby West Ham United wanted him. The Irons would have been well aware of his talents as he had graced Upton Park on more than one occasion. And in his granddaughters' photo albums there's a beautiful, faded and creased Barking Town team photo that's intriguing. Jack is sitting, hands on knees, shirt undone with the collar turned up, looking every inch the footballer who knows he's got it … not arrogant, but confident. An incredible piece of history in itself, but on the reverse, neatly scribed in pencil, is a list that reads: Fulham, Plymouth, Portsmouth, Notts Forest [sic] and Bury. These must be the teams who were expressing interest, as the *Western Morning News* reports at the time of Jack's signing for Argyle that he was 'secured in the face of competition with London and up-country clubs'.

It's fair to ask the question: Why didn't he join a 'bigger' club? Most of the others mentioned were First or Second Division outfits and you might think this would be more attractive and lucrative. A Plymouth fan's gut reaction to that is, 'What do you mean a bigger club? Argyle are massive! You can shove your Tottenham Hotspur up your a**e!' In truth, most of these clubs are in higher tiers with silverware in their trophy cabinet, and our current owner's genuine, realistic ambition is to be a sustainable Championship team. I can always dream, but there are no outlandish claims to future success. In the post-war period, however, Plymouth Argyle had a clear and public goal to be a top-flight team and were doing everything they could to achieve this, starting with the players. For Plymouth to compete in the Premier League feels like a pasty in the sky pipedream, but the fans and club hierarchy in the 1920s genuinely believed that reaching the top tier in England was possible.

It's important to give a little context here. Professional football had emerged in the mill and colliery towns of the north in the later 19th century and, given Plymouth is at the other end of the country, it's no surprise that it took a while for the professional game to kick off down in Devon. The amateur club that called itself Argyle FC had been established in 1886, and on 30 April 1903 became a professional outfit … Plymouth Argyle Football Club. And their first signing was one Robert Jack, a name that's synonymous both with the club and the Jack Leslie story. Bob Jack was a Scotsman who had played for Bolton Wanderers and Preston North End, both of whom were genuinely massive in the early 1900s. In just a few years he would become the club's manager and secretary. Robert Jack went on to serve Plymouth Argyle for 28 of its most successful years from 1910 until 1938.

Before the First World War, the club directors had assembled a team of well-known, seasoned pros to compete in the Southern

League, which they won in 1913. Plymouth Argyle tried to get elected to the Football League as war approached, but that global tragedy ended professional competition from 1915 until 1919. One first-team regular, William Baker, and six former players would never return to the game they loved. When football officially restarted, Plymouth Argyle would play, as before, in the Southern League. The team included Bob Jack's son David, who would go on to be a huge star. He would score the opening goal in the first Wembley FA Cup Final for Bolton Wanderers and captain England. Bob Jack may have made his home way out west, but here was a canny, connected patriarch of a footballing dynasty. He and the Plymouth directors wanted progress. In a bid to scale the Football League after the war, Argyle would be joined by an array of former and future England internationals and a player who would be selected for the national team while a mainstay at Home Park ... Jack Leslie.

The Football League structure was developing, and in 1920 a new Third Division was formed, with the Pilgrims elected to join. Jack Leslie's signing in 1921 coincided with Plymouth Argyle's entry into a new tier. Below the First and Second Divisions two additional leagues were created, the Third Division North and Third Division South, where Argyle joined the likes of Portsmouth, Southampton, Millwall, QPR and ... Exeter City. Only the champions of these two new leagues would be promoted, with two teams relegated from the Second Division. If the Greens were going up, they would need a bit of luck.

Bob Jack was happy to scour the entire country to push for success, and his approach was described thus in club history book, *All About Argyle 1903–1963*:

> Bob Jack was one of the old school of football secretary-managers that are sadly passing out of the football game ... and the game is all the poorer with their passing. He was one of those managerial giants of whom it has been said, knew the football game inside out. He and his contemporaries knew the true market value of every player in the game; they knew the location of all the breeding grounds of footballers from John-o-Groats to Land's End and scorned the bargain basement

technique of team-building: they made a study of the game from all angles, knew the League tables off by heart, and were respected in the boardroom as much as they were on the terraces.

Bob was building for the future and in Barking Town had found three players for his new squad. The manager knew he needed players to make an immediate impact as well as prospects for the future who would also gain experience by playing in the reserves. The second team would continue to compete in the Southern League, so the club would need a full squad with the ability to field two professional teams all season. Among 13 new signings for the 1921/22 season were Frank Richardson, Alf Rowe and Jack Leslie, who Bob Jack had seen in two cup matches for Barking at the end of the previous campaign. Richardson was a 24-year-old centre-forward and had lit up the London and Essex competitions with his goalscoring record. Many of the assists had come from Jack Leslie on the left wing, but with Alf Rowe at 25, Jack was very much the baby of the group and one for the future. The ambition of Argyle in its signings is clear but how did Bob Jack bring these bright prospects on board?

Bob Jack was an astute, charismatic man who cared for his players but in the best traditions of football managers wasn't averse to using slightly underhand tactics to get his man. Jack talked about his signing in the press a couple of times, and in the *Daily Mail* article explains how he was lured to the South West:

> Plymouth was crafty. I got home from work one day, and this man was in the front parlour. He'd got postcards spread all over the table and mantelpiece … Plymouth Hoe, the sea, the hills. Me mum and dad's eyes were poking out. In them days your holiday was a day just to Southend by char-a-banc. So Plymouth, all that green, was like the end of the world.

Of course, those postcards didn't come with the appropriate weather warning. The view from Plymouth Hoe is spectacular and a walk to take in the expanse of Plymouth Sound is obligatory. This natural harbour, with Drake's Island to the west and the yachting marinas and fishing fleet to the east, is a sight to lift the heart. A stroll down to the cobbled streets of the Barbican for a well-earned pint in The Dolphin is a joy that never tires. But that stroll often requires waterproofs. Umbrellas will be rendered useless due to high winds.

The thought of their young son moving hundreds of miles away from the family home didn't put Jack's parents off, and I love that they were on board with the idea. Jack's dad had run away to sea and his mum had married him, a black sailor from Jamaica. In their own ways both had made brave, adventurous, positive choices that made their life better. Now their son had his trade to fall back on, they encouraged him to go west and fully supported his decision to leave Canning Town to pursue this unpredictable but exciting career. They were excited about the idea of visiting him too. If Jack had already embarked on his relationship with Win, as it seems, then that would have made this an even tougher decision. It was a testament to the couple that their burgeoning relationship didn't fall victim to geography. But distance and absence wouldn't always make the heart grow fonder in the future.

Jack Leslie said in the *Daily Mail* that the signing wasn't about money. Earnings were a constant tussle between players and the Football League and there was a maximum wage that had recently been reduced from £10 to £8 in the season and £6 across summer. Jack says he was on £5 and £4 as a youngster, although he would be up to the maximum within a few years. Plymouth weekly, the *Sunday Independent*, interviewed Jack in 1972, and he recalled: 'A number of London clubs were interested in me. Argyle offered ten shillings a week more and that was a lot in those days. The idea of living by the sea also appealed to me.' Incredible. Not every player would want to leave their hometown if there were options nearby but, for Jack Leslie, Plymouth Argyle was an enticing and exciting prospect. I wonder whether he felt any of the pressure. The signing of the trio was trumpeted not just in the local press but nationally in *Athletic News*, which commented on Jack's young age and achievements: 'Leslie who is only 19 years of age, has represented Essex in eight inter-county games and has also played for that county and the London League in Paris.'

Training would begin on 4 August 1921, and as Jack Leslie, Frank Richardson and Alf Rowe travelled to Plymouth, their chests would be bulging with pride at becoming professionals. Jack's young head must have been filled with anticipation of the season ahead and, understandably, a little apprehension. Yet he and his older comrades were confident players who had achieved honours as amateurs and played in front of crowds of up to 15,000. The first team would be a step up, for sure, but it may not have been as intimidating on the pitch. Playing for Barking Town in local leagues meant opposition supporters were able to come in droves, so touchline barracking must have been fiery. Jack Leslie on the wing would have borne the brunt of it. He talked later about how the colour of his skin led to abuse and targeting. Jack never complained or protested but stood his ground and refused to be intimidated. He doesn't make a big issue of it in his later recollections, but it happened. However, away fans would be virtually non-existent at Plymouth's Home Park, so it would be a breeze compared to Barking's Vicarage Field or the many London and Essex pitches he had graced.

Jack must have known that his chances of first-team action would be few and far between compared to the more mature Richardson who came to the professional game with a big reputation, having scored more than 70 goals in the previous season. Local press such as the *Western Morning News* described the centre-forward as 'a mild sensation ... He was probably the most sought-after amateur in the country.' The paper also recognised how promising Jack was and that he 'plays a fine wing game with a lovely, easy centre, and combines well with other men. Richardson notched a lot of goals from Leslie's centres last season.' But with the arrival of William Baker, a 29-year-old left-winger signed from Derby County at the peak of his career, Jack would have been well aware of the challenge ahead.

Bob Jack had been desperate for a new set of forwards after finishing mid-table in 1920/21. The top scorer for the season only bagged seven. Even his son, the great David Jack, who moved on in December, only netted three in 14 matches. We'll discover how the manager always did his best to keep hold of the players he wanted, and with player power nowhere near what it is now, he was well able to in most cases. But it seems he made an exception for his son. Maybe David was so desperate to leave the parental clutches that he was giving his dad a hard time. More likely, Bob Jack put family over club and allowed his son to fly the nest and progress his career. And it was Bolton Wanderers, a club he had played for, who picked David up, so the connection was personal. The very decent fee of £3,500 helped create a new-look Plymouth team that would herald some of the most successful and consistent years in the club's history.

Having two team-mates from his previous club must have helped Jack Leslie settle into his new home. But it was quite a culture shock. He had just turned 20 and this would have been the first time he had lived away from his family. The football trips away would have helped, but aside from the cross-Channel tours, Jack hadn't travelled outside the South East. And now he would be in digs in Plymouth, living in a new community, not in the rarefied homes of today's big-money signings but alongside Janners, as Plymothians call themselves.

As he set up home in the residential streets of Peverell near Home Park, Jack would have been a novelty to locals. There wasn't anything like the numbers of black people compared to East London, although it would be wrong to say they were unheard of or unseen. Some black immigrants who wished to return home after the First World War were sent to Plymouth to board ship, and one of the town's most famous residents had a similar tale to Jack's. Bill Miller was the son of a seaman from Sierra Leone who settled in Plymouth and married an English woman. He was a remarkable figure who served in the Royal Flying Corps during the First World War and became a Labour councillor, wielding influence in Plymouth for decades to come. Jack found he had someone local to look up to.

In the most part, Jack was welcomed in Plymouth and became very well loved, especially as he became more successful with Argyle. He said settling in was no problem: 'It was a good move for me. Argyle treated me well, and I had a great respect for the club's supporters. I found Plymothians a fine bunch of people and I still have a warm regard for the place.' To think that he didn't face any discrimination, abusive or negative comments, particularly as a newcomer, would be naïve, but Jack would have been used to this while growing up, and the streets of Plymouth would have been a little less scary than the East End. That positivity towards the place, its population, the football club and its fans remained throughout his life. Plymouth and Argyle were always in his heart. And the feeling was mutual. But when he got married and his wife moved to Plymouth, it did expose attitudes that in some ways made life much tougher for Win than Jack.

Jack would soon get stuck into his new day job with a pre-season practice match on Saturday, 20 August, just three days after his 20th birthday. Argyle squad members played each other as Greens vs Whites and Jack is pictured for the first time in a green jersey playing in searing heat before a 6,000-strong crowd. He's snapped taking a shot stopped by 'a fine save from Cook', and the *Western Morning News* says his claims to a first-team spot 'merit consideration'. Pundits expected the experienced signing Baker to start but Jack Leslie was already getting attention.

Those initial waves of excitement in pre-season training and practice matches didn't develop into a storm and there must have been a bit of frustration at the start. Jack Leslie knew he was a good player, but instead of being an automatic first-team choice, as he had been for both Barking Town and Essex, he would have to fight for his place. He also saw his team-mate Frank Richardson get off to a flyer by walloping a hat-trick in his first match, with Jack on the side-lines. Richardson would score 31 goals that season. You can imagine the banter between them, even though Jack would have been pleased for Frank, and it was definitely a good thing that Argyle were doing well. Fortunately, Jack had Alf Rowe with him in the reserves, so they could console each other, and with Rowe a mature 25 it must have been more frustrating for him. But it was still early days in their professional careers.

It's fair to say that Jack's first year was full of promise but didn't see a spectacular breakthrough. His performances for Argyle reserves were an instant hit but transferring that potential to the first team wasn't a simple task. Any frustration or jealousy had to be tempered by the fact that he was playing competitive football in the Southern League. It's incredible to read the reports and find that Jack and Argyle's second string were greeted by huge crowds. Can you believe these reserve team match-ups would attract thousands of fans to Home Park? We're talking gates of more than 6,000 for Luton, 7,000 for Swindon and even 9–10,000 for Reading, all in the autumn of 1921, the first months of Jack's professional career. Astonishing. I've been a part of smaller crowds at Home Park watching the first team.

Jack's exploits also made the pages of the local press every week, and on 17 September a striking head shot of a young Jack Leslie appeared in the *Football Herald*. Sure, the good-looking Frank Richardson and Jack's rival, experienced outside-left Billy Baker, were pictured the week before, but this must have been a lovely piece of recognition so soon after joining the club. This would mark his burgeoning celebrity status in Plymouth.

It might have been easy for Jack's head to swell a little. I talk a lot about his grounded personality but even the calmest of minds can be lifted on the crest of a wave of praise. The *Football Herald* and its stalwart through Jack Leslie's time, 'Pilgrim', wrote: 'Argyle have discovered a winger of exceptional promise in Leslie, whose keenness for the game cannot be mistaken.' The reserves were performing brilliantly, marking their card as leading goalscorers in the Southern League. A week later 'Pilgrim' picked out an individual effort in a 3-3 away draw with Bristol City reserves, 'One of the finest features in a hard-fought game was Leslie's goal, which has been described by a Bristol critic as one of the best goals ever seen on the City ground.' The *Western Morning News* detailed the strike: 'A beauty and an individual achievement. He took the ball up the left on his own, bore in and sent the leather swiftly and obliquely into the corner of the net.' I would have loved to have seen that. The joy goals like this give a fan are unbridled. Seeing a talented young attacker express themselves on the pitch lifts the heart of even the most jaded among the crowd. And this would have given Jack the confidence to think he could make it in the first team. 'Pilgrim' certainly thought that Jack was one of the club's best summer signings: 'Whenever he is called upon to serve the premier side he will certainly fill the position with credit.' His chance would come, but would Jack grasp it with both hands or fall foul of the commentator's curse and fluff his first-team lines?

Before any opportunity could present itself, Jack had other duties and a chance to return home. Part of the deal when he and his mates were signed by Argyle was that the Devon club would travel up to Essex and compete in a friendly with Barking Town on Monday, 26 September 1921. The amateur club did well despite losing those three key players. They managed to keep goal machine Richardson at bay, but not Jack, who scored the first goal in a 2-2 draw in front of 5,000 fans. The match was a financial success and there was a nice touch as the unemployed were admitted free of charge. The event was followed by a slap-up dinner at The Bull Hotel and a warm toast by Barking chairman, D.T. Jackson, who said it was a pleasure to state that 'in securing Richardson, Leslie, and Rowe, the Argyle manager had not only got three players who would be a credit to the club, but he secured them in a thoroughly legitimate manner.' Postcards of the sunny seafront aside, it seems Bob Jack and the Argyle directors were straightforward, honest operators and suggests that perhaps other football club bosses behaved otherwise. Surely not?!

It's also interesting, and not surprising, to see that a key FA official was in attendance, Mr T.H. Kirkup, secretary of the London FA. Tommy Kirkup, originally from Durham, was a long-serving FA Council member from 1897 until 1947 and instrumental in the development of the amateur and professional game in the capital. As such, he would have been aware of Jack Leslie's talent and heritage even before the Barking Town vs Plymouth Argyle friendly. Kirkup never served on the International Selection Committee but was one of many senior well-connected officials who saw Jack play, probably on more than one occasion. This only makes the story of Jack's England selection more intriguing as we'll discover. These administrators and club managers and directors who sat down to eat at The Bull Hotel talked about the sport. They discussed players, their qualities and personalities. They would have talked about Jack.

For the new young professional, this was a chance to return to his old stomping ground, catch up with friends and talk about his progress so far. He must have been fairly satisfied, while anxiously awaiting his first-team opportunity. Jack's parents and Win might even have been at the match, and with his next outing being the following Wednesday at Home Park, he would have spent some time with them in London before his return.

Bob Jack's promise of sunny skies was proving surprisingly accurate so far as there was some phenomenally hot weather in the autumn of 1921 in Plymouth. It wouldn't last. Playing on pitches more suitable for cricket would have their own physical challenges but Jack would be out in the wind, rain and occasionally snow, very soon. I wonder what his hopes and fears were at this stage? Considering the support they gave him, I'm sure John and Annie would be proud of the start their son had made. Jack knew that football wouldn't make him rich, but he must have been desperate to grasp any opportunity for first-team action. This could open the doors to a long-term career and give the family he might be pondering with Win a decent start.

Jack didn't have long to wait. An injury to Billy Baker meant he would be in the team to face Merthyr Town at Home Park on 19 November. This should have been an ideal match to start. Plymouth were riding high at the top of the Third Division South, were yet to lose a home match, winning all but one, and had never failed to score at Home Park during this campaign. 'Pilgrim' was excited at the prospect. He criticised the lack of goals from the first-team wingers as opposed to Jack Leslie who was banging them in for the reserves with six already. The Welsh club were ninth in the league but were on good form. The 14,000 who came out to watch the Greens would have been excited to see their new signing in action. Could he reproduce the exciting form he had shown for the second string …? No.

Jack's first match for Plymouth Argyle was far from a disaster. The result was a disappointing nil-nil, but at least it wasn't a defeat. And the match report told how he was involved in many of his team's more promising moves, but 'Leslie's debut at outside-left was not the success his admirers had anticipated. He lacked confidence, and seldom displayed the skill which has characterised his games with the Reserves.' 'Pilgrim' seemed to think the understandable nerves of this first outing got to Jack and he didn't quite do enough to break through just yet: 'On Saturday's showing Baker must have preference, but in his absence, Leslie would be worth persevering with.' So, at least it wasn't a total write-off.

Billy Baker's injury was serious enough to leave the manager little option but to give Jack a run in the team, and in the return match at Merthyr he showed what he could do. A combination with a pal did the trick as Jack crossed from the left wing, beating the offside trap, allowing Frank Richardson to pounce on it and score. The commentary on this match was the first time Jack's skin colour was mentioned by the local press since he had arrived on the scene at Plymouth, with 'Pilgrim' commenting, 'It was from the "Darkie's" centre that Richardson made a fine opportunity to dash in and net the ball while everybody was shouting for offside.' 'Pilgrim' became an admirer of Jack so what prompted this comment? If he had any issue with Jack's skin colour, then surely he would have mentioned it sooner? Perhaps after writing this, he reflected on his words and chose not to in future.

Jack managed a nine-match run in the first team, which included the traditional Christmas fixtures against local rivals, Exeter City. Back in the 20s teams would often play the home and away matches in succession, and the Devon derbies frequently took place on Christmas or Boxing Day. With an away fixture at Southend on Christmas Eve, there wasn't much chance to enjoy the festive season and Jack would have been keen to keep impressing. Argyle were doing well but had dropped from top to second during this spell.

Throughout this time, Jack was winning regular praise for his exciting play, but he wasn't the finished article. Critics said he 'needs to be a little more resolute in his tackling'. And the packed festive timetable took its toll as Jack excelled in a brilliant 2-0 win away at Exeter on Boxing Day but was the weakest forward in the return fixture, a nil-nil the following afternoon that was a veritable Yuletide let-down for the 22,000 who thronged to Home Park. Too many pints of brown ale to celebrate the win or perhaps the congested fixtures proved just a bit too much for a young, developing player.

Either way, Billy Baker was fit for the New Year's Eve match and Jack was back to the reserves.

On the one hand Jack must have been gutted. To play consistently as a youngster in a team that was vying for promotion would have been exciting. To be among old hands such as Moses Russell and crossing the ball to his mate in the centre, Frank Richardson, who was having a hell of a season up front, would have been exhilarating. But Jack had to learn to cope with the pressures that top-flight football presented. No matter your natural ability, your place wasn't guaranteed. This would have taken man-management from Bob Jack. His retention of players and the many kind words said of him suggest that the gaffer helped keep Jack's head straight. Sure, he was out of the first team, but Jack Leslie knew he would get another chance if he continued to show his best in the reserves.

Backroom support may have been there, but criticism was writ large in the press and no doubt on the terraces and in the pubs of Plymouth too. From the Saturday nightspots of the Barbican to the hostelries surrounding the dockyard and naval base where people gathered for an after-work pint or three, football would be a big topic of conversation.

One wordsmith for the *Football Herald* called himself 'Tuan', which either means 'master or lord' or 'a small flesh-and-nectar-eating marsupial'. Probably the latter. Anyhow, 'Tuan' was frustrated by Jack's run of performances:

> Leslie ought to make a fine winger – he has speed and natural ability for the game – but he is developing on the wrong lines. How often on Tuesday did he get clean away only to centre yards behind the inside men? And that irritating habit of passing back to the half! It was all so purposeless.

Give Jack a break, 'Tuan', he's only 20 and he hasn't even found his best position on the pitch yet. If that was a football writer's verdict constrained by the polite norms of the day, just imagine what it was like when a group of blokes talked Argyle in The Dolphin.

Nowadays, you only have to go on social media to see how young players get it in the neck while they're still finding their feet, even when teams are having a decent season. And I've no doubt Jack's skin colour would have come into that. Not necessarily always negatively and it wouldn't have been seen as racism at that time. However, the white supporters' views of black players' capabilities was often tied to an existing narrative. If you look at the judgements the military hierarchy made about colonial service personnel, you see exactly this. Jack would eventually break through and prove so many of those stereotypes wrong over the next decade. He hadn't had time to yet and he got stick for it.

Disappointment at his return to the reserves wouldn't have lasted long as Jack immediately hit the form he had shown before. While the first team was gripped in a promotion struggle, the seconds were flying in the Southern League and wrapped it up by the end of April with two matches left to play. A 6-0 win at home against Southampton reserves with two assists and a goal for Jack made sure of the championship.

The big rivalry in the Third Division South was with the same club's premier players but this one was going down to the wire. Championship and promotion would rest on the final match of the season. Argyle were away to Queens Park Rangers, who they had convincingly dispatched 4-0 at home the previous Saturday. Southampton lay in second, two points behind, and were at home to Newport County, who they had already beaten away. Plymouth had the tougher test but were on a 16-match unbeaten run, would field an almost unchanged team and only needed a draw. Even losing Billy Baker again through injury shouldn't be an issue. The enforced change even garnered attention in the *Daily Mirror*, which was aware of Argyle's talented young replacement. Jack Leslie would take the left-wing berth for the final league fixture. It was only the most important match in Plymouth Argyle's history.

It wasn't Jack's fault, honest. The *Western Morning News* match report, while perhaps leaning towards the Pilgrims' favour, tells a sorry tale of misfortune, with shots blocked and a clear offside for Rangers' first goal. It was a shock 2-0 defeat for Argyle. As for Jack

Leslie, he did his job well, putting in an excellent performance to no avail. This would hurt. It was characterised as 'PLYMOUTH ARGYLE'S DRAMATIC FALL FROM GRACE' in the *Sunday Illustrated*, which called it thus: 'Rarely has there been such a dramatic eleventh-hour surprise since relegation and promotion were first established.' No doubt, Jack's thoughts on luck began to form after this match. How did Southampton do? They won 5-0, leaping to the championship above Argyle on goal average. Plymouth were stuck in the Third Division South.

Bob Jack praised his players as they hung their heads in disappointment, while also doing a bit of classic managerial blame-shifting. He criticised Welsh clubs such as Newport County for their poor showing against Southampton during the season. But that's football and Argyle would continue to be the unluckiest team in the league for the rest of the decade. Jack and his team-mates didn't know it yet, but they would become accustomed to disappointment. At least the season had ended in London, albeit on the wrong side. After commiserating with his team-mates, Jack could head east to spend time with his family.

While the finale was a gut-wrenching disappointment, Jack had done his best to help his club and won the Southern League with the reserves. He'd had a pretty good first season as a professional and Bob Jack was delighted with his decision to sign Jack Leslie. He had also had some fantastic experiences in front of big crowds. Even that final match was something to learn from and would stand him in good stead for the adversity ahead. Jack would have plenty of good times to enjoy too. The close season would be spent in London, and the family home in Canning Town was still his permanent address. There would be time for trips to Southend, cricket and courting Win.

Chapter Six

On the Fringes

JACK RETURNED to training in August 1922 and was just as excited as he had been the previous summer, if not more so. Sure, he hadn't made that first-team place a certainty and was yet to find the net for them, but he hadn't let the side down. Jack was, however, a breakout star of the reserves, scoring regularly and often spectacularly from the left wing, helping the team walk the Southern League. As the new season approached, the *Western Morning News* concluded that Jack and the other new players had proved valuable. Jack probably assumed that his task ahead would be simple. Either grasp the opportunity if experienced winger Billy Baker got injured again or play so well for the reserves that he replaced him.

As it transpired, it wouldn't be quite so straightforward. Frank Richardson scored an incredible 31 goals, but no other forwards had even come close to double figures. The manager and directors who would pick the teams by committee spent the next two seasons shuffling their forward pack. These experiments would eventually work out for Jack, but it meant two years in and out of the first team with a succession of different partners up front. Jack Leslie needed all his reserves of patience and resilience.

There are more reports about the players' activities outside their day jobs later in Jack's career as he became more established. It looks as if the better the player he became, the more fun he had, but that's probably because more was written about a first-teamer. How was life for Jack Leslie in these early years? He was a promising, young, good-looking footballer in Plymouth and would have been noticed for that alone. But he would also have attracted attention because of the colour of his skin, of that there's no doubt. It wasn't all negative but there must have been times after a poor performance where it would have been difficult to have a quiet pint. Jack wouldn't have had a local nearby as he was, along with many of the other players, in digs in Peverell. It's a quiet, residential area – well, it's not so quiet on matchdays given its proximity to Home Park, but there are rows and rows of Edwardian houses and ... no pubs. The land was sold at the turn of the 20th century and the seller, who favoured temperance, stipulated there should be no licensed premises. So, Jack would have to make an eight-minute trek to the well-known hostelry, The Hyde Park on Mutley Plain. It has always been a peaceful pub compared to others in Plymouth, so hopefully Jack never had any issues when buying his brown ale at the bar.

Players in the 1920s were placed on a pedestal because they were elite sportsmen playing in front of thousands each week. Just like today, it was a status many boys aspired to, one that only a tiny percentage would ever attain, and to do so took talent, hard work and a few slices of good fortune. Unlike today, even the highest-profile players lived among us, not behind the gates of a mansion. Lower league players may live in less rarefied circumstances, and many do get involved in their communities, but there's still a separation that didn't exist in Jack's time. The maximum wage for a professional footballer was being cut in the early 1920s and by 1922 was £8 a week during the season and £6 across the summer: that's less than £600 and £450 in today's money. The players did also get £2 for a win and £1 for a draw. Jack was earning less as a junior player, but still pulled in a very decent wage compared to fans who worked in the dockyard or Jack's mates back at Beckton Gas Works. In 1924 a boilermaker was at the lower end of the wage scale for skilled workers on £2 4s. Jack was doing well and had some disposable income, but he wasn't on crazy money. Eventually he would earn the maximum wage and certainly by 1928 because his contract exists. I would imagine that by then he had been on the top wage for a few years, having been a permanent fixture in the first team and been the subject of offers from other clubs.

Jack was affable, friendly and well liked wherever he went. One 97-year-old fan, Charlie Trevethan, says the fans loved him and never thought about Jack's colour: 'We just thought of him as a footballer and a damn good one at that.' He was a great player for Argyle and that's what mattered. Of course, this is wonderful to hear and reflects the view of the majority of Plymouth fans. But the fact that Jack faced adversity and abuse, on and off the pitch, should never be forgotten.

Jack's personality helped him settle. He was a generous soul. Too generous perhaps, as his time as a pub landlord in the late 1930s when he gave away a few too many free drinks shows. But that spirit of bonhomie meant that making friends with his team-mates and neighbours came easily. If he were to take a slightly longer walk or the tram beyond The Hyde Park pub, Jack would very quickly be in the town centre. A short hop up a hill and he would be on Plymouth Hoe looking out to sea. There's the odd pub around there, but he would want to head east to the Barbican, which is one of the few areas to have survived the Blitz. The delights of many historic hostelries can still be enjoyed to this day, including The Dolphin Hotel, made famous by Beryl Cook, and The Minerva, tucked away on Looe Street. 'I really loved the old Plymouth,' Jack said in the 70s, comparing it to the reconstruction after the war. 'I must say I am impressed by the way the new modern city has been planned and built, but there was something beautiful, even rustic about the old Plymouth, and I had no difficulty in settling there.' Jack quickly fell in love with Plymouth, and Plymouth would soon fall in love with him.

At Barking, Jack was playing so frequently while also working full-time that his only training was the occasional 'trot'. Plymouth was a big step up and physical training was the focus. Strategy wasn't high on the agenda and, in general, British clubs didn't prepare tactically for matches, and Jack said that was the case at Argyle. The committee would choose the 11 players to turn out and then it was up to them to work it out. Physical fitness was important, and this was key to his development as a player. You only have to look at his vital statistics to see that. The *Plymouth Argyle Football Club*

Hand Book was a publication that came out ahead of each season, and the 1921/22 edition stated that Jack was 5ft 9in and 11st 10lb. No weakling, but by the next season he was up to 12st and in 1924 he had apparently grown an inch to 5ft 10in and was 12st 4lb. He went up to 12st 7lb by his late 20s and maintained this to the end of his career. For a player like Jack, who would move from the wing to a more central, combative, attacking role at inside-left, this physical development can only have enhanced his on-field progress.

Below the manager, Plymouth Argyle had two trainers, Tommy Haynes, and recently retired player Septimus Atterbury. With a name like that you would think the team used quidditch as a training technique, but Atterbury was a popular and sturdy defender who took physical fitness and stamina very seriously. This was seen as unconventional at the time, which seems surprising given how hard-fought each season was and the stresses the game put on players' bodies. Pictures of the team in training show Jack and his mates running along the sidelines of the Home Park pitch and jumping over outstretched hands or long pieces of rope. It's been written that training in England at the time was basic, with the theory being to starve players of the ball between matches so they were hungry for it come Saturday.

But there are plenty of images that prove this wasn't quite the case. There's a great series from January 1924 with a very chilly-looking Jack Leslie pulling his jersey down over his hands in front of a goalmouth with barely a blade of grass to be seen. He's with a group of first-team regulars, which shows that, even though he was still in and out of the starting XI, Jack was already a key part of the set-up. There's also an amazing archive film of Plymouth Argyle in training from 1935, just one agonising year after Jack's retirement through injury. It features players such as his legendary partner Sammy Black, cheekily yet somewhat uncomfortably grinning at the camera. It's an endearing insight into a character who wasn't unlike Jack – hugely talented but never one to boast about it. In the video the first team play a training match against the reserves in an empty ground. The team clearly did practise technique but didn't go deep into formations and strategy.

Archive video of Hull City in training from 1930 shows the players lying on their backs, lifting their lower torsos up and doing those bicycle exercises with their legs. This was a system 'to develop their abdominal and gluteus muscles' apparently. You can hear the faint sound of laughter in the background as if some people thought these kinds of new-fangled methods were ridiculous.[16] At Plymouth, Bob Jack wasn't sitting down with the players preparing a plan to exploit their next opponents' weaknesses and counter their strengths. He was busy keeping an eye on the squad and who might come in and out while also dealing with admin and correspondence as he was club secretary as well as manager. The day-to-day workouts were with Tommy and Sept, while Bob was in the office, where Jack would be called one October day in 1925.

The manager's two key staff were clearly popular. One reserve match Jack played in was a benefit for Atterbury for which 7,000 fans turned up to boost his bonus. And in 1926 there's a promo photo with Tommy Haynes comically dressed as a police constable pointing a smiling Jack and his team-mates towards a sign saying, '2nd Division'. It didn't help, but there was clearly great team spirit. Having said that, it was taken at the start of training when the weather was good and everyone was full of hope for the season ahead.

The West Country weather didn't always mean training would go to plan. In January of 1924 the team were about to take a walk across Dartmoor, ending with tea in the village of Yelverton. But this was cancelled due to inclement weather. Dartmoor is beautiful but bleak and it can sometimes be impossible to see your hand in front of your face. Stepping into a deep bog and sinking up to your armpits wouldn't be ideal preparation for a professional football match. Bob Jack also didn't want his players enjoying themselves *too* much and told *The Snooze* that he had banned them from throwing shapes in local nightspots. 'Dancing in itself may be a useful physical exercise, but the late hours accompanying it are not conducive to the best interests of a professional footballer.'

The straightforward nature of training and preparation was in line with how the English saw the sport. It was all about guts and glory, hard-fought physical battles, thundering tackles and fearsome shots, rather than beautiful passing, moving and probing until you created an opening. This took its toll on the players, and match reports show how often they were stretchered off the pitch or hobbling on, exacerbating their injuries. Players would often be patched up and return mid-match. There's a movie from 1931 called *The Great Game*, starring Jack Cock, who played with our Jack for a couple of seasons, and it's a great insight into the life of a professional. As a film it's not the best but the changing room scenes are evocative, and Cock's performance stands up. One of the trainers says of his team, 'Most of them are wounded heroes before they get on the field.'[17] The players sup cups of tea and light up cigarettes as they sit in their mud-stained kits. Jack Leslie smoked Player's all his life and Sammy Black sometimes ran on to the pitch with a tab tucked behind his ear. It was a simpler time when men were men, who were totally unaware of the health risks of smoking tobacco and heading a heavy leather football.

As for playing conditions, the pitches could be baked into solid concrete in the summer, become a quagmire in the autumn and spring or a frozen wasteland in winter. There are pictures of Jack throwing himself around in lakes of mud and on pitches covered in snow. It would take a tsunami to call off a match and most of the fans would be getting soaked too. Grandstands and coverings did go up at Home Park in Jack's time, but many supporters were out in the open and one press report complains of how those in the cheap sections were essentially standing on rubble. Jack may have been earning well for a young man and enjoying life in Plymouth, but it wasn't easy. The job itself was something he loved, but his body was on the line just as much as it would be when his hands were hard at work on metal at the gas works or the docks in East London.

The next two football seasons were frustrating yet formative for Jack. For much of the 1922/23 campaign he remained understudy to Billy Baker on the left wing but would very quickly see a fellow second-stringer, inside-left Bert Batten, break through. They had played four times in the first team together previously and there's no sense of any personal enmity, but they would soon be fighting it out for a place. Spoiler alert ... the good guy wins. Bert was a few years older than Jack and had come from Bristol City. While Jack continued with the reserves Bert grabbed his chance and played 32 times to Jack's seven, including one cup and one league match together as partners on the left. Unfortunately, in the 1-1 home draw to Norwich in the league the pair 'did little which inspired confidence', according to the *Western Morning News*, although the *Football Herald* said they 'combined in good style' for a period of the second half, at least. *The Snooze* seemed harsh as it also said supporters would be pleased that players would return to force Jack back to the reserves again! So, he would have to sit it out for a while, and during the spring of 1923 also picked up an injury that kept him out for a couple of months.

But something changed on 31 March 1923. Argyle decided to try Jack Leslie at inside-left for the reserves. He was a revelation, 'repeatedly sending in hard shots' and scoring two of the team's three goals with no reply from Bath reserves. When Bert Batten picked up an injury after a run that produced an excellent 11-goal return, Jack took his place. And he did it in style, scoring three times in five matches and playing exceptionally well.

Jack's breakthrough into the first team came at a time when Plymouth Argyle were getting plenty of attention from the press and the FA bigwigs. Much of that fell on their exceptional defender from Durham, Jack Hill. He towered above his peers at 6ft 3in and was an immense presence. Argyle may have been in the Third Division South, but they had Moses Russell, who regularly turned out for Wales, and in February 1923 Hill came to the attention of the English FA's international selectors who chose him for 'The South' team in a trial against an England XI. Although his team lost 1-0, Hill did enough to be chosen for another trial match for England vs 'The North'. That second match was postponed, and Hill didn't make it into the next international fixture. But he had made his mark and on 12 March 1923 this Plymouth Argyle player was selected as a reserve to travel for the England vs Belgium match to be played at the Arsenal ground a week later. This was a player who Jack Leslie had worked alongside several times.

Hill's selection was a huge honour, and Home Park was buzzing with praise and banter bouncing around the changing room and training pitch. Jack Leslie would have been aware of exactly what this accolade meant to his team-mate. 'Pilgrim' in the *Football Herald* hailed Jack Hill's talent and was convinced he would win his cap. And the news he had been hoping for came on Friday, 13 April 1923, an auspicious date for Plymouth Argyle. The International Selection Committee met at The North British Hotel in Edinburgh and picked Hill to play for England against France in Paris on 10 May.

After he had received that incredible news, Jack Hill and Jack Leslie would play three first-team matches together. On a squally April night in a total quagmire, 2,000 diehard fans huddled together under the covered areas. They forgot the rain in the 87th minute as they rose expectantly to watch Jack Hill thread Jack Leslie through with a neat pass. Anticipation turned to joy as their man sealed a 2-0 victory against Gillingham with his left boot. It was Jack's first goal for Plymouth Argyle.

How poignant that a young man, chest puffing with pride as he was about to win his first England cap, should pass that career-defining ball to Jack Leslie, who would be on the same path to international glory two years later. Bob Jack, the Argyle directors and the supporters must have been over the moon to see this accolade bestowed upon one of their players. They may have been in the Third Division South, but the Pilgrims were winning fans across the country for their play. Jack Hill was instrumental in this, and Jack Leslie surely congratulated him. Maybe a spark of ambition and hope had been ignited too. He was good enough to play with England's Jack Hill. He was good enough to play for England.

Sadly, for Jack Hill and Plymouth, he didn't play that match for England. To this day no Argyle player has won a full England cap while registered with the club. Hill picked up an injury and missed the trip to Paris as well as Argyle's final fixtures of the season. Absolutely gutting for a young player hitting his peak, but this wouldn't be his only chance. Hill had rightly been given the opportunity in trial matches, then joined the squad as a reserve before being selected to start. Jack Leslie saw how progression to full international recognition might work and would soon see Jack Hill move on to another club and England glory.

Jack Leslie's end-of-season form in his new position must have given him a huge boost after months on the sidelines. He was hailed by 'Pilgrim' at the end of the season:

> Taking the place of Batten, the ex-Barking player formed a happy combination with Baker ... Leslie has not been in the picture much this season, but in his recent games with the chiefs he has shaped remarkably well, and it would be no surprise to find him a strong candidate for the position another season.

Jack had done enough to show he was well worth sticking with and he was still just 21 years old. And he proved adaptable, switching from inside-left to centre-forward at half-time in the final match of the season. Jack couldn't overturn the one-goal deficit away to Newport but was praised for his efforts.

Plymouth Argyle finished second again, but at six points behind promoted Bristol City it wasn't the tense finish of the previous season. This was still a time that would have contained plenty of excitement for Jack and his team-mates, with incidents they would all reflect on. That included the departure of his Barking mate Frank Richardson. He had been comparatively disappointing during this campaign and was allowed to leave when Stoke City came in for him. Frank went on to have a decent career, particularly with Reading.

One big question is why Jack Leslie never moved to a bigger club. The simple answer is that Bob Jack wouldn't let him. Plymouth's manager was well known for keeping hold of players that he wanted to retain. As we'll see, transfer rumours were frequently floated in the years to come, particularly where Jack Leslie and Sammy Black were concerned, but Bob Jack knocked them all back. So why did he sell Jack Hill? Hill must have been a very different character to Jack Leslie. Football League players didn't have any real power with the retain and transfer system that operated until 1963. It was in a football club's gift to keep or sell a player at the end of each season. The club could accept an offer during the season, but it wasn't something the player could actively choose. The only option if they wanted to leave was to be such a pain in the arse that the club would eventually want rid of them. There are examples of players just telling their managers they wouldn't play, failing to stay fit, or even turning up for training drunk. In the case of Hill, it seems that he was desperate to head back up north.

In the 1923/24 Argyle *Hand Book* the writer laments on Jack Hill's departure:

> Whatever may be said to the contrary, however, it must be insisted that the local directors were powerless in the matter of Hill's removal to the First Division Club. For reasons of his own the player was bent on leaving Plymouth and was even prepared to sacrifice his own football career had the club persisted in their refusal to release him and been supported in this by the Football Association.

The fans were obviously not happy but the transfer fee of £5,750 from First Division Burnley softened the blow. This was at the very highest end across the divisions and still in the top 20 prices paid in the early 1930s.[18] Hill himself managed to top it, being sold to Newcastle United for £8,000 in 1928.

Jack Hill is one of the finest players ever to wear the green jersey of Plymouth Argyle. He went on to win 11 England caps and captain his country eight times. Jack Leslie saw the pride Hill took in hearing news of his selection. He must have wondered too about Hill's rejection of Argyle, the progression that followed and if he too could make such a move in the future. Jack saw a Plymouth Argyle team-mate getting the nod for an international cap and that stoked his own aspirations. He was four years younger than Hill and looked to a bright future ahead. Jack Leslie believed that he too could play for England.

As Jack mulled over the fortunes of his fellow players and those who had moved to pastures new, he hoped the 1923/24 season would see his breakthrough. 'Pilgrim' tipped him from the off: 'Two players of ability in Batten and Leslie are candidates for the inside-left position. Leslie came out of his shell in the latter part of the season and as he has played well in the trial games he gets his chance.' The practice matches were tedious affairs by all accounts and the biggest cheer went up when a police constable neatly caught a ball behind the Devonport End goal. Still, they worked out for Jack, and this would be the first time he started a season in the first team.

That pre-season bubble of hope was soon burst. Jack proudly took to the Home Park pitch with the Plymouth Argyle first team on 25 August to face Portsmouth. But chances went begging, including a header that missed by inches. Plymouth were a team with an enviable home record in recent years, but they lost 2-1, and after a 1-1 draw with Brentford away, Jack was dropped and the team started winning. One report suggests Jack may have been injured as it was a few weeks before he next played for the reserves, but he was yet to make the position his own. Bert Batten was back in.

Promotion-tipped Plymouth – well, they always were in the 1920s – were off to a shaky start and the board tinkered with the forward line, switching players and their positions, desperately trying to make something happen. In Jack's first reserve match he was centre-forward, but it seems Bob Jack concluded that inside-left was the best use of his talents. The shuffling of the forward pack moved Batten out to the left wing, and in December Jack came back to partner him on the inside. The move worked and the team went on a five-match winning streak, which included serving Exeter City a double helping of Christmas stuffing courtesy of two 4-0 victories. Jack scored in the home fixture on the 25th and he and Batten were rampant in the away derby on Boxing Day. Bob Jack had found his No. 10.

The merry toasts didn't last, as Jack tore a ligament in his thigh and was out for the start of 1924. The injury meant he couldn't even enjoy some illicit 'Auld Lang Syne' dancing away from Bob Jack's prying eyes. Jack returned on 16 February, replacing Batten for the Luton home match but the 'treacherous turf' was unforgiving: 'Leslie had practically an open goal when he lost his footing.' Jack wasn't a happy man and knives were out in the press as Plymouth slipped to seventh in the league. While things were shaky for our Jack, the gaffer's son, David Jack, who left Argyle in 1921 to become a star at Bolton, was about to be capped for England against Wales. The Welsh team included Plymouth stalwart Moses Russell. Jack Leslie was watching players he knew get their chance at international level while he was still pushing to play regular first-team football for his club.

It was early April when Jack got the nod once more. If this were a film, our hero would be called into his manager's office and Bob Jack would say, 'If you don't score today, son, you'll be on your way back to Barking.' But I don't think he was quite in the last-chance saloon; he was only 22. Bob Jack knew he had a special talent who was performing brilliantly for the reserves. Jack had scored a hat-trick just before his recall and had shown glimpses of that form in his first-team appearances. Yet, Jack would have to make it count at some point and show he was fulfilling his potential. Thankfully, he did.

Jack played the last eight fixtures of the season and hit the back of the net four times to help Plymouth move from fifth place to ... runners-up ... again. This time it was another south coast team who won promotion, Portsmouth. More end-of-season disappointment for the Argyle, but an upturn in Jack Leslie's fortunes. He bagged five goals in 17, which compared favourably to the other inside-forwards and wingers. Bert Batten scored the same number in 34 appearances, for example. And Jack was winning over the press. 'Pilgrim' in the *Football Herald* said he had been in fine form in the run-in, and the paper's away correspondent, 'Traveller', picked Jack as the star man in the 1-0 win at Charlton Athletic. He was swiftly signed on for the next campaign.

As the sun set on the football season, Jack Leslie had a sense that it was rising on his professional career. If he kept this form going, and he knew he could, then he should be first-choice at inside-left next season. Two things would change his career magnificently ... the arrival of the player who would forever be mentioned in the same breath as Jack Leslie, and the adventure of a lifetime.

In May 1924 talk abounded that Jack and his team-mates could be on a boat to South America. The Argentine Football Association had extended an invitation and Argyle were negotiating terms. Wow. Plymouth Argyle were lining up one of the most remarkable escapades in their glorious history. The ever so slightly patronising idea was that the English club would be showcasing its superior brand of football as part of the nation's global sporting export plan. We invented the game, and we knew how to play it best. It's true that the British had taken association football to South America, but by the mid-1920s that continent was developing its own style and telling its own story. We all know how South America's World Cup-winning countries of Argentina, Uruguay and Brazil have compared to England over the last century. But what a prospect for Jack Leslie. He was a young man approaching his 23rd birthday and would surely learn as much as he might teach, both on and off the pitch.

Chapter Seven

Plain Sailing

THE SUMMER of 1924 was a heady period when everything finally seemed to fall into place for Jack Leslie. But it involved an adventure as risky as his dad's voyage as a 12-year-old the previous century. Sailing to South America with the Plymouth Argyle team was momentous but foolhardy. Not on Jack's part ... he was hardly going to say no! But for almost the entire close season to be taken by weeks on ships, strenuous competitive matches and an enormous amount of beef and red wine seems reckless. So why did the club agree to it? The exotic notion was enticing to directors and players alike, but essentially it was all about cold hard cash. They were being paid to go. A boost to Argyle's finances would be useful and the players must have pocketed more than their usual reduced summer wage too.

As Jack Leslie and his team-mates left the pitch for the Home Park dressing rooms on 3 May 1924 having finished the season in style with a 7-1 win, they were probably wondering what the summer would hold. The tour would have been the talk of the team, but it wasn't even publicly mooted in the press until two days after the final match and the players had no idea yet whether it was going to happen, although it was said to be a probability. There were some difficult discussions at home to be had. Jack would usually be returning to London to see his family and his future wife Win. They would get married the following summer, so perhaps the tour meant their wedding had to be put on hold. The boost in Jack's earnings would help ease the blow.

By Tuesday, 13 May what was a probability was now 'almost certain' as the *Western Morning News* announced that the contract should be signed in London that day. A referee would be going along for the ride with Bob Jack, a director, a trainer and 19 players. They were due to sail from Southampton on the liner *Arlanza*. Better get a farewell gift for Win and pack your bags, Jack!

But the next day things seemed to be touch and go. Bob Jack had gone to London to sign the contract, but nothing had arrived from Argentina. While the departure had to be postponed, there was still confidence that it would happen. By the following Monday it was all sorted. Bob Jack told the *Western Evening Herald* that 'satisfactory arrangements have now been concluded'. The touring party would meet in London on Friday of the following week and sail from Southampton on 31 May on the Royal Mail steamer *Avon*. They planned to return from Buenos Aires on 9 July, arriving home on 28 July. At least Jack had a few weeks in London once the league was done, but it must have been a little discombobulating with the constantly changing plans.

You can imagine how the fans and press in Plymouth regarded the tour. With just a little suspicion. Jealousy? Surely not …! Writers looking forward to the season ahead would speculate on the impact the tour might have. 'Observer' in the *Devon and Exeter Gazette* said, 'I opine, the tour will do the players more harm than good in regard to the winter programme.' Typical Exeter, raining on Plymouth's parade. Ironic, given the Devon rivals had their own summer jolly to South America in 1914. Within the pages of Argyle's own handbook for the coming season Henry Rose, editor of the *Football Herald*, pondered: 'We must not blink at facts. One of two things is the case. Either they have become stale, or playing together during the summer will have resulted in a better understanding having been brought about, and also in the elimination of that beginning of the season stiffness that usually follows the close season rest. We shall see!' Seems a bit down on the whole affair. It's understandable that supporters would be unsure, but what kind of misery guts would deny players who weren't earning a mint such an adventure?

Throughout the tour Bob Jack sent letters home to the *Western Evening Herald* and *The Snooze*, which paint a wonderful picture of the whole affair. There's a beautiful team portrait of the party on board the *Avon*, so smartly decked out in blazers that you couldn't wish for a more dapper bunch to represent the English game. They all look well. Bob Jack reported that after a few days' sailing the seas had been calm and there had 'only been a few cases of mal-de-mer and they were temporary'. He allayed any fears of slacking by reporting that the team would begin training in earnest the next morning as the players needed to find their sea legs. They still had more than two weeks on board.

It was important for the manager that his team represented Plymouth Argyle and England well. The Argentine Football Association representatives in London had spread word of the club's talent, with glowing accounts sent to *The Standard*, the English paper in Buenos Aires. Could Jack and his team live up to the hype? They would have a couple of weeks' sailing before they found out. It seems that the first week or so of the journey was a relaxed affair and, although there had been 'a few luggards when the bugle sounds', no one missed a bath before breakfast, so they weren't overdoing it.

Bob Jack trusted his players enough to revoke his dancing ban but reassured that:

> For the sake of peace at home, I may say that the married men are content to be lookers-on, which is just as well as there are not enough ladies aboard to go round, unless it were permitted to fetch up a few of the Hungarian peasants, who are already beginning to amuse themselves in this way on their own deck.

The Hungarian women would, no doubt, be delighted to hear about discussions of their being fetched up. Sounds like they were having more fun on the lower deck in any case. And, although Jack Leslie wasn't yet married, he was keeping himself to himself, possibly sporting the same ring he wore to France a few years before to ward off any overtures from the Eastern European passengers. Or the Western ones for that matter.

As the journey progressed the party became a tad bored with the long trip to the South Atlantic. But they found ways to entertain themselves and 'pretty well swept the board' at the deck sports, according to Bob Jack. Our Jack reached the final of the men's singles deck tennis competition but lost to 'Mr. G.', a Manchester City supporter, for shame. Meanwhile, Bob Jack reported on social events at stopping points: 'At Pernambuco leading townspeople, including many ladies, came aboard to take tea and exchange courtesies with the passengers.' Sounds a bit dubious but all was above board on board, 'This apparently is a popular custom of the Europeans, and one they seem to thoroughly enjoy.' Bob Jack also told readers how he enjoyed looking up at the tropical sky 'ablaze with stellar glory', but thought the famed Southern Cross was a total let-down and 'scarcely worth writing home about'. The manager was more excited about the prospect of the smoothness of the bowling greens of Brazil when they had a short stop at Rio de Janeiro. Apparently, they were a joy compared to the lumpy turfs of Devon.

Jack Leslie's review of the constellations didn't make the papers, but he did enjoy a game of bowls. Player and manager would play bowls together on Plymouth Hoe just like the city's most famous historical figure, Sir Francis Drake, whose own sailing trips to South America were a little more violent than Argyle's. Only a little, however, as we'll discover. Perhaps Jack bonded with his manager over their shared love of a beautiful and true lawn. That may sound flippant, but he was a popular young man who was part of a smaller squad journeying for this long summer tour. It seems that Jack had his sea legs as, unlike some, he didn't suffer from motion sickness or side effects from the vaccinations they required. What an opportunity then to cement his position in the team and forge a stronger relationship with the manager. Bob Jack would be intensely busy throughout the season and contact was brief and focused. The manager might have been travelling in first class while the players were in second – can you imagine that today? – but Jack was able to hang out with him and senior players such as club captain, Moses Russell, far more than during a campaign. Jack clearly grasped this and, knowingly or not, had the kind of personality that works in a team sport. Having the confidence to be a major part of the team would only help him play more freely. It's not just about being a nice guy, it's about those connections being reflected in success on the pitch.

Although Bob Jack was keen to ensure propriety at all times, they let their hair down in Rio. And who can blame them? One member of the party turned £3 into £200 at the roulette tables of the Copacabana Palace Hotel and Casino. The manager was a paragon of discretion and avoided revealing the identity of the lucky man, but hopefully he bought the drinks for the rest of the journey. The lads rolled back on board at 4am and Bob Jack hoped the readers would understand that 'we may never have the good fortune to revisit this most beautiful city'. It's very true. We can hardly begrudge the players, although many a dockyard worker reading *The Snooze* did. Fair enough, this was a time before foreign holidays to Spain, let alone such exotic locations, were accessible to most. Even today a trip to Brazil isn't something many can afford. For Jack Leslie the boilermaker, who broke this career with a 13-year spell as a professional footballer, this was an experience to cherish. Who could blame him for pulling an all-nighter? While revealing their party antics, Bob Jack was also keen to reassure supporters at home that the group were 'a most temperate lot' and no one had put on weight.

Disaster struck at Santos when the players stopped for a few hours and slipped on their football kit to train on a pitch. While the Argyle players were having a kickabout, Frank Sloan's coat and shoes were stolen, or 'lifted by one of the numerous black boys who gathered around the field', as relayed by Bob Jack. How do you analyse that comment through the prism of today and the last century? If every child around that pitch was black, then it's simply an observation. But would it have been mentioned if they were all white? No. It must have been quite an experience for Jack to be playing in front of a crowd of young black onlookers. But was he inspired, or did he feel the pressure to inspire and show how good a player he was?

While this was another difficult experience for Jack that his colleagues could never understand, for Frank Sloan it was just bad luck. His passport was in his coat. Argyle should have taken a leaf out of the Essex FA's book and had one official in charge of everyone's credentials. Santos would repay the debt when the city's famous football team with the world's most famous footballer, Pelé, visited Home Park for an exhibition match in 1973. That's a story in itself, and saying they repaid the debt is stretching it a bit when you find out that Pelé's team, having seen the size of the crowd, refused to play just before kick-off unless they got a bag of extra cash.

The party finally docked at Buenos Aires on 19 June to a 'hearty and expressive' welcome from a large crowd. The Argentinian capital had a British population of more than 60,000 and there were many connections with Plymouth. Canon Brady, who used to work at the Devon town's main Anglican church, St Andrew's, oversaw the entertainment. Having a priest probably reassured Bob Jack that there would be no Rio-style nights out. One of Brady's first trips was an educational and healthy jaunt to the British American Tobacco Company's factory. The smoking mecca was managed by a former Devon rugby player … it's not what you know.

On Saturday, 12 July, Plymouth Argyle took on Argentina. Let's just take that in … Plymouth Argyle were playing Argentina. Bob Jack was told that the South Americans would be quick in their movements, speedy and enterprising. There's no doubt that a different style of play was developing that countered the direct, physical, English approach. And it's the clash of these styles and England's tactical and psychological difficulty in dealing with this that seems to have hampered the national team on the global stage ever since. Except in 1966, of course.

Incredibly, Argyle won that first match at Sportivo Barracas with a single goal from Percy Cherrett. The manager reported that Jack Leslie 'schemed cleverly without however attempting to cut through on his own, which I am sure would occasionally pay here as elsewhere'. Bob Jack felt they had given a good impression of their skills but noted that 'charging is taboo in Buenos Aires' and 'neither the players nor the crowd like it'. Sounds like Argyle had a rough reception when they showed their brand of good, honest, tough-tackling, shoulder-barging, English football. The gaffer said the teams they were to face would just have to deal with it and felt the lack of charging meant they would lose against any professional

English team whenever anything was at stake. This was just the start of a few weeks of fireworks.

Bob Jack is a huge figure in football history, but this shows how stuck in its ways the English game could be. It's also amazing that he didn't fear crowds that were famously hostile. He clearly had no idea until he got to Argentina, when expats told him it was 'not long ago when the knife and revolver were resorted to on the least provocation'. Officials and players were threatened, assaulted and even shot. Bob seemed rather blasé given there was a knife attack at a match in Buenos Aires the day before he wrote this letter home. The crowd at Argyle's first match became so incensed that a fight broke out after the final whistle between some English sailors and local fans. Luckily, only fists were thrown in anger, but this wouldn't be the last explosive incident before the tour was out. Jack Leslie and the Argyle team would see crowds and players behave unlike any they had seen at home. Would they succumb to this just as David Beckham would in 1998? Yes, they very much would.

The tour consisted of nine fixtures against representative sides from Argentina and Uruguay, as well as club sides and combined league teams. An amazing run of matches, and while the national line-ups Argyle faced varied in their quality, they all contained genuine internationals who represented their countries on more than one occasion. Argyle went on to win three, draw three and lose three, a record that meant they could leave with their heads held high. Or could they? It depends on who you believe.

Argyle faced high-quality opponents who had a different approach, but for Jack Leslie and the players the atmosphere must have been the most remarkable thing. Temperatures for that time of year in Buenos Aires and Montevideo are around 15°C but, while playing conditions were ideal, the crowd's mercury could rise rapidly. Bob Jack complained about pitch invasions when a player scored and fans throwing oranges or, worse, stones, at officials when decisions went against them. And all the while aeroplanes would circle overhead taking photos and dropping advertising flyers or toy balloons 'in shoals'. Worse, small boys would run on to the pitch during play to grab the colourful balloons. There would be no club fines for this kind of behaviour so Jack Leslie would be dribbling around leaflets and bobbing latex inflatables as well as South American players. All the while fans chanted in a language they couldn't understand at full volume. It must have been intense and frightening, but brilliant.

The most farcical incident with the potential to trigger mindless violence came against a combined team representing the Liga Rosarino de Football. Argyle had seen out a hard-fought goalless draw against them in Rosario on 6 July. Bob Jack claimed the Rosarinos played rough and said Jack Leslie was the best player on the pitch, 'holding on to the ball in bewildering style'. A banquet followed this match, but the manager's missive said that his players disappointed the hosts with their moderate alcohol consumption. Jack and his team-mates were clearly taking it seriously and needed to be on top form for the rematch. The two teams travelled together to Buenos Aires to face each other again at Boca Juniors' ground on 8 July. Whether or not the two teams got on well during the trip, there was certainly no love lost by the end of the next match.

It was tight, with Argyle one down at the interval, and it must have been very physical. Defender Fred Cosgrove was injured so badly he was replaced at half-time, something that was allowed in this 'friendly'. Substitutes weren't introduced in the Football League for decades to come. The previous match had been refereed by a local but now touring party official, Fred Reeve, took charge. His awarding of a penalty to Plymouth in the 68th minute didn't go down well. According to Bob Jack, not an unbiased witness of course, it was a case of 'glaring handling' in the box. A defensive prequel to Maradona's 'Hand of God' on the turf the Argentine legend would later grace. The Rosarinos decided to march off and all hell broke loose.

Reeve was sticking to his guns, and fortunately none of the local supporters or players fired one. The gate was one of the lowest of the tour at 6,000, but that's still a lot of anger to cope with, and it took 20 minutes for the police, many of whom were on horseback, to clear the pitch. While the crowd was forced back, a group of Argyle players hatched a plan. Winger Patsy Corcoran would deliberately squander the spot kick. They tried to keep this scheme quiet from tough-as-old-boots captain Moses Russell. The defender had been praised in the South American press, but his popularity would plummet sharply. Before Corcoran could take the kick, Russell shoved him aside and whacked the ball into the net. Cue more chaos as another pitch invasion ensued.

'The game concluded in a fever of excitement and semi-darkness,' wrote Bob Jack. Sadly, it also concluded with a winner for the Argentinian team just before the final whistle, which was probably about half an hour into added time. Jack was still a junior member of the first team so it's unlikely he was consulted on the penalty kick. But as someone who hated injustice on the pitch and who made his presence felt, he was surely on Moses' side.

Whether or not the South American tour was a sensible move only time would tell but, taken as a whole, it was a great experience. And in football terms the players must have learned a huge amount from seeing the game played in a different way. But it left Bob Jack a little sore from the mixed press his team received. He was incensed by 'the "Standard's" "sporting" reporter' – those are Bob's pointed inverted commas, not mine. The writer had been damning of Argyle's rough play in the 0-0 draw against the Rosarinos, but of the report on the 0-0 Boca Juniors match, well, 'This latest effusion of evident spleen is the limit!' The manager couldn't believe what his players were being accused of and felt the only dangerous play was coming from Boca's left-back Ramón Mutis, who was putting in some wild tackles. The only misdemeanour from a Plymouth perspective was when a player got so frustrated that he walloped the ball out of play after the whistle had blown. That was 'decidedly wrong' admitted Bob Jack, but didn't warrant 'the reporter going out of his way to blackguard the team or even the particular player'. Wouldn't it be great if that had been Jack Leslie booting the leather into touch? That would be so out of character and show they must have been as infuriated as Peter Shilton at the Azteca in 1986.

By the end of the tour Jack and the Plymouth team were at the end of their tether. *The Standard*'s report on the penultimate match, a one-nil victory over Argentina, chastised the visitors' 'deliberate roughness, spiteful displays of temper, and a desire to indulge in fisticuffs on the football field no matter what the provocation, should have been held in check as much as possible'. The expat writer feared Argyle had sunk to the level of the locals, bringing down the English reputation for fair play. He feared the worst: 'The consequences may be serious if the crowd make up their mind to take a hand in reprisals, and the finish of the tour may well end in tragedy.' Although Argentina's president and his minister of war came to watch and the crowd swelled to 30,000 fans, the final match was peace personified. Argyle lost one-nil, but no one died. *The Standard* was much nicer about Jack and his team this time, and the Plymouth party could leave with their heads held high.

For Jack Leslie the tour was a baptism of fire but undoubtedly a footballing success. He took part in every match and won plaudits from his manager. Before Jack embarked upon the *Avon* bound for Buenos Aires, he was a useful squad member who was yet to be sure of a starting position. When he stepped off the liner *Andes* at Southampton, he was a bona fide first-team player. Bob Jack was impressed by how Jack handled these tumultuous conditions. 'Pilgrim' wrote that he had been the best forward on the tour and had been commended in that otherwise hated Argentinian expat journal, *The Standard*. In Jack's success there are echoes of another pioneer's progress. Walter Tull travelled with Tottenham Hotspur on the club's tour of Argentina with Everton in 1909. He left England as a triallist, scored in a showcase match between the two English teams in Buenos Aires and earned his first professional contract on his return to home soil. Before the tour, the *Tottenham and Edmonton Weekly Herald* wrote, 'We are told that if Tull shines at all he will be made much of, as darkies get a good show at Buenos Aires.' This just shows how much attention there would have been on Jack, with crowds and pundits quick to praise and to criticise.

Jack had mostly played at inside-left but switched outside when others were injured or sick. The team recorded one win, one loss and a draw against the Argentina XI but were, stunningly, unbeaten against Uruguay. Jack Leslie sealed a 4-0 victory against the Olympic champions with an 86th-minute penalty (we don't have a record of the crowd's reaction to that one, but at 3-0 down maybe they had already been stunned into silence). In the rematch Jack hit another late goal, this time an 87th-minute equaliser, with the match ending 1-1. This was a different line-up to those that had won the Olympics that summer, but it did contain future World Cup winners. Whatever, forget the nuance. Plymouth Argyle beat Uruguay.

Let's say it again. In 1924 …

PLYMOUTH ARGYLE BEAT URUGUAY.
JACK LESLIE SCORED TWICE AGAINST URUGUAY.
AND … PLYMOUTH ARGYLE BEAT ARGENTINA.

These two countries would compete in the first FIFA World Cup Final just a few years later in 1930, and some of the players Plymouth Argyle faced took part in this historic international match, including two of Uruguay's goalscorers. They were Santos Iriarte, and the incredible Héctor Castro, a one-armed, hard-living, hard-loving, football legend.

If this was a film, then Jack's goals against the future World Cup winners would be the climactic redemption, but this is real life and we're nowhere near the third act. Jack Leslie was on the up. The highs he felt on the football pitch were followed by another long voyage, which must have sent the adrenaline levels below zero. While he was able to reflect on an experience and a job well done, he was missing England and Win and was itching to get back home. That three-week journey ate into Plymouth Argyle's pre-season too, so Jack and the team couldn't take their feet off the gas. Those early morning deck sprints would be of even greater importance as they were homeward bound.

The tour lasted almost two weeks longer than originally planned, and it was 11 August by the time they reached Southampton. Thankfully, all the players were fit and well, as the season opener was less than three weeks away. Jack's first few campaigns with Plymouth had been a roller coaster and the cards hadn't fallen in his favour. But this summer, fortune favoured the brave.

Chapter Eight

When Jack Met Sammy

IN 1924 the pendulum was only just starting to swing in Jack Leslie's direction. He was establishing himself in the Plymouth Argyle first team on his own merits and had been backed by Bob Jack and his staff. But he had been making his mark amid the constant switching of team-mates and positions. Something was about to change things magnificently ... the arrival of a mercurial Scottish left-winger. He was a diminutive demon with size four boots who became possibly the best outside-left in the league, and his name was Sammy Black.

While Jack Leslie and friends were off on their overseas adventure, crucial work was going on behind the scenes at Plymouth Argyle. The ups and downs of building a football team that could finally win promotion was on the directors' minds as well as the manager's. Former club secretary, Louis Crabb, was on scouting duties, looking for talent in clubs where big fees wouldn't be needed. He found three likely targets in Scotland and brought Sammy Black from East Dunbartonshire's Kirkintilloch Rob Roy. Young Sammy was as swashbuckling a player as that origin name suggests and was introduced to Argyle fans in the season handbook as a 'regular box of tricks'. But he was bashful and unassuming. Black was a mere 5ft 6½in and just 19 years old when he travelled the 485 miles to Plymouth in the summer of 1924. What a find.

Quite how the partnership came alive they didn't know themselves, as Jack recalled in 1972: 'I have never really fathomed what made us click as a wing. Certainly, we never talked deeply on tactics. I suppose we had an instinctive understanding.' Jack and Sammy had their own styles and physiques, which clearly complemented each other. They had a similar humility and gentleness off the pitch, but outwardly Sammy was less confident than Jack. Like Jack, Sammy had one daughter, Gloria. Holding the most incredible photo of her dad, full-pelt and mid-air, having left a defender for dead, Gloria laughed at the memory of what he was like in normal life: 'He was so slow, so laid-back, he never hurried for anybody. He could be meeting the Queen and he wouldn't have hurried.' And he was completely unassuming too: 'He'd sit behind his paper, and I'd bring my friends in and say, "Dad, this is so and so."' Gloria mimed how he would lower his paper a little, 'And he'd go, "Alright," and back to his paper. I used to tell him, "You're rude!" He would look miserable too, but he wasn't. He was just a very quiet, shy man and you wouldn't think he had been a famous football player.' These were two very special players who never boasted about the talent that made them household names.

If his old partner came up in conversation, Jack's granddaughters could see how much that relationship meant: 'Whenever he spoke about Sammy Black, you always felt the affection he had for him.' You can sense that in his own words: 'Sammy was, of course, a brilliant winger – a natural, two-footed player. You could give him the ball on either foot. It made no difference to Sammy.' But Jack Leslie was typically gracious in wanting others to get credit too: 'Mind you, there were some very good players in that team who helped to make us a wing partnership.'

The pair clearly struck up a rapport and were great to have in the dressing room. They loved the game and didn't need smoke blowing up their backsides to perform. As well as being a reliable partner on the pitch with a few years' experience at the club to share, Jack would have been able to empathise with Sammy coming to a new town as a young man and help to show him the ropes. The Jack Leslie and Sammy Black partnership would make headlines across the nation and the two names were inextricably linked in the minds of fans for decades. Many in Plymouth and beyond believed they were the best left-wing in the country, and that both should play for their respective countries.

What helped establish the relationship was the unexpected and unwanted exit of experienced left-winger, Billy Baker, the man who kept Jack out of the first team for so long. Across the summer the angst around his situation had been reported in the press as the 32-year-old refused to agree terms. Like Jack Leslie a few years before, Sammy Black had been signed as an understudy to someone described by 'Pilgrim' as 'one of the idols of the crowd' whose 'absence would seriously jeopardise the chance of winning the championship'. Little did our soccer scribe know that within a season the understudy would replace the old campaigner in the fans' hearts ... and some.

With Baker in limbo and eventually out of the picture, Argyle followers and local sports writers were concerned. 'Pilgrim' was withering about the South American tour, feeling it may well have been 'a much needed fillip to the club's exchequer' and the players 'have spent a jolly good time – off the field', but worried it may harm the club's chances. There were even rumours that the club hierarchy didn't want promotion. That seems madness. To have the league success Plymouth enjoyed during the 1920s without promotion must have been as painful for the players and staff as it was for the supporters. The team's consistent performances meant paying out more than £7,000 in bonuses across the decade, higher than almost any other Football League club. Going up would probably save them money, given it would be harder to win matches.

Sammy Black impressed in the practice games of August 1924, as did Jack Leslie, who looked in good shape. Jack's vital statistics were reported in the Argyle *Hand Book*, the South American diet having obviously worked its magic. At 12st 4lb he had reached fighting weight for his more combative and creative inside-left role, and Jack said later in life that his size was one reason the manager switched him from the wing. Jack's rival Bert Batten started at outside-left for the first couple of matches, a draw and a loss away from home, but Sammy had done enough in training to win the confidence of the committee.

The Argyle manager and directors threw caution to the wind and introduced him to the Home Park crowd on 6 September against Brentford. It wasn't the finest start for Sammy, and the crowd's energy dipped when Plymouth went a goal behind after 20 minutes. But Jack Leslie pulled up his bootstraps and hit back with a brilliant individual goal. He left the Brentford defence standing and, with just the keeper to beat, finished with aplomb. From then on it was all Argyle. Sammy Black showed what was to come by scoring on his debut with a magnificent shot to put the Greens ahead. The match became a rout, ending 7-1, including a brace from Jack.

Within weeks the first whispers of the partnership that would write records in Plymouth Argyle's history books were being heard. The pairing was a revelation that 'served up some delightful football', said 'Pilgrim', and his praise was effusive from the off: 'Nothing has been more pleasing than Leslie's brilliant work,' and Black is 'as elusive as the proverbial eel'. Jack was Baldrick to Sammy's Black Eel, providing cunning plans aplenty. Like Jack, the local press didn't spare Sammy if there were criticisms to be had. They loved his speed and ability to beat defenders but wished he would quicken up his centres. But it's clear that even our friend 'Pilgrim' knew he was nit-picking and that Argyle's new outside-left was a real find, while the combination with Jack Leslie was unstoppable. It seemed that way when Argyle had reached the top of the table by the end of September, where they would stay until the middle of December, with eight home wins in a row.

Although Plymouth had finished runners-up the previous three seasons, the last two were sketchy to say the least. Even with Jack and Sammy Black firing on all cylinders, there remained question marks over the forward line, particularly in the centre. It's hard not to feel sorry for Bert Batten, who was moved to centre-forward and then dropped, even though he scored six goals in seven matches. But it was Jack and Sammy who showed the most consistency and they would play together 37 times in Black's first season with Plymouth Argyle.

There were inevitable dips in form for Sammy, just as there had been for Jack in his first campaign, and Argyle had a little wobble around Christmas with a loss to promotion rivals Swansea Town. Jack was injured in the festive fixture at home to Exeter City, which meant he didn't get to see Sammy's first hat-trick at Home Park against Norwich. But critics be damned, this newfound partnership was on to something, and the report of the 2-0 home win against Gillingham on 31 January 1925 gives an insight into the understanding the pair quickly developed. As Sammy skipped inwards with the ball, Jack slipped to the outside-left position to receive his pass. Jack then crossed but the shot was tipped over the bar. You get a real sense of instinctive movement that wasn't constrained by formation. Maybe that South America trip had something to do with it, but this pair knew how to play to each other's strengths.

Sammy Black is rightly revered as the leading goalscorer in Argyle history with 184 goals in 491 appearances. Plymouth's famous political son, Michael Foot, also comfortable on the left wing, writes about the joy of watching Black as a teenager in the early 1930s:

> He was not alone, however much he might appear to be riveted by some distant, disconsolate revery of his own, as he would amble along the touchline; he kept all his speed and spirit in reserve for the moments of tension. Then he was the greatest outside-left in the age of outside-lefts. But where would he have been without Jack Leslie beside him, the first black footballer in English football to show us the way.[19]

Jack wasn't the first black footballer in England, of course, but it's not surprising that Foot wrote this, as he was the only black player in the Football League for much of his career, and stories of other pioneers such as Arthur Wharton and Walter Tull had, like Jack's, failed to be celebrated until recent years.

Sammy was a fast-paced, whirling dervish of excitement that would send the Home Park crowd to fever pitch in expectation of another thundering shot. He didn't get stuck in like Jack. It wouldn't have made sense for him out on the wing, but he was no coward. In his first season, opposition defenders were singling him out, and if fair means couldn't stop him, they would use foul. And it became so commonplace that writers such as 'Pilgrim' became weary at the opposition's targeting of him. There's the lovely story of camaraderie that Jack's granddaughters recount about Jack's reaction when opponents tried to intimidate Sammy before a ball had even been kicked. Jack let them know he would be giving them a taste of their own medicine if they had a go at his mate.

Jack and Sammy's personalities complemented each other. Like Jack, Sammy never boasted about his ability. He was down to earth, liked a flutter and the pair would play cards together on the long journeys to away matches. Their friendship and on-field relationship were swiftly cemented and would stay long in their memories and in those of fellow players and supporters who never saw the like again. Charlie Trevethan remembers sneaking under the fences into Home Park as a lad and occasionally carrying Sammy Black's kit bag for a shilling tip: 'Sammy Black and Jack Leslie, now they were players. They'd get the ball forward, not like today passing it around the back and to the keeper.' And Bill Stephens recalled how this partnership lifted the fans spirits: 'Whenever one of them got the ball there was a real rustle in the crowd, they knew it, there could be a goal.'

If Sammy Black didn't know the blood and thunder of the English league yet, 14 February 1925 would be a fine tutorial. Brighton & Hove Albion were the visitors for a veritable Valentine's Day massacre, if you can say that about a match that finished 1-0. It should have been two though. Jack and Sammy worked another opening, but as Black's boot thundered into the leather, sending it goal-bound, the ref blew the half-time whistle. The shrill parp of the official's instrument still hung in the air as the ball hit the back of the net. Taking hints from the South American teams, Argyle players surrounded Mr Grimstead. They eventually marched off and the referee later claimed he blew three or four seconds before the ball crossed the goal line.

The weather was the opposite of Jack Leslie's picture postcard promise, with rain, sleet and hail creating horrific ground conditions and players sliding dangerously across the mud. It was a curious match all round. With the match still goalless, the Argyle players, all except Jack Leslie, came out for the second half wearing blue shorts. This fact attracted no other comment in the papers, but it seems very odd that either he wasn't included in the prank or refused to get involved in such silliness. He was a serious professional on the pitch but not devoid of a sense of humour. Whichever, the change of kit didn't calm the atmosphere as two players were sent off after a heavy tackle. Well, one report makes it sound like more of an assault on an Argyle player who had slipped in the mud. Fisticuffs followed and no doubt Jack got involved. He was fair and kind, but in that situation he would back up his team-mates. That was the type of man he was. Fortunately, Frank Sloan got a goal for a home win.

Throughout this first season together, Jack and Sammy were contributing to Argyle's push for promotion. Jack, however, could do with scoring more frequently, and Sammy needed to improve his crossing. As ever, that's the critical analysis of 'Pilgrim', but that was his job. What the team really needed was a consistent centre-forward. Over the previous few years, they'd had players who would bang in 20 or even 30 goals in one season but go off the boil the next. So, Plymouth Argyle made their intentions clear in March 1925 with the signing of one of the biggest celebrity players of the time. He could act, he could sing, and he could score. Enter triple threat Jack Cock. The Cock of the South.

It was a clear message to the footballing world and their own fans that Plymouth meant business. Signing Jack Cock was a massive coup. The 32-year-old was still in his prime and came from Everton, where he hit 29 goals in 69 matches. Before that he had bagged 47 in 99 for Chelsea. He was a Cornishman, supremely fit and a decorated war hero who had won two caps, scoring twice for England. Not only that but he had starred in football movie *The Winning Goal* in 1920 and would feature again in that brilliantly terrible feature, *The Great Game*, in 1930. In Jack Leslie's granddaughters' collection there are a set of postcards of Cock's Hollywood-style head shots, signed by the man himself and looking every inch the Beckham of his day, or maybe Cantona, because he could act.

The arrival of big names at smaller clubs doesn't always work out and can have a habit of unsettling the dressing room. Jack Cock would apparently sing before trotting on to the pitch, which sounds annoying. He did score three in his first three matches, so at least he was singing when he was winning, and Argyle were soon topping the division. Our Jack certainly seemed to enjoy the introduction of this quality player. He had a decent voice himself so maybe they did a duet. On 10 April 1925 Jack Leslie scored his first hat-trick wearing a green jersey in a 7-1 home win that sent the fans into raptures. As the climax of another season approached, 'Pilgrim' wrote that Jack Leslie had developed a 'happy understanding' with the superstar signing, Cock, and complemented his brilliant work with Sammy Black.

With these big wins, Jack Leslie and his team were doing their best to avoid what happened in 1922 when they missed out on promotion through goal average on the final day. In their last match of the season on Wednesday, 29 April, Plymouth did all they could by beating Southend United 6-0, with Black, Cock and Leslie all on the scoresheet. But this must have left Jack with the weirdest of feelings. The last kick of the season had been taken, they had scored 77 goals, way ahead of any other team in the division and were top. But Swansea Town were just three points behind with two matches left to play. Plymouth were in purgatory.

To leapfrog Argyle, Swansea needed a clean sweep to collect four points or the unlikely combination of a win by four clear goals and a draw. Jack Leslie could be satisfied that he was now a major first-team player in a forward line that was winning matches and plaudits. With 14 goals he was the top scorer for the season, while his new partner Sammy Black hit 13. Now they had to wait for the reports to come in, and the next day Swansea were at home to Reading. The Welsh team scraped a late winner.

Saturday came and Swansea's visitors were none other than Exeter City. Come on Grecians, do it for Devon. A wire was sent to City claiming 20,000 London Devonians were urging them to assist their neighbours. But the pleas fell on deaf ears. Former Argyle striker Jack Fowler put the Welsh team ahead and a second came before half-time. Exeter pulled one back but it was to no avail. This was a new feeling for Jack Cock and Sammy Black, but it was all too familiar for Jack Leslie and the players who had been with Argyle for a while. This must have been worse, though, sitting on your hands knowing you should be celebrating promotion and then seeing it slip away. It's the kind of sinking feeling you really don't want at the start of your summer break.

Jack Leslie would have been praying for Swansea to slip up. After all, it was the penultimate match that did for Argyle. Their rivals visited Home Park on 25 April where a crowd of more than 30,000 turned out for this huge and crucial fixture. A win and Plymouth would be virtually home and dry. What happened sounds a bit like that awful moment when Ronald Koeman put paid to England's hopes of going to the World Cup in 1994. Argyle were one up when Jack committed what was apparently 'a trivial infringement'. From the free kick Swansea's Deacon lifted the ball towards the left corner, while Plymouth keeper Fred Craig was at the other side of the goal. The impertinence. 'Probably no one experienced the greater surprise than Deacon, for as soon as he noted the success of his kick he jumped for joy.' At least the fans didn't have Brian Moore's brilliantly prophetic commentary to compound the misery: 'He's going to flick one now, he's going to flick one.' Swansea dug in and held out for the next 65 minutes to secure what would prove to be a championship-winning away point.

Four times in a row. Four times the bridesmaid and never the bride.

Jack Leslie would have to shake off the disappointment quickly, because he had important matters of the heart to attend to. One of the best bridesmaids of the Third Division was soon to be a groom.

Chapter Nine

Five Goals and a Wedding

HE WAS just 23 but Jack Leslie had sailed to South America, set out his stall with Sammy Black and finished in second place with Argyle once again. As his summer birthday approached, he could put another promotion near miss for his team behind him. The last year had been a major success for Jack personally. He had established himself as a first-team player and forged an on-field partnership that was pleasing his manager and the fans. If he could keep clear of injuries, Jack would have many years ahead as a top footballer. Now it was time to forge the off-field partnership that would truly define his life. Jack was getting married.

Lavinia Emma Garland, our Win, was from a big family, and while Jack's childhood was hardly a bed of roses, hers would have been a struggle just to find a bed. She was born in 1899, the fifth of eight children, and grew up in a house where 11 people shared five rooms. Jack's home, a half-hour walk away, would have felt spacious in comparison. Making ends meet was a constant struggle, with her father, William, unable to hold down a job due to his brain injury. The 1911 census shows that her dad and eldest brother were unemployed. Win's 18-year-old sister, Sarah, worked in an electric laundry, while 32-year-old Uncle Albert was out hawking coal, but they were the only ones bringing in any cash. Things were so tight that Win's younger sister Maud was living with an aunt elsewhere. With her dad in and out of Goodmayes asylum and household members desperately trying to find employment, Win had to develop the same inner strength as the man she would marry.

Why didn't Jack and Win get married sooner? The answer could lie in Jack's profession, her family circumstances or both. Win's parents relied on others in the household to help earn a wage. William was so desperate that he went to war aged 43, so she might have felt an obligation to stay at least until her youngest brother, Richard, was old enough to go out to work. Richard was only 13 when Jack signed for Argyle. And for Jack, while he had fulfilled his ambition to become a professional footballer, he had no idea how it would work out. He might be back in London within a year or two, either with another football club or back at Beckton riveting metal.

Jack and Win didn't *have* to get married in the way couples often felt they should. It's abundantly clear that each had found their soulmate. Jack's granddaughters say, 'He was a handsome young man, and he was idolised in Plymouth. So, he would definitely have had admirers, but he was besotted with her, she was the only one for him. Throughout their life they certainly loved each other.' And the fact that their daughter, Eve, didn't come along until 1927 shows this was no shotgun wedding. The couple were married on 27 June 1925 at St Matthias Church in Canning Town, where Jack had been baptised.

The wedding pictures are wonderful. Standing side by side, the young bride and groom clasp hands tightly as they look warmly to the lens. Jack is wearing a fine three-piece suit with what looks like one of his football medals on a waistcoat chain, while Win in her white dress, veil lifted, holds a bunch of lilies. In a joyful group photo, Jack's mum, dad and sister look on proudly. Alongside family there are many young men in suits, including current team-mates Patsy Corcoran and Jack Cock, and an old Barking and Essex comrade who was now at Millwall, James Dillimore. It shows how important friendships were to Jack and how well regarded he was.

There wouldn't have been much of a honeymoon. Win might have joked that her new husband could take her on a cruise to South America, but Southend for a couple of days was more likely. Embarking on a marriage is a heady adventure and Win and Jack were a young couple very much in love. Not only that, but they were in a good position in life. Jack was earning more than any family member ever had, and they would be living away from the London pea-soupers by the sea in Plymouth. The newly-weds settled in Glendower Road in Peverell, the quiet and sober residential area where Jack had already been lodging.

Having lived most of his time in the town for the last four years, Jack wouldn't have had the same trepidation that Win might as they embarked upon this new stage of life. It sounds like an idyllic move to leave a cramped house where money had always been tight for the sea air of Devon. And Win was marrying a footballer. Being a WAG didn't come with quite the trappings of today, but Jack had status and was an honoured guest at local events and football functions. He had dined with the upper classes in France and London and was now hanging with the glitterati of Plymouth. Not quite the same as champagne with Jules Rimet but exciting, nonetheless.

The Plymouth Argyle *Hand Book* for 1925/26, previewing the season, warmly congratulated Jack on his marriage. The late summer of 1925 was happy and carefree for the newly-weds. Celebrating Jack's 24th birthday that August must have been a sweet moment for the young, successful footballer and his beautiful wife. Neither could predict what adversity they would face within months. Jack and Win Leslie would need all the resilience that growing up in the poverty-stricken East End of London had imbued them with.

As Jack and Win prepared for their new life together, Plymouth Argyle made ready for another assault on the Third Division South and the game of football itself contemplated a new era. I won't bore you with the machinations of how the offside law has developed since the dawn of time, but ... before 1925 an attacking forward was offside if the ball was passed to him when there were fewer than three opponents ahead. With the formation being two backs in front of the keeper, this meant attackers couldn't run beyond defenders to receive a pass. After some experimental matches ahead of the 1925/26 season it would now be just two defenders (the keeper and one outfield player) ahead for an attacker to stay onside. The idea was to avoid endless stoppages and disputes. I mean, since when has the offside law been an issue in the last century? Jack Leslie would look at VAR and weep.

Being what we would now call a No. 10, this rule change was manna from heaven for Jack. His defence-splitting passes were more likely to come off, and with Sammy Black to the left of him, Jack Cock to the right, he was getting stuck in. In fact, they all got stuck in. Jack Leslie scored the season opener within four minutes of the starting whistle in a 6-2 win over Southend United at Home Park on 29 August 1925. He pounced on a rebound from a shot by Sammy and, as the ball thundered into the back of the net, making it bulge towards the rapturous supporters behind the goal, Jack Leslie wheeled away, his arms outstretched in celebration. A photographer captured the moment and it featured in the *Daily Mirror*'s collection of images highlighting that opening Saturday goal-fest. The photo has gained poignancy given the events that would soon follow, but it also inspired the positive image of Jack Leslie now captured in bronze outside Home Park. What it also shows is that both Jack and his Argyle team were winning plaudits beyond the local press. They had done so before, but the timing is significant.

On 21 September 1925 the FA International Selection Committee discussed England's forthcoming matches and decided to put out a call:

> The Secretary was instructed to issue a circular to Members of the Council inviting them to bring to the notice of the Association the names of any players whom the Members considered showed marked ability, with the view to arrangements being made for the players to be seen by Members of the International Selection Committee. [20]

Jack Leslie had no idea this was even happening, let alone that his name might be floated at such a high level. He had seen friends and colleagues get an England call-up, understood the enormity of the honour and hoped it might one day happen for him.

Jack was winning enough fans to be thought of as a future international, that's for sure. In the previous season he fully established himself and had now played nearly 100 matches for his club. When the message asking for candidates was circulated by FA secretary, Frederick Wall, Argyle's free-scoring play had attracted national press attention. With five goals in five matches immediately prior to this call for nominations, Jack was garnering more praise than ever for his shooting, link-up play and commitment. The FA had representatives in every county and Jack Leslie was known by FA Council members from his time with Barking and Essex. Now he had professional credentials in Plymouth and the backing of his manager Bob Jack, a very well-connected football man. Jack Leslie didn't know it, but his name was put forward as a potential England player.

It was probably a good thing that the spotlight on Jack Leslie was, to mix a metaphor, in the shadows. The pressure on him was no greater than usual at Home Park, and while the selectors were contemplating their choices for international honours, Jack's team ran riot. Argyle beat Brentford 4-0 and Aberdare Athletic 7-2 in the space of three days. Jack only scored once in those victories but his season tally had already hit six and he was providing his fellow strikers with plenty of chances. Argyle travelled to Brighton, one of the other top teams in the division, on 3 October and beat them 2-1. Jack Leslie had played his way on to the longlist of candidates the England selectors should seriously consider. Would he make the shortlist? He certainly hadn't done his chances any harm.

Jack Leslie and his fellow Argyle players knew the famous Charity Shield match was coming up in a couple of days. The man Jack was now keeping out of the Plymouth first team, Bert Batten, was due to be involved. In 1925 a team of Amateurs competed against Professionals for the trophy and the latter were the team that had recently returned from the FA summer tour to Australia. Bert had scored a hatful against the leaky Antipodeans. But the Professionals were players their clubs were prepared to release for a long tour on the other side of the world rather than full internationals. It was Monday, 5 October, and the Amateurs won the Charity Shield at White Hart Lane 6-1. Bert Batten didn't play, through injury, but his involvement demonstrates how well the FA knew Plymouth Argyle's squad. They had, of course, selected Jack Hill for England just two years previously.

While Jack knew about the match in London and might have known the England selection was happening, it didn't cross his mind that he was in the frame. With the FA bigwigs gathered at Tottenham Hotspur's ground, the International Selection Committee would meet after the final whistle. The 14 men's task was to pick the England team to play in Belfast later that month. The fixture was listed as against 'Ireland' but was effectively Northern Ireland. England refused to recognise and compete against the Irish Free State. All Jack Leslie had to worry about that Monday evening was tomorrow's training and the visit of Watford next Saturday.

A young Jack Leslie in pristine Plymouth Argyle kit. This was surely popular with his many admirers.

One of Jack's few surviving medals from his time as a youngster at Fairbairn House Boys' Club, which produced many sporting stars.

Sat beside Barking Town FC's president having won trophies in his first season. Jack has the ball and the world at his feet.

The Essex team on tour in Normandy in April 1921. War hero Baden Herod affectionately cradles Jack, the baby of the side.

In Normandy again, Jack curiously sports a ring on his wedding finger four years before his marriage.

This faded Barking Town team photo contains an incredible piece of history ...

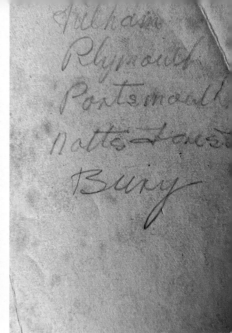

... on the reverse, Jack noted in pencil the professional clubs who were chasing his signature.

Readers of the Football Herald in Plymouth see Jack pictured for the first time in September 1921.

LESLIE, OF ARGYLE.

Leslie, the promising young outside left, who is figuring prominently in Argyle's Reserve XI.

Plymouth Argyle lured Jack to the club with postcards of a sunny seafront!

From 1922, this is one of many cartoons depicting Jack that reference his colour. It's from a local publication and while not designed to be offensive, is of its time and shows how he was often portrayed.

Looking every inch the dapper Englishmen abroad, Jack and the Argyle team on the Avon bound for South America in June 1924.

Diminutive, yet explosive. Goalscoring outside-left Sammy Black forged a partnership with Jack that became famous throughout the land.

The happy couple on 27 June 1925. They loved each other deeply until the end.

The opening day of the 1925/26 season and Jack's goal makes the Daily Mirror just before he was picked for England. His celebration inspired the statue that now stands in his memory.

ENGLAND TEAMS

ARGYLE PLAYER RESERVE AGAINST IRELAND.

The International Selection Committee at Tottenham yesterday selected the following amateurs to represent the Football Association against the Royal Air Force at Cranwell on October 21st:—J. F. Mitchell (Manchester City); R. chipperbottom (Old Boltonians) and E. R. Woodhouse (King's Lynn); W. I. Bryant (Millwall), F. Scott (Bury Amateurs), J. W. Booker (Nunhead); R. L. Morgan (Clapton), Gordon Dale (Handsworth Old Boys), J. Blair (Liverpool University), W. R. Donald (Bishop Auckland), and Hall (Lowestoft Town).

The following team was chosen to represent England against Ireland at Belfast on October 24: B. Howard Baker (Chelsea); Smart (Aston Villa) and Wadsworth (Huddersfield Town); Kean (Sheffield Wednesday), G. H. Armitage (Charlton Athletic), Bromilow (Liverpool); Austin (Manchester City), Puddefoot (Blackburn Rovers), C. T. Ashton (Corinthians), Walker (Aston Villa), Dorrell (Aston Villa). Reserves: Ruttall (Bolton Wanderers) and Leslie (Plymouth Argyle).

Jack Leslie named in the England squad in papers nationwide on 6 October 1925.

READER & WAYS OF THE F.A.

Reserve for England, Leslie or Earle?

"When the English team to meet Ireland was first published" writes a London reader, "Leslie, of Plymouth Argyle, was down as reserve (to travel), but for some reason, not made public, Leslie played for his club on Saturday, while Earle, of West Ham United, travelled to Ireland instead.

"Cannot you, in the columns of Labour's only daily newspaper, make a stand against the snobbery which is like a blight in first-class football? I refer to instances which are continually cropping up, such as the selection of Ashton, of the Corinthians, to captain an English team. It is fairly obvious that on merit he is a long way from International class.

"I would also mention the glaring injustice of that scratch team, the Corinthians, being exempt until the third round of the English Cup up to the present they have played only two matches this season, when such renowned cup fighters as Swindon, Barnsley, etc. have to play in the first round.

"I feel sure that you would give great satisfaction to thousands of fair-minded sportsmen if you brought these matters out into the daylight and fought for a square deal for the man who has to live on what he earns, whatever the occupation happens to be."

WAS LESLIE CHOSEN?

In an endeavour to discover why Leslie did not go as reserve to Ireland, we rang up the Football Association yesterday, and were informed that Leslie had not been chosen. Upon making a similar inquiry at the offices of the Press Association, we were told that at the meeting of the Football Association Leslie was announced as a reserve, and his name appeared in many papers which published the English team the same evening and the following morning.

The 1920s equivalent of a media storm as the Daily Herald asks the FA what happened to Jack?

Chapter Ten

Knocked Sideways

WHEN JACK Leslie walked to work on the morning of Tuesday, 6 October 1925, he was looking forward to a day of training with Sept Atterbury and Tommy Haynes. It was a warm, dry autumn morning and the ten-minute stroll from the home he shared with Win, through Plymouth's Central Park to the ground he knew inside out, was pleasant, carefree almost. Football is a game that throws plenty of surprises at a young player, but with no match until Saturday there was nothing to get stressed about. He was working with a fantastic group of lads, and they were top of the league. Home Park was a happy place to be.

Bob Jack sat in his office bursting with excitement. The Plymouth manager had nurtured many a young hopeful and took pride in developing players rather than buying a team. He brought Jack Leslie down to Devon from the East End and turned him into a match-winner. Bob was proud of what this young man had become and now he was about to give him an incredible piece of news.

That morning, Jack was called into his manager's office. This wasn't a common occurrence and, although he had a good relationship with his gaffer, Jack must have wondered what this was about. His nerves were calmed when he saw his boss and mentor peering over his glasses and smiling. Jack was dumbfounded when his manager opened his mouth:

He stands up and puts his arm on my shoulder. 'Johnnie' – that's what he called me – 'Johnnie … I've got great news for you. You've been picked for England.' Well, you can imagine. I'm a level-headed sort of man ... sort of bloke who'd sell matches for a living if he had to. But this really knocked me sideways.

Bob Jack embraced him. The manager knew what this meant to a young lad. His own son, David, had been named as a travelling reserve in 1923 and followed that with his first start for England a few months later.

What a feeling that must have been. The surprise and the smile that immediately appeared on Jack's young face, his heart pounding with pride and in his mind the instant desire to tell Win, his family and friends. 'He must have been absolutely over the moon,' say his granddaughters. 'It's what every footballer must dream of, to play for your country. It's the pinnacle.' He knew his team-mates would be proud and pleased for him too, just as he had been pleased for Jack Hill and for his captain, Moses Russell, who was a regular in the Welsh national team. Jack wasn't a big head and would get his fair share of ribbing in the dressing room, but he was a popular man throughout his career, and the overwhelming emotion at Plymouth Argyle Football Club was delight for this talented, decent young man.

That morning the England team was announced in virtually every newspaper in the land from the *Western Morning News* in Devon to the *Liverpool Echo*, *The Scotsman* and the *Northern Whig* in Belfast, where the match would be played. The list is identical in every single one and includes Leslie (Plymouth Argyle) as a travelling reserve. Jack Leslie *was* named in the England squad, one of only 13 players chosen to represent his country. This was massive news for him and for Plymouth. Jack Leslie was the talk of the town:

> Everybody in the club knew about it. The town was full of it. All them days ago it was quite a thing for a little club like Plymouth to have a man called up for England. I was proud – but then I was proud just to be a paid footballer.

These words are an old man looking back at events, but at the time it must have filled his head with that rare feeling only the biggest accolades can. Think how high he must have been and the joy that was coursing through his veins when you consider what followed.

The excitement at the prospect also brought nerves, but Jack had plenty of people he could look to for advice. His attacking partner Jack Cock for one. He was an experienced player with two England caps. In his first match, against Ireland in 1919, Cock scored after 30 seconds, the fastest England goal at the time; it's still in the top ten. Jack Cock had attended Jack's wedding and gave his pal postcards – all pictures of himself. Well, he was a movie star. They're signed 'From your Pal, Jack' and, 'Many Happy Days from Jack.' This was also a happy day, and I can imagine Jack Cock winding his friend up, betting he couldn't score as quickly for England as he had. For the next week or so, Jack Leslie's selection was on everybody's lips, and while this could have gone to his head, he seemed to take it in his stride.

That doesn't mean to say there was no negativity locally. There was, no doubt, some discussion in the pubs and coffee houses. There would have been people in Plymouth and beyond who believed that a person of colour shouldn't represent England. But the sense from the immediate reaction in the press and from Argyle fans who remembered Jack Leslie for decades to come is enormous pride. This man who had made Plymouth his home was becoming a club legend and had been given this almighty nod. His success was theirs to share. It's sad to think that as that generation chock full of heroes fades into the distance, a sad rump of the generation that followed denies this history, claiming it's part of a woke agenda.

In the days to follow, as Jack was on cloud nine, his selection attracted commentary in the press, but no surprise or criticism. On Wednesday the *Western Daily Press* wrote:

> An interesting feature to Southerners of the England XI chosen to oppose Ireland at Belfast on 24 October, is the selection of J.F. Leslie, the Plymouth Argyle inside-forward as reserve. Leslie, a man of colour, was one

of three players persuaded by Mr Robert Jack to leave Barking Town for professionalism at Plymouth [...] Leslie has improved tremendously since changing his status. Last season he made 40 league appearances and was top scorer for the Argyle with 14 goals.

'A Deserved Honour For Argyle Player – Leslie in the Running for a Cap' wrote 'Pilgrim' a few days later on the day of the Watford match at Home Park, which Argyle won 2-1. The *Football Herald*'s star writer had become a sure-fire Jack Leslie fan by now. He was bursting with local pride at Jack's recognition:

> I don't wish any of the chosen forwards any harm, but I should very much like to see Argyle's clever inside-left gain his place in the team. In any case he has attracted the notice of the International Selection Committee and therefore it is not too much to expect that he will win his cap on some future date.

That Jack had been picked as a reserve was by the by. He had been chosen for England and people were delighted. Jack knew 'Pilgrim' personally and, although he was never one to court attention, this kind of praise elevated the excitement as he considered the trip to Ireland.

Just imagine Argyle fans stopping Jack in the street to congratulate him just as they love to get selfies with players today. Plymouth embraces the footballers who show commitment to the place and the club. Jack Leslie had done that. They would remind him about Jack Hill, David Jack and all the others who had got the nod in recent years and who had progressed. His next step would be a starting place and a full international cap. Jack Leslie didn't just feel it in his bones, it had been confirmed on paper and by his manager. He would finally get to do his bit for his country.

From the moment he had been given the news, Jack was dreaming of his England debut. Like 'Pilgrim', he would never wish ill on any other player, but he knew the reality of the game. The likelihood of someone getting an injury was high and he would be ready to step up. Filling his head were thoughts of stepping out with the other England players, getting his first touch, making his first run, showing the Belfast crowd what he could do with both feet. And scoring. A thundering shot from distance, a diving header, an overhead kick even. Jack could see himself knocking in goals for his country. And with two weeks until kick-off an opportunity for Jack to make the starting XI did open up. After the Huddersfield left-back Sam Wadsworth picked up an injury, the *Western Daily Press* on 12 October said, 'A substitute, of course, will now have to be found, and it is not unlikely that Leslie, the darkie forward of Plymouth Argyle, will fill the vacancy.' While Jack Leslie was a versatile player, this turned out to be speculation. Jack had no idea what plans the FA had for him, because they hadn't yet been in touch. He expected to travel with the squad and could be forgiven for thinking, like 'Pilgrim', that an injury or some other mishap might give him the chance to play. At first, the FA pinned their hopes on Cope of Notts County as left-back. When he was also ruled out, Newcastle United's Frank Hudspeth was drafted for his first and only cap at the ripe old age of 35.

The press saw Jack's selection as noteworthy. He was an emerging player, and the consensus was that he was a justified selection for the England squad. It's also interesting that only at this stage was Jack's colour mentioned frequently. The local press had rarely referenced it and, although the language is sometimes uncomfortable, there's no sentiment of negativity towards him. To be a part of the set-up and meet other players and officials would be another experience that Jack Leslie, the future England player, could chalk up. It was all good preparation for when he pulled on the famous shirt with those three lions that would rest against his beating heart. The time that would surely come when Jack Leslie would play for his country.

For Win, seeing her husband selected for the national team not only made her proud but also gave her hope. She had to cope with constant looks in the street and even abuse for being in a mixed marriage, and this news could only have a positive impact. In October 1925, future England player Jack Leslie and his wife Win thought they were about to be truly accepted at last.

Chapter Eleven

A Second Look

ONCE THE fuss and initial excitement died down, Jack was thinking about how he should prepare for the Ireland trip. He had plenty of experiences to fall back on: the South America tour and his forays to France as a teenager. These were meticulously organised affairs, and he would expect the same from the English FA. After a hard-fought 1-1 draw at promotion rivals Reading on Saturday, 17 October, his thoughts must have turned towards packing his bags for Belfast. But as the date of the fixture drew nearer, the silence grew more deafening. Young Jack had been left in limbo: 'Then all of a sudden everyone stopped talking about it. Sort of went dead quiet. Didn't look me in the eye.' Jack was getting a nagging feeling. Something wasn't right and he was beginning to realise what had happened. He knew.

Jack's dreams of glory were slowly turning to dread and disappointment. The first sniff came on Monday, 19 October when the team was printed in *Athletic News* and the travelling reserves were now listed as Harry Nuttall and Stan Earle. Nuttall was then injured and replaced by Alf Baker of Arsenal. But what of Jack Leslie? He had suffered no injury, nor was he serving a suspension. This was just two days before the England party was due to travel.

Within two weeks of being given the career news of a lifetime, an honour only a select band of players would ever be granted, Jack Leslie's name was nowhere to be seen. The position he was now in was incredibly difficult. Nobody was talking about the England selection anymore, so how could he find out what was going on? Jack tried but no one gave him a straight answer:

I didn't ask outright. I could see by their faces it was awkward. But I did hear, roundabout like, that the FA had come to have another look at me. Not at me football but at me face. They asked, and found they'd made a ricket. Found out about me Daddy, and that was it. There was a bit of an uproar in the papers. Folks in the town were very upset. No one ever told me official-like, but that had to be the reason, me Mum was English but me Daddy was black as the Ace of Spades. There wasn't any other reason for taking my cap away.

The euphoria, the embraces and back-slapping from the Plymouth Argyle players and staff turned to embarrassment and awkwardness. There's a sense in Jack's quote that, while he 'didn't ask outright', he did try to broach the subject. How his heart must have sunk during those uncomfortable exchanges when he realised he wasn't going to get to the truth, even from those he trusted such as Bob Jack. That the colour of his skin meant the denial of his dream was a truth to be avoided and Jack felt his only option was to bottle it up too.

Jack Leslie reflected on the events in 1978 and his words show what a quiet and humble man he was. Talking to Brian Woolnough, he simply said, 'They must have forgotten I was a coloured boy.' Players such as Clyde Best, Sir Trevor Brooking and Harry Redknapp, whose boots were tended by an elderly Jack Leslie at West Ham United, remember him fondly. They also tell of a modest man who never spoke of his footballing achievements. His testimony when finally asked to tell his story is all the more remarkable.

The only person he could have discussed this with was Win, and she wasn't surprised. As a white woman in a mixed marriage, she was treated appallingly on many occasions, so she knew people looked on her husband differently, even though they loved him as a player in Plymouth. Her hopes were dashed too that month and she was incredibly upset by how her husband had been treated. 'She was very shy and reticent when it came to meeting people,' say her granddaughters, 'but if Jack had that recognition as an English footballer, perhaps with that status she might then have been more accepted. The fact that she was living with a man of colour would have been more acceptable because he was an English hero, or he would have been.' Being chosen for his country meant so much to Jack and his family. England should have been proud to have Jack Leslie on their team.

When the final team came out, Jack recalled, 'Then the papers came out a day or so later and Billy Walker of Aston Villa was in the team, not me.' Billy Walker was one of the finest forwards of his generation, playing 18 times for England, so Jack might have found it difficult to oust him from the starting line-up for a while. He was a sensible choice as inside-left but was also an occasional centre-forward, so England could have tried the pair together. And Billy Walker didn't play in every match. After winning his penultimate cap in February 1927 there was a gap of nearly six years before Billy had one final outing at the age of 35. This was the period when Jack Leslie was in his prime and was, for many, the best inside-left in the country.

That rejection has stayed with the family. Jack knew it wasn't right, you can just feel it from his words. He never spoke out in anger, but what happened enraged his daughter, Eve. She spoke to the BBC in 2004 about her frustration:

> He probably had a lot of disappointments because of his colour. I don't know if it bugged me more than it did my dad, because I think that it was the icing on top of the cake. It was his career and that would have been the top accolade wouldn't it, and it was taken away from him.

Eve passed away in 2022, and the passion she felt was there until the end. In fact, her initial reaction to the statue campaign was that it was all too late. It's understandable. In the end she was happy that her dad was finally recognised, but her fury shows the impact such treatment has beyond the moment and the individual.

Jack wasn't someone to dwell on the negative and didn't discuss the situation with Win at length. They were trying to get on as a newly married couple and she didn't have it easy. Alone in Plymouth with no close friends, and a husband who was away half the time playing football, Win saw the judgemental looks of neighbours and passers-by that would sometimes turn to vocal abuse and threats. Like Jack, she would no doubt reflect on what happened later in her life. After the dressing room banter surrounding the elation of his selection, Jack couldn't bring himself to talk to his team-mates about it now. Any commiserations they had would have been brushed off. And as the only black professional in England at the time, how could he possibly raise an objection? The wall of silence and inability to discuss the matter is heart-breaking.

On 24 October 1925, England limped to a nil-nil draw against Ireland with the amateur who was given his only cap and the captaincy, Claude Ashton, putting in a lacklustre performance. Ashton had been picked after performing well in the Charity Shield and was a fine sportsman, but Jack Leslie couldn't have done any worse. That afternoon Jack scored after just ten minutes and hit a second in a 7-2 victory against Bournemouth and Boscombe Athletic. Jack Leslie never let that crushing disappointment affect his game, but his strength should never take away the reality for him, as his granddaughters believe: 'I think he just shut it down, because it was too painful to face.'

Jack didn't know exactly what the FA bigwigs had said to each other, but he knew why his name had been struck off. And he tried to shrug it off, just like he did when he was regularly taunted by opposition supporters and players: 'I used to get a lot of abuse in matches. "Here darkie, I'm gonna break your leg," they'd shout. There was nothing wicked about it – they were just trying to get under my skin.' This is a man who didn't complain and just got on with his work on the pitch. But Jack Leslie was robbed of his chance to make history for England. How did it happen?

In the aftermath of the Ireland international, the controversy was reported, both locally and nationally. In the *Daily Herald* on 28 October, a London reader wrote in asking:

Leslie, of Plymouth Argyle, was down as reserve (to travel), but for some reason, not made public, Leslie played

137

for his club on Saturday while Earle, of West Ham United, travelled to Ireland instead. Cannot you, in the columns of Labour's only daily newspaper, make a stand against the snobbery which is like a blight in first class football?

This was a left-wing paper, so was this reader a proto-woke virtue signaller? Maybe. 'WAS LESLIE CHOSEN?' the *Daily Herald* asked:

In an endeavour to discover why Leslie did not go as reserve to Ireland, we rang up the Football Association yesterday, and were informed that Leslie had not been chosen. Upon making a similar inquiry at the offices of the Press Association we were told that at the meeting of the Football Association Leslie was announced as a reserve, and his name appeared in many papers which published the English team the same evening and the following morning.

The denial was bold, given the Press Association had been handed the team news. There's no suggestion anywhere in the days after Jack's name had been circulated and printed nationwide that there had been a mistake. This was the uproar that Jack remembered but the journalists weren't able to dig any deeper at the time.

The FA minutes for 5 October note that Nuttall and Earle were selected as reserves to travel. But this is a typed, not handwritten record made after the meeting had taken place and only signed off in ink by FA president Charles Clegg on 19 October. At a meeting that day the minutes inform us that Baker of Arsenal was chosen in place of the injured Nuttall. It's ludicrous to think the FA officials would keep a written record of a controversial reason for reneging on their earlier decision. It was struck from history and any questions rebuffed and allegations denied.

While Jack Leslie was trying to process what was happening to him, it's devastating, but not surprising, to read that his club and the local press were forced into a corner. Plymouth Argyle released a statement that dumbfounded Jack, as 'Pilgrim' reported on 31 October:

> My readers may be expecting from me a comment upon the Argyle Club's announcement that Jack Leslie was not chosen as reserve forward for England. Unfortunately, my pen is under a ban in this matter, but I may say that a mistake was made in London and transmitted to me. Anyway, Leslie was at that time playing quite well enough to be chosen.

There was no mistake, just denial, and this is a telling quote that backs up Jack's own testimony. People were not allowed to talk about it.

In the same edition of the paper, on the same page, is its 'Chatterbox' column, a series of brief news and gossip items, and there among that week's tittle-tattle sits a remarkable pointer: 'Jack Leslie, Plymouth Argyle's inside-left, is the only "gentleman of colour" in present day League Football.' 'Pilgrim' may have had his pen banned but here he gives readers a clue. In all the years leading up to this moment, Jack's skin colour had only been mentioned once in the *Football Herald* in 1921, at the very start of his Argyle career. 'Pilgrim' is doing exactly what *Popbitch* and *Private Eye* do today to avoid the lawyers, cleverly leading us to the truth without breaching the ban. And, at least, in describing Jack, 'Pilgrim' is being more respectful than most rather than tacking on an epithet we would no longer use today. Jack was too busy helping his team beat Bristol Rovers 3-2 away that day to dwell on this 1920s media storm.

The decision was accepted by Jack in the sense that he could see no way to make a stand and no point in doing so, but it would stay with him for the rest of his life. The irony of the story is that the FA selected him on merit and yet they dropped him for this shameful reason. How and why could this happen? Like so many questions and stories around the treatment of people of colour at the time, it's far from simple. One thing is for sure, it's unfathomable that none of the 14 selectors knew Jack was black.

The FA International Selection Committee was chaired by the FA's president Charles Clegg and made up of: Charles Wreford-Brown (Oxford University), S.R.B. Cowles (Norfolk), Arthur Joshua Dickinson (Sheffield Wednesday), B.A. Glandell (Amateur Association), Henry J. Huband (London FA), Harry Keys (West Bromwich Albion), Arthur Kingscott (Derbyshire FA), John Lewis (Lancashire FA), John McKenna (Liverpool FC), H.A. Porter (Kent County FA), George Wagstaffe Simmons (Hertfordshire FA), J.A. Tayler (Gloucestershire FA), Tom Thorne (Millwall FC) and Harry Walker (North Riding County FA).

Of those 14 long-standing football administrators, Henry Huband of the London FA, J.A. Tayler based in the West Country, and Tom Thorne, director of Millwall FC, must have seen Jack play. He had turned out for Argyle against Millwall several times, including the recent 2-0 win at Home Park on 12 September in which he scored 'a very pretty goal' according to 'Tamar'. His former Barking and Essex team-mate and friend James Dillimore, who attended Jack's wedding just a few months previously, played for the Lions that day too. Huband had visited Plymouth in March when Home Park hosted an amateur international. Several other officials on the wider FA Council who had been asked for recommendations would have seen Jack play for Argyle, Barking or the Essex FA team. His county had awarded him a senior cap, so he was on the roll call of honours.

The selectors' meeting on 5 October can't have been a long one, as it was scheduled between a match and a fancy dinner with players who had taken part in the Charity Shield, and they were, no doubt, all eager to get cracking into some decent food and wine. Jack Leslie's name was put forward at that meeting, agreed and signed off verbally by Charles Clegg, then released along with the 12 other names to the Press Association.

Once named, why did the FA renege on Jack's selection? There's no footballing reason as Jack continued to play without injury for Argyle and he wasn't suspended. The FA records show that he never faced suspension in his career. What grounds could there be, other than the one Jack himself stated in such a matter-of-fact way when asked later in life? If there was a different explanation then he would have been told, it would have been made public and he would have been given a chance in the future.

There are only two sensible explanations as to how it happened. Either one or more of the committee members put Jack Leslie's name forward, backed up by his stats and got the agreement to select him without mentioning his colour, and then he was dropped when other members discovered he was black. Or, more likely, Jack was recommended and any argument came out in his favour, but then an objection was raised later by a committee member or an external party. Once Jack's name was on the England team sheet in the press and commentary about his colour was seen by a wider audience, that would, no doubt, elicit a response from anyone minded to object on grounds of race. There was no groundswell of public opinion that a man of colour shouldn't be selected for England. Whatever objections were raised were done so privately and by a person or people of great influence. That's what persuaded the FA officials to cave in.

Frederick Wall's call for new talent in September was to get players seen before the 5 October meeting. In Jack's case Tom Thorne might already have seen him and confirmed his potential, had he been in Plymouth to watch his club Millwall on 12 September. Officials might have travelled to Brighton to watch Argyle's visit on 3 October. Jack said that the FA came to have 'another look at him' and it's possible that more committee members took the opportunity when Argyle played at Reading on 17 October. When the committee met again on 19 October, they had team matters to discuss, with injuries that had occurred to other players in the meantime. The decision may have been made beforehand or discussed at this meeting. Either way it was ratified and the minutes from 5 October were typed up, omitting Jack's name, and signed in ink by Charles Clegg. The new team was released and printed in *Athletic News* that day.

It has been suggested that it's scandalous to accuse the FA committee members of racism when they're no longer here to answer the charge. Whether or not any selectors spoke out in that way, the irony is that one or more argued in favour of Jack. That's clear from the outcome. He was selected. Even Charles Clegg, the most senior

FA official, wasn't an obvious candidate for proposing the reversal. He was 75 at the time, teetotal, deeply religious and mourned the onset of professionalism. But he was also a straight-talking northerner who was liberal-minded in other ways and considered some of his southern counterparts 'snobs'. The members either changed their mind as a committee once they all became aware of Leslie's heritage or they were pressurised to conclude that his inclusion wasn't appropriate. Whoever pushed back against his selection and whatever the process, it happened because of the colour of Jack's skin, and the FA allowed it to happen. But then, so did everyone, because it was simply accepted.

Knighted in 1930, Sir Frederick Wall was the archetypal FA administrator and wrote a memoir about his time in football with the usual praise for the gentlemen amateurs of the game. His words on how committees were viewed are tellingly defensive and contradictory:

> Some people seem to have the strange idea that the Football Association meets with all the secrecy of the Star Chamber of centuries ago. There are those who hold that the FA love to punish and instil fear into directors and players; that they are a modern form of the Inquisition, with Sir Charles Clegg the Grand-Inquisitor. If these feelings remain, I can assure those who suffer from such delusions that they are quite wrong. It is true that commissions are held in private. Only those who have business there, or are concerned with the proceedings, are allowed to be present. [21]

So, the people who complain that these are private meetings are wrong. But the meetings are, in fact, held in private, and so they should be. Thanks for the reassurance, Sir Frederick.

When seen in the context of race relations at the time, you begin to understand why and how Jack Leslie was dropped. We've been fed the narrative that racial tension exploded in the post-Windrush years when immigration from the Caribbean and elsewhere increased. But in Jack's youth in Canning Town and in other areas with significant black populations, riots targeted those communities. There was undoubtedly tension and racist abuse and attacks, alongside integration, camaraderie, friendship and marriage. It was no different for Jack on the pitch and in life.

The attitude towards black men who wanted to join up and fight during the First World War, as Jack Leslie wanted to do had he been a little older, is indicative. Some recruiting officers let black candidates sign up, others turned them away. Principal Clerk at the Colonial Office, Gilbert Grindle wrote, 'I hear privately that some recruiting officers will pass coloureds. Others, however, will not, and we must discourage coloured volunteers.'[22] The official approach as set down in the *Manual of Military Law* of 1914 is as murky as the FA's treatment of Jack. It states that 'any negro or person of colour, although an alien, may voluntarily enlist', but this relates to the lower ranks, and the manual 'prohibits their promotion to commissioned rank'. The inference here is that being black meant you weren't British, which is exactly how Jack explained the FA's thinking when he was denied his England chance.

The exception of Walter Tull proves the rule. As a fit, famous player for Northampton Town, he joined the Footballers' Battalion, half of whom were killed in action. Having served heroically, and with the army in desperate need of men with ability and experience, Walter was given a commission, something that was usually reserved for men of 'pure European descent', said the military manual. So, you could be half-German but not half-Jamaican. There was an attitude writ through the military top brass that black soldiers shouldn't be killing white men, but some, like Walter, broke through that colour bar. He was killed on 25 March 1918 during the Second Battle of the Somme. A born leader who, like Jack, let his deeds do the talking. His commanding officer recommended Walter Tull for the Military Cross, but he was never awarded that honour. Jack Leslie's story is a peacetime echo of brave Walter's.

This military colour bar continued into civilian life. After the war, the Liberal government introduced the Aliens Order of 1920, and this was followed in 1925 by the Conservatives' Special Restrictions (Coloured Alien Seamen) Order of 1925, which required all black seamen living in Britain to register with the police and prove their nationality. That included British subjects. If you couldn't demonstrate your status you would be forced to register as an alien. The response to disturbance and rioting that targeted the black community was to further target the black community. On the left of politics, unions were no better. Of course, there was both tolerance and bigotry across the political divide, just as there was in society and football through the players, supporters, club hierarchy and administrators in the Football League and FA. In this maelstrom of unrest and paranoia, there would have been a fear at governmental level that seeing a person of colour promoted to the national football team could be destabilising.

Jack's treatment was pandering to those fears. A young man's dream was about to become reality and then it was silently shattered without a word.

Chapter Twelve

On with the Job

JACK LESLIE reacted in the only way he knew how and in the only way he felt he could, by continuing to perform for Plymouth Argyle. But the issue returned throughout his career because Jack hadn't even hit his best form yet. If at the age of 24 he was good enough to be selected for England, and he was, then he would be good enough for many years to come. The partnership with Sammy Black was just a season old and they would go on to perform spectacularly together until Jack's career ended through injury in 1934.

When racism is discussed today, it's often about equality of opportunity and levelling the playing field. The chance to be a part of the England set-up, once denied, spelled the end of opportunity. At that moment in October 1925, the gates to an international career effectively slammed shut on Jack Leslie. A consistent player for more than a decade, he should have been in the running for many more matches, but Jack was never allowed to show what he could do.

It has been suggested that Jack was overlooked because he was playing in the Third Division. That wasn't the case because he *was* selected and other players in that tier had been given the nod too, including his former team-mate and future England captain Jack Hill. And bigger clubs wanted to sign him. In November the *Football Herald* reported rumours that a club 'not 100 miles from the Mersey' – a not too subtle hint at Everton – offered £9,000 to secure Jack and Sammy Black. But Argyle were 'not biting'. What a combination the pair could have created with that club's star striker Dixie Dean. It would have made Jack part of a First Division title-winning team in 1927/28.

The Everton bid was the first of many, and in January 1927 *Chatterbox* included this:

> It will interest the Argyle supporters to know that Jack Leslie, the popular inside-left, is attracting considerable attention amongst managers of league clubs in the First Division, and two well-known club managers watched him perform at Luton recently. Argyle, however, are not prepared to part, for the club know his value quite well.

Later that year 'Pilgrim' protested that the powers that be should consider Jack for international matches. He must have known that his plea would fall on deaf ears.

There would still be plenty for Jack Leslie to achieve in life, but it's important to understand that he wasn't a player who had a short run of good form, piqued the interest of the England selectors and then faded. He went on to have a stellar club career and in a different era would have moved to a bigger club. At Plymouth Argyle he would earn the maximum wage available to a footballer, and when the offers came in from clubs higher up the league, Bob Jack and the directors knocked them back. They also, as we'll discover, refused to listen to Jack on the subject of a transfer.

From the moment he hit his stride in the year leading up to the England selection, Jack Leslie made headlines locally and nationally. In November 1931, *The People* described Jack as 'one of the greatest schemers in English football', and reported a Second Division manager as saying, 'England's dearth of really good inside-lefts appears to me to be merely imaginary. Have the selectors, by any chance, run their rule over Leslie, the Plymouth artist?' The following year, a writer for the *Daily Telegraph* speculated on England's choices and reports on the 'CLAIMS OF LESLIE', saying, 'I believe the best inside-left at present is Leslie, of Plymouth Argyle, but I doubt many of the selectors have seen him play often enough to realise this.' Jack is in the journalist's dream team that he suggests the FA pick. Of course, the selectors had taken a second look at him. They wouldn't take a third.

It's remarkable that through the Jack Leslie story the one national paper to contribute so significantly is the *Daily Mail*. Its 1978 interview provides us with a rare journey into Jack's mind but the paper at the time he was playing has some key commentary too. In 1932 it called him a 'coloured genius', and the following year Geoffrey Simpson wrote about the 'Coloured Stars of Football' when Frank Soo was about to make his Stoke City debut. Frank was born in England, the son of a Chinese immigrant and a white English woman. While serving in the RAF, remarkably, Soo did play for England in unofficial wartime matches. Simpson's commentary on Jack Leslie, 'the best known of the coloured stars', is incredible. He boldly states, 'Had he been white he would have been a certain English international.' Now, I don't believe the *Daily Mail* was embarking on a campaign for Jack to be recognised. It was purely making a statement of fact. Football writers, supporters and the selectors with the power to make him an England player knew he was good enough.

For the Plymouth Argyle fans the treatment of Jack Leslie stuck with them. It's not something Jack could talk to them about or vice versa. If he was ever asked about it, he would have brushed it off in the same way he did in that 1978 interview. But members of the Green Army who saw him play and were alive when the events happened felt he had been badly wronged. I struggle to comprehend why some people would deny the story when the generation that was there remembered the events with such sadness. When Jack returned to Home Park for a visit in 1965 along with Sammy, who still lived in Plymouth, the matchday programme said, 'Why they were never "CAPPED" is still a sore point with Argyle supporters of the time and still rankles with a lot of them.'

As a boy, 97-year-old Charlie Trevethan watched Jack play at Home Park just a few years after the call-up and it still rankles with him today: 'He was one the best players we've ever had and to be picked and dropped like that. We are supposed to be a Christian country and to do that to a young lad like that, it's disgusting.' But

Jack Leslie had little time to reflect on this era-defining decision. The football season is relentless and its demands intense.

As the winter of 1925 closed in and Jack Leslie's England chance had been quashed, the outlook for Plymouth Argyle was bright. They were sitting pretty at the top of Third Division South. Surely 1926 would be their year. Jack's team didn't lose at home until Chelsea, then in the Second Division, came to Home Park in January for the FA Cup. It was a tight 2-1 encounter in front of a bumper crowd of 31,025. But a few wobbles followed. They should have won at Millwall when Jack played brilliantly but Argyle had two goals ruled out for offside. It ended 0-0, and a rare 4-2 loss at home followed against Northampton Town. The rigours of league football and his now constant targeting by opponents meant Sammy Black was out for this run of matches.

That February, Bob Jack decided to strengthen the squad with a handful of signings. One of them, Fred Titmuss, would become Jack Leslie's best friend in the Argyle team for the years to come. Fred had played for Southampton since 1919 and was a well-known full-back with a masterful sliding tackle. He was in the team that pipped Argyle to promotion on the last day of Jack's first season. He had a humble background like Jack, although it was a rural upbringing. Fred was a farm labourer from Pirton near Hitchin before finding football. His great nephew, Pete Lake, says it was no surprise to find out he was mates with Jack: 'He was a smashing fella who would treat everyone the same.' Fred won two England caps before joining Plymouth and that achievement is still commemorated to this day in Hertfordshire. Just think how Jack would have been celebrated in Devon throughout his life had he been given that honour.

Meanwhile, Jack's old rival for the inside-left position, Bert Batten, was allowed one final outing at Home Park and scored in a 5-3 home win against Brighton in February before being sold to Everton. Bert was tired of playing second fiddle to Jack and was keen to move on. While Bob Jack wouldn't part with his key pairing of Leslie and Black, he was happy to give Bert the chance of first-team football elsewhere and the £1,000 fee helped towards the £1,750 paid out for Titmuss.

Although Argyle bounced between second and third place in the league in the early months of 1926, they were very much battling for promotion again. The excitement of the season end included a visit from First Division Everton, but it was a bittersweet affair. The match on 19 April was a benefit for Jack's old comrade Patsy Corcoran. The Scottish outside-right had suffered appendicitis and been rushed into a nursing home back in January. The 32-year-old never played for Argyle again and only notched a handful of appearances after returning north of the border. Patsy had gone to South America with Jack and joined him and Win at their wedding, so they were good pals. It just shows how transitional the game was. It still is, but in those days it was harder to keep in touch, so Jack and Patsy knew they may not see each other again. These benefit matches were a vital part of footballers' earnings as their wages were limited, and bagging Everton's visit was a coup. Bert Batten returned for the match, but more exciting for fans was their famous centre-forward Dixie Dean. The Toffeemen won 4-3 but reports say Jack Leslie and Sammy Black were the equal of Dean.

As Jack said farewell to Patsy Corcoran with four matches to go, Argyle hit a monumental milestone … 100 goals for the season. How can a team score more than a century and not get promoted? Plymouth Argyle would find a way. They beat QPR 4-0 away, Jack scoring one with his head. He was the star player in a performance that made them look like champions. After a home win, 1-0 against Charlton Athletic, while promotion rivals Reading lost 3-0 at Crystal Palace, Argyle looked favourites. They were level on points but on top with a whopping goal average that would never be a factor. And they had a match in hand. On Monday, 26 April, Jack and the team travelled to Brentford and drew 2-2. Top on points and with goals galore, Argyle only needed a draw at Gillingham while Reading hosted Brentford. It was within their grasp and even Gillingham fans were wishing them luck, assuming Plymouth would at least get a point.

On Saturday, 1 May, Jack and his team travelled from London, where they had stayed overnight, and were met with telegrams wishing them good luck and a trainload of Argyle fans who had made the long journey to Kent. The *Westminster Gazette* had concerns about the defence, but was certain Argyle would score 'with Leslie, the old Barking boy, about as neat a dribbler as there is in the country'. But a bleak wind blew from one goalmouth to the other, and when Argyle lost the toss the omens were against them. Behind after 11 minutes, the team reacted well and did everything but score, an overanxious Sammy Black even missing a penalty. When keeper Fred Craig failed to punch a corner clear and it dropped to Gillingham's inside-right, Marshall, Plymouth's promotion dreams came crashing to the ground. 'Bitter Hops for Argyle' read the rueful headline of 'Pilgrim'.

News must have been coming in that there was no catching Reading, who beat Brentford 7-1 that day. By the end of the match Jack and Sammy were broken men on the pitch. It's rare to read about Jack Leslie giving up, and this is the only time it's written in ink. He had turned matches around with his grit and determination, but in the last ten minutes of that season-defining encounter, as news filtered on to the pitch, the trials of a long campaign took their toll. For this to happen for the fifth time in a row when they had played such brilliant, swashbuckling football was a sucker punch. Sports writers across the land, including the nationals, reflected on yet another calamity for Argyle. How tough must this have been for Jack Leslie, given what the sport he loved had done to him that season? He kept his emotions in check for the most part, but at this moment they would be laid bare in front of the most committed of Argyle supporters and his team-mates. In a classic piece of football knife-twisting, Jack's old Barking and Argyle mate Frank Richardson was playing for Reading and scored four that day.

Jack would reflect on the opportunities that went begging that season. The England chance he could have no influence on, but for Argyle maybe he could. That's what would go through his mind even though he'd had a cracking season. Jack and Sammy hit 27 goals between them and helped Jack Cock to a record haul of 33. The team had scored 107 league goals. That tally has only been equalled once by a Plymouth squad, in 1951/52 when they played four more league matches. It was the highest total in all divisions that season and 30 more than Reading, although Argyle conceded 15 more. What could have made the difference? Well, Jack's team managed a useful draw away to their rivals back when he thought he was in the England team. But the home fixture in February was a rare and disastrous 3-1 loss. Jack was injured and missed that crunch match. Frank Richardson wasn't and scored.

The *Daily News* couldn't have summed up the season better with its headline 'Alas for Argyle'.

Alas for Jack.

Chapter Thirteen

Head Turned

IN THE summer of 1926 Jack Leslie could look forward to the first full summer break he was able to spend with his new wife Win and to celebrating their first anniversary. Her companionship helped ease the end-of-season heartbreak and the devastating blow to his hopes of playing for England. As he approached his 25th birthday, Jack's best years as a player were still ahead of him. Commentators would continue to suggest that he should be in the running for an international cap. Yet, from this point on, Jack knew it was never going to happen.

Plans for relaxation were tempered by the fact that this was a time of huge social anxiety and unrest. Within days of the season ending, the General Strike took hold of the country. With his working-class roots and trade union membership, Jack was a man with staunch left-wing views, so would have been on the side of those who downed tools. Whether or not he and Win were still in Plymouth or up in London for a visit, they would certainly have been aware of events. The quiet streets around their Peverell neighbourhood were disturbed on 8 May by thousands of strikers heading for Home Park. But the marchers weren't demonstrating their anger at the pampered footballers living there – Peverell is hardly Alderley Edge, and players themselves had their wages cut in the 20s – they were going to watch a match. The chief constable's wife stood at the centre of Home Park and swung her leg at the leather for the ceremonial kick-off to an extraordinary encounter between Plymouth Police and Strikers. Strikers won 2-1.

It must have been strange for Jack and Win living comparatively comfortably during this turbulent period. It wasn't a life of luxury but was a contrast to their childhoods, especially for Win, with her large, impoverished family. And it must have also been a wrench for her to leave them in London. Jack and Win had a strong marriage but that doesn't mean it was always easy. A lifetime partnership is an achievement that's often hard-won. While marrying Jack meant Win had a little more money, it also meant travelling far away from her parents and seven siblings. She was thrust into a situation where her husband was idolised in Plymouth while also being treated differently due to the colour of his skin. People would also treat her differently because of the man she married.

We've seen how rioters a few years previously had targeted the black community and how commentary on mixed marriages was often not only damning, critical and downright racist, but also horrific in how it viewed the women who fell in love with men of colour. This is in no way to diminish how Jack was treated. The England selection affair was clearly appalling, and he suffered abuse on and off the pitch. But while Jack became accepted into Plymouth society, something that's clear from the fact that he became Argyle captain and a Freemason, mixing with local VIPs, Win was often shunned. Her granddaughters have been told of the shocking abuse: 'She was spat at in the street and people would call her scum for marrying a black man, which is really difficult to come to terms with.' This was incredibly tough for Win, although she loved Jack deeply. In the aftermath of October 1925, she knew that some people would continue to treat her that way. This was an added pressure on the marriage and had a profound impact on how Win viewed her own choice to marry a man of colour.

Jack also had a job that involved constant away trips and commitments connected to Plymouth Argyle. His views on social issues were, not surprisingly, of their time. Women were expected to become homemakers when they married, while Jack worked and socialised with his team-mates. Jack was out with the lads frequently, and his granddaughters tell stories of how the players would hire charabancs to race along the quiet but narrow roads across Dartmoor.

Chatterbox dishes the dirt on practical jokes, such as one of the players being served up a cold kipper as a prank. The anonymous victim promised to 'get his own back!' In May of 1926 it asked a curious question: 'What did the married men do with the shillings offered for every goal scored by them?' There's no suggestion of anything untoward. Maybe they were having a flutter unbeknown to their wives, but they were certainly getting up to hi-jinks and Jack was included in that.

In the first year or so of the marriage there was the afterglow of the wedding and the excitement of the move. The couple's immediate neighbours in Glendower Road seemed a progressive bunch too. A solicitor who lived in the same house had been secretary of the Socialist Democratic Federation, Britain's first socialist party. That didn't always equate to enlightened views on racial and gender equality, but it's more likely to have skewed in that direction. Of course, not everyone disapproved of mixed marriages, so friendships were formed in Plymouth, but compared to the adoration of Jack Leslie the footballer, Win was isolated. She found her new life increasingly challenging as the reality of being the wife of a professional sportsman in a town far away from her home began to bite.

Meanwhile, the football season didn't get off to quite the same start as 1925/26 and there was even talk of changing the club colours of green and black, as if that must be the reason for this run of bad luck. Thankfully that never happened. Where would the Green Army be without the very colour of the blood flowing through their veins? Jack was playing well until he broke his toe in a 3-0 home win against Coventry City. He had to limp through to the end, and with Sammy Black out for a run of six matches, it's no wonder they weren't flying. Once the left-wing pair recovered, things began to pick up and they were fifth by the end of the year after a Christmas double over Exeter City. Jack was approaching his peak as a player and interest in him was hotting up, with managers of two well-known First Division clubs making enquiries.

Jack Leslie loved Plymouth Argyle and the club stayed in his heart forever, but had Bob Jack not been hell-bent on keeping him, Jack would have joined one of the bigger London outfits who had been keen to sign him. This would have gone down well with Win for sure. Whatever the debates at home about their situation, Jack and Win were thinking about the future and a family of their own.

It was early 1927 when Win sat Jack down and told him that he was going to be a dad. Perhaps the spring in his step inspired the hat-trick he scored in a 7-1 home thrashing of Crystal Palace on 12 February. The timing of Win's pregnancy was also good from a financial perspective because this was Jack's first benefit year. These matches were crucial in giving players a nest egg from their short and uncertain careers. Plans for the fundraiser show what a popular player he was both with his manager and team-mates. Bob Jack pulled some strings to bring his old club Bolton Wanderers down to Home Park. This was a real coup as they were a top First Division team and FA Cup holders. It would also be a reunion with the gaffer's sons Rollo and David, the latter being one of the biggest stars of the game in Jack Leslie's time. The Argyle players also organised a dance for Jack at the Pier Pavilion to boost his finances, perhaps knowing he had a child on the way. Previewing the event, 'Pilgrim' hoped that Jack Cock would belt out a few tunes and that Sammy Black might do a turn on the dancefloor. *Chatterbox* flagged the dance to, erm, interested parties by writing that Jack's 'numerous admirers should bear this in mind'. Just imagine what a pregnant Win made of that. It emphasises the attention this good-looking young player received and points to the pressure that would have put on his marriage. This must have had an impact on the couple, no matter how humble and attentive a husband Jack was when he was at home.

In the end Bob Jack came to Win's rescue. When a Devon Cup match against Exeter City was scheduled for the following day, he banned players from attending the dance. The promoters were gutted as their star guests were forced to pull out. The disappointed Argyle players lost 3-1 in any case and the manager couldn't even blame it on the boogie.

A few weeks later, on Monday, 28 March 1927, Bolton Wanderers came down to Plymouth for the benefit match, which Jack shared with the long-serving Fred Craig; it was the Argyle keeper's second fundraiser. 'Pilgrim' encouraged fans to attend, saying both players deserved the support. Bolton brought their first team, so a galaxy of international talent was on display. Argyle boasted Welsh internationals, Moses Russell and Jack Pullen, as well as England cap holders, Jack Cock and Fred Titmuss. The Trotters had six internationals, including David Jack and Harry Nuttall, who was originally named alongside Jack as a travelling reserve for the Ireland match in October 1925. Nuttall's absence that day was clearly and very reasonably explained; he picked up an injury and was replaced. Unlike Jack, Harry *would* go on to be a squad member ten times and win three full England caps.

Sadly, Jack had picked up a knock before his benefit match. In a hard-won 3-2 home victory against Bristol Rovers, Jack played through the pain, switching to the left wing to see the match out. But it meant he was a mere spectator for the Monday night friendly in his and Fred Craig's honour. The match didn't attract the bumper crowd 'Pilgrim' hoped for, and while 5,000 seems pretty good to me, Jack Leslie's journalist fan was hoping for 12,000. Bob Jack suggested in the match programme that supporters send in cheques to supplement the gate receipts. The result of that plea isn't on record, but the difficult times the country was going through affected both the crowd and subsequent donations.

Jack and the Argyle were always chasing the pack through the 1926/27 season, but their home form was staggering. They didn't lose a single match at Home Park. However, both Jack and Sammy Black missed quite a few fixtures through injury, and as the season end approached, Argyle performed better with Jack Leslie than without. Jack Cock had rarely missed a match and had been on fire again, with 33 goals, while Jack hit 14 in 34 and Sammy scored 10 in 37. Strong contributions but not quite enough to close the gap on Bristol City, who won the Third Division South championship by two points, with Plymouth runners-up again. That would make it six seasons in a row that Jack Leslie's Argyle team finished second and missed out on promotion. Lady Luck was grimacing from above.

Jack would have other things on his mind. Win was in the second trimester of her pregnancy and through the summer the couple made plans for the birth of their first child. When the 1927/28 season began this certainly didn't affect Jack's football. His brilliant performances so impressed 'Pilgrim' that he berated the international selectors for failing to come and look at Jack. But the FA had looked at him and already decided his England fate for good. Being frequently tipped for England throughout the peak years of his career must have been more than frustrating. Whenever he had a chance to reflect, it hurt.

While Win would have been in his thoughts, Jack's approach to her pregnancy was of its time. Childbirth was something that should be left to the women in the family to deal with, while he supported them by earning a wage on the pitch. As the event drew closer, Win went to London to be with her sister and other members of her large family, who would be on hand to help. Jack was with his Plymouth team-mates down in Devon preparing for their mercifully short away trip to Torquay United.

Evelyn Winifred Leslie was born in Poplar, East London on 4 November 1927. It was a difficult birth, and baby Eve would be their only child. It was still joyous news for the couple and Jack celebrated the following day with a 2-1 win against Torquay. He would have travelled to see his new daughter but it would be a flying visit as Jack had to be back in Plymouth to train for the match against Southend the next Saturday. Win had the support of her mum and three older sisters, which must have been invaluable in those early days and the years to come. Jack's job meant he was constantly on the move and playing every weekend for much of the year.

While Jack was wetting the baby's head after the victory and continuing to win plaudits for his performances, Win was learning to cope with a new baby while recovering from a traumatic birth. Jack can hardly be criticised for failing to take Eve out for walks in a papoose while sipping a flat white like the new dads of today. He was just 26 and truly hitting his stride as a footballer, so his day-to-day focus was on his job. But at times he took his eye off the ball when it came to his marriage and responsibilities as a father. Some of this was out of his control. The fact that he couldn't be with his family for Eve's first Christmas was due to the packed festive schedule. A home match on Christmas Eve was followed by the Exeter derbies on 26 and 27 December. But Jack wasn't as mindful of Win's hardships as he might have been and that put pressure on the young parents' relationship.

Jack's form continued to be inspirational, but two things dealt Plymouth a major blow. The first was the loss of Jack Cock, who 'left under a cloud' shortly after Eve came along, although the two events weren't related! Cock hadn't started a match that season and wasn't happy. The Torquay match would be Cock's last for Argyle. Jack Leslie was saddened to see this talented forward leave, but this was the politics of football and Bob Jack didn't tolerate players whose ego outstripped their usefulness. Millwall came in with £2,000 for him, the biggest fee they had paid to date, and Cock was out. There are hints that the previously supremely fit Cock was a yard or two off the pace as he approached his 34th birthday but the stats show that selling him was one of Bob Jack's few big mistakes.

Jack Leslie must have questioned his mentor's judgement for once. Millwall went on to win promotion and the star striker scored 83 goals in 126 matches, while Bob Jack couldn't settle on a regular centre-forward. Jack Cock was an entertainer and his quote on taking penalties is great: 'My record in that branch of football endeavour is 100%. But then I've never taken one, never been asked, and never want to.' But what kind of striker doesn't want to take a penalty? The quote is served with lashings of ego, and cocky characters can have a negative impact in the dressing room. Maybe Bob Jack had just had enough and thought it was for the best, whatever impact it had on Argyle's goal tally.

The Plymouth manager had no such concerns around Jack Leslie. He had been working his socks off and the influence he had within the team was about to be recognised at club level in a big way. When Plymouth travelled to play Norwich, the old stalwart Moses Russell was laid up with food poisoning, and senior pro, Fred Titmuss, had an ankle injury.

Jack Leslie was about to make history.

On 10 March 1928 Jack Leslie became the first black player to captain a Football League team. There wasn't the fanfare that greeted moments such as Viv Anderson's first England appearance but, as we look back, the significance is huge. It took exceptional people such as Jack Leslie and Walter Tull to win these accolades on exceptional merit when so often there was push-back and denial. This was breaking new ground and a bold decision by Bob Jack and the Argyle board. Most of all it was a remarkable achievement by team captain for the day, Jack Leslie. Jack led his team of Pilgrims on to Norwich City's pitch at The Nest. Conditions were dazzling as Jack won the toss. He took full advantage, choosing to play with the sun at their backs. Snow blizzards occasionally came in to obscure the blinding sunlight, but Argyle failed to make their initial advantage pay and the fairy tale ended. They lost 2-0.

Jack finished the season with a creditable 15 goals in 41 league appearances, missing just one match, while Sammy Black hit a remarkable 16 in 29. Opposition defences were constantly targeting Jack's mercurial mate and he was laid up several times. Sammy's injuries and the lack of a consistent centre-forward put paid to Argyle's chances, and they finished third, with Millwall 12 points ahead. Jack and Sammy Black discussed their plight. They were two top-class players who had raised eyebrows among First Division managers, and after a closing 2-0 away win at Crystal Palace, *The People* rumoured that the pair 'would not be against a change'. But it reiterated that Bob Jack wasn't prepared to part with certain players.

The transfer system that gave all the power to the clubs was described as a 'Crying Injustice' by *The People*, as they could either demand ludicrous fees or simply refuse to sell players while not even paying them the maximum wage. Plymouth Argyle didn't mistreat Jack and Sammy in this way, and Jack was earning top whack by 1928 and probably earlier, but there were other factors. In the summer of 1928, with baby Eve still in her first months, attempting to move on from Plymouth must have been a point of discussion. Win had found it hard away from her family so the prospect of being stuck there indefinitely with a baby was a heavy cross to bear.

In the early years of parenthood, Win and Eve spent most of their time in London while Jack got on with his job. Through the 1928/29 season any issues they might have had didn't get in the way of his football and Jack had his best season to date. He and Sammy Black played 45 times, each missing just a solitary match. Jack was joint-top scorer alongside emerging centre-forward Ray Bowden with 22 goals, and Sammy netted a solid 13. While Jack was earning a regular wage with win bonuses coming in handy, it was hard going for Plymouth financially. Argyle rarely lost at Home Park in all his years in the Third Division South, but fans were as fickle in the 1920s as they are now, and missing out on promotion was taking its toll on gate numbers. Jack recalled, 'Plymouth didn't have much money. We were practically owned by the local bank ... The players lined up for their pay outside the bank every Friday. But it was a grand life, and a good living ... especially at times like the big strike.' The club is in a comparatively good position today, but it has always been a tightrope as Argyle's tumble into administration and perilous teetering on the edge of the Football League in the early 2010s shows.

Crowds for league matches bounced between 10,000 and 16,000 and were at the higher end as Argyle topped the division at Christmas. The only hint at disharmony was on the trip back from a 1-1 draw at Walsall, which they should have won. As the team arrived in the town, half-back Norman Mackay played the banjo, apparently creating 'weird sounds', but 'Pilgrim' reports that Jack dealt with his team-mate: 'Unfortunately, the prospects of an harmonious return journey after the game were rather spoilt by Leslie settling on the "G" string as he would upon a goalkeeper who fumbled a shot.' The gate at Home Park was swelled by FA Cup excitement on 12 January 1929. Plymouth had failed to get very far in the competition to date, but 30,358 fans saw Sammy Black hit a hat-trick to send Second Division Blackpool packing and Argyle into the fourth round.

When Plymouth drew Bradford Park Avenue, who were also in the tier above, the match hit the headlines. More than 33,000 supporters would fill Home Park as Jack and Argyle made their furthest progress in the prized competition. But there was another reason for the strength of the spotlight on the match. Park Avenue had recently signed Eddie Parris, which meant Jack Leslie was no longer alone. There were now two players of colour in the Football League. Parris's father was a sailor from Barbados who married a white woman, and Eddie was born in Pwllmeyric, near Chepstow in Wales. Knowing this, the papers fixated on the link, with one picturing the pair as 'Coloured Cup-Tie Rivals'. The *Daily Mirror* also picked up on the connection: 'There is the somewhat unusual prospect of two coloured young men, both thoroughly British, appearing on opposite sides.' It's progressive, or is it pointed, of the paper to state unequivocally that the two men were UK citizens? In the end, Eddie didn't play in that cup tie, but in 1931 he did win one cap for Wales, becoming the nation's first black player. Turns out Eddie Parris was accepted as a bona fide born-and-bred Welshman, but for England's selectors, Jack wasn't British enough. In the cup tie, Argyle did everything but get the ball in the net in a 1-0 defeat and a dream died.

And yet another promotion dream died that season. Despite a late surge and some superhuman efforts from Jack, it was, again, not to be. As his team faced a rare defeat at Home Park against Northampton Town on 6 April 1929, Jack limped off injured. He was patched up and returned at outside-left, where he would be less exposed to danger. But when a cross looked out of reach, Jack stretched his leg to score with an overhead kick. Incredible that given such efforts 'Pilgrim' wrote of 'unnecessary barracking' and that one player 'almost dreaded playing at Home Park for fear that he played a bad game'. I don't think Jack Leslie was a player who would ever dread a match but there are several reports of fans targeting him, even at Home Park. It would be no surprise to find some fans turned on him before others, because there are always those who are quick to find an excuse to target a black player.

On the final day of the 1928/29 season Argyle had a mathematical chance of promotion but it was highly unlikely. Only 5,000 turned out, which shows how weary the fans had become despite the sparkling play of Jack and Sammy. Their left wing was the one area of the team commentators said shouldn't be touched. When other scores came in at half-time there was brief excitement, which helped the team push for victory. Jack and Ray Bowden scored, and Argyle beat Bournemouth and Boscombe Athletic, but 'Pilgrim' lamented almost as if it were the passing of a nonagenarian relative: 'We have been prepared for disappointment, so that the end came peacefully.'

Although the season ended in failure, it seems madness to view almost a decade in that light when you look at the goals scored, the stars who passed through Home Park and the winning streaks Jack Leslie's team built. They remain in the history books to this day. The recognition Plymouth Argyle received was remarkable for a Third Division club, and Jack was frequently at the centre of this. He stood out for his talent, while his skin colour was also often mentioned. National papers, including the *Daily Mail*, *The Times*, the *Daily Mirror* and *The People*, frequently referenced Jack during this period. In November 1927 his headshot appeared in a *Mirror* cup tie preview, praising him as one to watch out for: 'One says "of course" in regard to Leslie, for he has been giving some brilliant displays this season.' In February 1929 he was a question in the *Sunday Mirror*'s crossword in relation to his skin colour, and in January 1930 Jack was referenced alongside other notable athletes of colour, including the boxer Len Johnson. The middleweight was himself prevented from competing for British championships due to a colour bar that existed in the sport from 1911 to 1947.

As the decade reached its close Plymouth Argyle fans seemed weary and exasperated. The Green Army is a fantastic fanbase that stretches from the city across the globe. But there are always fans who berate the team. Even in the good times there are dips during matches or periods in a season when things aren't quite firing, and the crowd can be quick to get on players' backs. The complaints they, the manager and 'Pilgrim' made about supporters needing to get behind that 1920s team, on occasion, echo around Home Park today. At the first home match of the 1929/30 season only 12,161 supporters turned up to see a 1-1 draw against Brentford. Not a great start.

Jack Leslie and the senior players who had seen such misfortune in the 1920s, such as Moses Russell and Fred Craig, would wonder whether it was ever going to happen for them. This would be the toughest campaign for Jack since the trials of 1925.

Chapter Fourteen

Pull Your Socks Up

TWO BRILLIANT away victories preceded the disappointing opening home fixture against Brentford, and as summer turned to autumn in 1929, Argyle were again tipped for promotion. 'Don't jinx it!' thought Jack. He had heard it all before. Jack Leslie and Sammy Black were touted as the pair to make it happen this time. On 1 September *The People* said, 'One of the minor mysteries in football is: Why isn't this duet playing in the Top Drawer?' And writers began to suggest that Sammy deserved a Scottish cap. While the experts and fans fawned over Jack and his partner, the new dad was struggling to juggle parenting with professional life.

On the pitch, the away form was making all the difference this time and Argyle didn't lose a match until Christmas Day at Coventry. They only lost four times away and were unbeaten at Home Park that season. Yet, while 3-0 up against Bristol Rovers in January, the Plymouth crowd turned on Jack as they demanded more goals. 'Pilgrim' wrote, 'There even being a suspicion of barracking where Leslie was concerned.' Sammy missed that match through injury so perhaps the creativity didn't come quite as easily, but Jack had scored and Argyle were easily ahead. It seems strange that Jack was targeted, and while there's no mention of race, the phraseology of 'suspicion' is telling. It demonstrates how quick people were to judge him harshly compared to others and how he had to go beyond other players to prove how good he was.

Despite the team's success, Jack was getting a hard time from the Home Park crowd and opposition supporters and players who would always try to needle him, and often because of his skin colour. But some problems off the pitch were more of his own making. By the spring of 1930 he was a 28-year-old married man with a two-year-old daughter. It's fair to say that he hadn't considered what pressure that would put on Win. While Jack was on the train to and from away matches singing songs and playing cards with Sammy and his mates, Win was either in London with her family or in Plymouth looking after Eve on her own.

As a popular, established player, Jack had a built-in social life and commitments in the community. In April 1930 he was involved in charity matches between the Plymouth and London branches of Fairbairn House Boys' Club where he began his football journey. Jack helped at the Plymouth club encouraging local youngsters, which is laudable, but meant more time away from his family. He was often out having a beer with his pals if there was a break between matches, great for team spirit but not so great for his relationship. There are several photographs in the family album of Jack hanging out with his good mate Fred Titmuss in Plymouth's Central Park where the stadium stands, and in the countryside. Sometimes there's a woman in the picture who must be Fred's wife. Win is nowhere to be seen. Win doesn't appear in any group photos with Jack and their West Country friends until Eve is a little older.

The isolation, judgement and absence of Jack began to get too much for Win. It was early in their marriage when she decided she'd had enough and couldn't take it anymore. Win read Jack the riot act and left him, and she made it clear that it was for good if he didn't buck his ideas up. In the spring of 1930, Jack suffered a loss of form, and on 1 March 'Pilgrim' believed he needed a rest. These two events may well have coincided because this would have been a particularly tough time for Win as a young mother. After the trauma of childbirth and the first months of looking after their new baby with her mother and other family members on hand, Win had returned to Plymouth with Eve. She expected to settle into normal family life. But when their daughter grew into a toddler, and Eve was a forthright character, well that would have been even harder to cope with on her own. It began to take its toll.

Knowing that it would make Win happy, Jack tried his best to force a move back to London. But his granddaughters say that fell on deaf ears:

> Granddad wanted to get back to London when he and nan were having an iffy time and he refused to play. I remember him telling me that and Bob Jack said, 'That's up to you Jack, but you don't play, you don't get paid.' So, obviously he wasn't going to be allowed to sign for another team and if he didn't play, he wouldn't get his wages and he had a family to look after, so he had no option.

Jack wasn't prepared to stand his ground any further. He needed his wages, so he got on with his job.

Win's move in giving Jack an ultimatum was as bold as Bob Jack's refusal. She had a large, loving family but they had always struggled for money, while Jack was earning a good wage. Jack's granddaughters were told that it was Jack's mum, Annie, who went to see her daughter-in-law to try to talk her round:

> She said, 'He will grow out of this, he will settle down,' and she went back and perhaps that might have been what shocked him, and he realised what he could lose. He settled down after that.

Jack's efforts and his mum stepping in helped win back his estranged wife. At least the effort Jack was making to consider her wishes and try to get a move back to London showed he could consider Win's situation:

> It was very brave of her to go back to be honest, but she did, and they stayed together for all those years and we could see the love between them. But the early years were very difficult for nan.

Looking back, Jack is seen as a true family man. And he was. But it's no surprise to hear that the life of a professional footballer put huge pressure on the marriage. It's to the couple's credit that they worked through it and Jack changed. He got his relationship back on track and luckily this time his team stuck to the task in his absence. As they pushed for the championship and beat QPR 4-0 on 5 April in front of nearly 19,000 fans brimming with excitement, Jack was back to his old self. He missed a few matches with a blistered knee but returned for the Easter Monday clash at Newport County. A win would secure promotion with three matches to spare. It was nil-nil at half-time, but then Sammy Black hit the net twice – 2-0. That was it. Argyle were up.

Victory would have been all the sweeter for Jack Leslie, having joined Argyle in the first of six crushing years as runners-up. Back in Plymouth the mood was ecstatic. That decade of hurt faded into the distance. What was only recently just a town was now a proud city and the streets were buzzing. For Jack Leslie, the personal and professional trials over that time and particularly in his recent home life could be put to bed. Win certainly wouldn't begrudge a celebration that Easter. The players returned to a heroes' welcome and a civic reception. Telegrams of congratulation came from other football clubs and supporters across the country and the globe, including Buenos Aires. Papers nationwide happily reported Plymouth's success at last, and even those in the towns and cities of promotion rivals agreed that the boys in green deserved it.

Plymouth Argyle ended the season at Home Park with a celebratory 2-1 win against Watford in front of 23,459 delirious fans and one giant pasty. The baked treat with 'congratulations' inscribed on its crust was stretchered on to the pitch and presented to captain, Fred Titmuss. There are no reports as to whether it was tastier than a Ginsters. Argyle finished the championship with a record total of 68 points, scoring 98 goals. Jack had a relatively quiet campaign with only nine goals, although he had only played 36 times due to injuries and his futile strike. Fortunately, Sammy had his back and hit 24 in 41, a remarkable tally for a winger. They were ably assisted by two talented young strikers in Cornishman Ray Bowden and army man Jack Vidler, who scored 19 goals apiece. Bowden would go on to play for Arsenal and England.

When the whistle blew on a successful season, at last, a pitch invasion followed and then a parade through the streets of Plymouth. Three charabancs with a military band, Jack and his team-mates and local dignitaries slowly made their way through streets lined with adoring fans flying the green and black Argyle colours. They ended with a slap-up dinner at The Duke of Cornwall Hotel along with musical entertainment including the dulcet tones of Jack Leslie. The next Monday, having shaken off his hangover, Jack took to the stage again at a Masonic Club dinner. For all their trials and tribulations, I guess Win felt Jack had earned a pass to celebrate such a momentous achievement.

With Jack Leslie's mindset, he could probably see the irony in this being the season his team got promoted. He'd had a year of ups and downs, but Jack was in no way past his best at 28. He was immediately retained, and the front cover of the *Western Independent*'s special promotion programme featured his caricature in the foreground. He stands next to Sammy Black with the ball bouncing between them. The paper's editor, W. Taylor, reminded readers: 'Many first league clubs have cast envious eyes on the two, but the Argyle directors, very wisely, have retained them.' 'Pilgrim' of the *Football Herald* agreed in his inimitable style: 'For the information of some who do not know, I shall now repeat that Leslie is the finest inside-left in the game.' Spare a thought, though, for Moses Russell. He had seen it all and for longer. He had only played a handful of matches through injury that season and at the grand age of 41 had reached the end of his Plymouth road. Bob Jack put him on the transfer list, asking for £100, which would at least be given to the veteran defender. He moved to Thames AFC in East London, who for two seasons played in Third Division South, from which Argyle had just escaped.

What a joyous summer it must have been. Jack, Win and two-year-old Eve spent time on the beaches and in the countryside relaxing before the rigours of Second Division football took hold. Family photographs show Win and Eve happy in the Devon sunshine in pictures taken by Jack. In July 1930 the most beautiful photo appeared on the front page of the *Western Evening Herald*. Eve crouches on the sand looking wistfully at a young lad, perhaps the son of one of Jack's team-mates. A stunning image that also shows they spent time together as a family between the seasons in 1930, repairing bonds that had fractured and forging memories that would hold them together for a lifetime.

The second half of the 1920s were some of Jack's best years in professional football. He had shown the country what he was capable of and had finally progressed to a higher tier. Commentators believed he should be playing at an even higher level. The city was exuberant. When a football club does well it can raise the spirit of a place and that was certainly true of Argyle's home. This had been a time of social and economic strife, so to have something to cheer lifted the heart. Jack was someone who was generally a positive presence, a force for good in the dressing room. But people looked at him in a different way and at times did judge him based on his skin colour alone. Some, as the international selectors eventually did, considered that he wasn't truly English, even though it was the country of his birth. That Jack largely stayed positive in adversity both in his professional and personal life is a testament to his grounded personality. It's also a testament to his commitment to football and his family. Jack Leslie deserved a slice of luck just as much as Plymouth Argyle and its supporters.

Chapter Fifteen

Captain Jack

HAVING SEEN bald warrior Moses Russell play for Plymouth into his 40s, Jack Leslie believed there was a chance to push on to the top flight before his playing days were over. The career high of promotion to the Second Division came for Jack after nearly a decade as a professional. He had just turned 29 and was at his peak. But stepping up to a new tier is never easy in football and the pre-season was no walk in the park either.

Plymouth Argyle were building a new grandstand and, with the help of the Supporters' Club, a new covered area at the popular Devonport End. It's where the loudest chanting can still be heard at home matches today. A labour dispute, so common in the inter-war years, put the pressure on, but once resolved teams worked night and day to finish before the big season opener. When training began in the early August heat, construction meant players had to practise at a ground with no dressing rooms or baths. Essentially, they were in a park. There are no reports of any complaints. Strongly worded emails from agents would be dropping into Bob Jack's inbox if that happened today.

At least Jack and his team-mates stayed dry as Plymouth had a surprising summer free of rain. By the first Saturday of the season, work was still needed on the Devonport End, but the state-of-the-art grandstand was ready. It was a sight to behold as Jack strode out on to the turf to face big boys of the division, Everton. Fans were throwing off their coats and collars and first-aiders had their work cut out. There were plenty of minor casualties as the crowd of around

34,000 were packed together like sardines in a tin left out in the sun. As the team trotted on to the pitch a mighty roar blasted out. They welcomed Everton in 'full-throated West Country style'. The crowd was gracious rather than booing loudly, of course.

Plymouth lost that match but surely showed enough talent and heart to please the home crowd and make it clear they were a force to be reckoned with. Everton had just been relegated and would go on to bounce back up that season. Argyle led at half-time before going 3-1 down until Jack Leslie scored with just a few minutes left to make it a nervous finale for the visitors. It might have been a rare home loss but against such highly rated opposition in a new league this was no disgrace. Throughout the 1920s Jack's Argyle had been appreciated wherever they went, and pundits predicted success. His old team-mate Jack Hill, the England star who was now at Newcastle United, thought Argyle would go up straight away. But the higher tier proved a tough, physical challenge and the travelling that Argyle teams through history have had to contend with was a constant factor. Even in the Third Division South there were many miles to go, but now there were a host of teams in the north, such as Barnsley, Bradford, Burnley, and all the way through the alphabet to Wolves.

It was a relegation battle for sure, but Argyle never looked beaten. Well, maybe they did on 27 December at Everton when they lost 9-1 … but let's get the excuses in. They arrived at 6am having travelled overnight from Plymouth on Boxing Day after beating Cardiff City 5-1 at Home Park. The lads were knackered. To counter that disaster, they did the double over West Bromwich Albion, who were promoted as runners-up. And there was the inspirational 2-0 win against Spurs after going down to ten men. Fred Titmuss had to take over as keeper and Jack Leslie dropped back to centre-half. Jack put in a captain's performance that day just as he did at White Hart Lane in similar circumstances two years later. And with Fred missing half the matches through injury, the team needed Jack. He would lead the side in his friend's absence, including the last 12 matches that took them to safety.

Jack was handed the captaincy with Plymouth Argyle in a perilous position, third from bottom, only one spot above the drop zone and level on points with Reading below. With Jack at the helm, they claimed valiant draws at Burnley and Stoke City, faraway teams in terms of geography and league position. After two wins in three across Easter, Bob Jack went public and heaped praise on his stand-in skipper. The manager noted how he was 'suffering somewhat from the crowd' during the home loss against Charlton on Good Friday. Clearly the Green Army didn't get the Christian memo on that holy day and again Jack was their target. Maybe he was their first point of attack because they had come to expect so much from him. Or was it because a man of colour in a position of authority must deliver without fail or face the consequences from those uncomfortable with his success?

Argyle beat Millwall 5-0 and then wreaked revenge on Easter Monday at Charlton with a 3-1 win, when yet again Jack had to drop back to midfield. To 'Pilgrim' he was 'the hero of the weekend', while 'Traveller' said 'he could not have been surpassed, and was just wonderful'. The manager said, 'Jack Leslie again stepped into the breach, and by his display perhaps not only won the game, but may have saved us from relegation.' Bob Jack knew his player was giving his all for the cause and refused to stand idly by while the crowd got on Jack's back. So much is unspoken yet plain to see in Jack's story, from the nature of the barracking to the inability of people to look Jack in the eye and tell him why he couldn't play for England.

Second Division football was secured with two matches to go by beating relegation rivals Reading 3-1 at home. Jack Leslie was on the scoresheet, one of only nine goals in that campaign. It may not have been his best season in terms of the record books but keeping your team up after promotion is tough and Jack had more than played his part. He had also created plenty of top scorer Sammy Black's impressive 19 goals. Plymouth Argyle had survived, and Jack could enjoy the summer with Win and three-year-old Eve with a deal of satisfaction and security. The club had come through some financial worries, he had been retained, of course, and everything was in place for a more successful assault on the Second Division. And with the Uniteds of Manchester and Leeds both relegated to join them, they would have even more famous names to pit their wits against.

Jack and his family were able to pass a relaxing couple of months together, although it was always incumbent on him to keep fit. Just before training began in August, Jack and at least one other team-mate took a 'novel holiday on a sea-going tug'. Apparently, it was an enjoyable trip despite terrible, nausea-inducing weather. That must have put a wry smile on Win's face, although she was happy for him to have a short trip away on his own after two full months together, such is the contrast between the season and summer. The football rumour mill didn't stop for the warmer months. Bob Jack had to scotch whispers that Sammy Black wanted to leave for a First Division team as 'rank nonsense'. He was probably getting the same seven-year itch Jack had a few years previously. But the manager remained steadfast and kept the pair at Argyle.

The summer had been particularly exciting and rewarding for young Cornish inside-right Ray Bowden. He had joined the FA's tour of Canada, scoring 17 goals in nine appearances. Although they didn't play an official national team, at an FA event back in England on 24 August 1931, Bowden was awarded an international cap. Jack Leslie congratulated the 21-year-old on his achievements and genuinely hoped this would buoy him up for the coming campaign. How ironic that the only player to be presented an England cap while an Argyle player was nurtured by Jack Leslie. The skipper knew his charge could go on to play for his country, but despite being the best inside-left in England, Jack never could. Ray Bowden was sold to Arsenal in February 1933, where he won the league twice and the FA Cup in 1936. He would gain six full England caps. Ray also ran a sports shop in Plymouth with his brother. I used to go there with my mum, trying to persuade her to treat me to the best football boots money could buy in a bid to improve my pitiful game. She disappointed Ray in going for the cheapest option and I'm gutted that as a child I never knew to ask about what he, Jack and his comrades had achieved in the 1920s and 30s.

With facilities firmly in place, pre-season training in August 1931 was a step up in professionalism as the players hit the gym in the new grandstand. It was a 'commodious hall ... furnished with all the necessary equipment, including punchballs, body exercises, a rowing machine and clubs'. Preparation felt good and there was a burgeoning sense of optimism for Jack Leslie and his team. And it really was his team now. Fred Titmuss was approaching the end of his career and would only make a few more appearances, so Jack was appointed club captain of Plymouth Argyle. He was a mature senior pro who would celebrate his 30th birthday that month and had filled in successfully as skipper many times. Jack had shown his mettle in the fight to stay up and was determined to let rip in this campaign with flair as well as grit. This was to be one of Jack's and Plymouth Argyle's most successful seasons in history.

Jack missed just one match and was joint-top scorer with future England striker Ray Bowden, both finishing with a fantastic haul of 21 goals. The season was full of highlights. Nearly 20,000 watched Jack score a hat-trick against Bradford City with each goal bringing his team back from behind to level the score. Four against Nottingham Forest was the difference in a 5-1 win at home. They beat Spurs away and followed that with a 3-1 home victory against Manchester United. They would face United a second time, in the FA Cup on 9 January 1932. What an occasion for the club and for Jack Leslie, leading his team out to be greeted by 27,000 ecstatic Argyle fans. The Supporters' Club presented him with a horseshoe, which brought better luck with the result than the weather. Heavy rain and wind made it a treacherous affair, but Jack guided his team to a 4-1 victory. The mud was so bad that when right-winger Tommy Grozier headed home from an opening created by Jack, he rose 'not like a phoenix from the ashes, but from the mud, plastered with it from head to toe. He had earned his hot bath and, what is more, he wanted it!'

In the extended coverage of the big match, Jack was as straight-talking as ever:

> It was a good cup tie match, but I think we clearly showed we were the better side, and well earned our entry into the next round. The conditions were appalling, but every man in the Argyle team pulled his weight, and I felt thoroughly proud to lead such a winning side.

Plymouth drew a plum tie in the fourth round ... Arsenal away. But the prospect didn't distract them from the league, and when famous Arsenal manager Herbert Chapman came on a scouting mission to Home Park, Argyle beat Millwall 8-1. As the FA Cup tie approached there was huge excitement in Plymouth. Around 8,000 fans travelled to North London, this at a time when away support was a rarity. Journeying with them was a giant, three-foot-long pasty. It had been baked and given a filling considered healthy in the 1930s ... cigarette packs. Decorated in green and black, the crusty carcinogen container was presented to Jack Leslie, who welcomed it heartily. Jack liked a smoke. The Arsenal mascot was less keen. It was a live swan that waddled away, shaking its feathery booty in disdain when members of the Green Army offered it a bite.

Preparations for the match were mind-boggling, with so much attention on the Argyle players that photographers pursued them to their hotel. Unbelievably, Jack and Sammy Black were snapped having their cup of tea in bed. The famous pair had been papped. You expect that swell of local enthusiasm, but there would be no such press intrusion even if Argyle reached the final today. But for the supporters of both teams this was huge, and more than 65,000 crammed into Highbury, with gates closing 20 minutes before kick-off to prevent a crush. Even so, there were injuries in the crowd and police had their work cut out to keep everyone safe.

The actual match is a classic in Plymouth Argyle history. A typical underdog performance, it was full of incident, with Jack Leslie at its heart. After just four minutes he thundered a shot from the edge of the area against the left post, and when Jack Vidler met the rebound, Plymouth took the lead. But for the remaining 86 minutes luck was against them. Argyle were denied a penalty when Sammy Black was cut down in the area. Arsenal equalised from a free kick that shouldn't have been awarded. In the second half the Gunners put two Argyle players out of action for a period. Keeper Bill Harper, who had just joined from Arsenal, had to drag a stricken Jack Pullen behind the goal line as the referee didn't stop play. Soon after Pullen had returned to the pitch, poor George Reed was laid out by the Arsenal captain, who had already got away with fouling

Sammy Black in the penalty area. The match was descending into a war zone, as Reed was carried off with a towel wrapped around his bleeding skull. He returned ten minutes later after the wound had been stitched up and his head bandaged like Terry Butcher in Sweden. That Argyle stayed in the match was largely down to Jack Leslie's morale-boosting stewardship as he 'took upon himself the double role of rover and left half-back'.

It was still level after 70 minutes when Arsenal scored a goal the Pilgrims were so convinced was offside that they employed tactics learned in South America. But the players' encirclement of the referee was about as effective as it usually is. Arsenal then went 3-1 ahead with a great, and fair, shot before Jack retaliated with a short-range effort to keep the tie alive. Argyle still had a chance to force a draw but their luck was as rotten as the matchday pasty filling. Argyle right-back Harry Roberts tried to pass back to Bill Harper and somehow managed to lift it over his keeper's head and into the net. 4-2. Gutted. Jack was 'bitterly disappointed' and said, 'Our boys put up the game of their lives, and we at least deserved to draw.' A replay at Home Park would have warranted a six-foot pasty full of Cuban cigars but it wasn't to be. The *Daily Mail*'s description of Jack as 'a coloured genius' in its match report would be scant consolation. Arsenal went to Wembley that year but lost to Newcastle United in the final.

Reading about such a legendary match and seeing the pictures not only makes you wish you had been there but also shouts out loud how tough, dangerous even, the game was in those years. The higher up the league, the harder the opposition seemed to be physically. Jack Leslie could compete and inspire in that arena. A loss like that was a gut punch but Jack could take heart from the performance and use the injustices his team suffered as a catalyst to push for promotion. They lay fourth in the Second Division, so this was looking distinctly possible.

The influence Jack had within the club on and off the pitch by now can't be underestimated. In February 1932 the president of Plymouth Argyle FC, Archie Ballard, held a dinner for players and officials. Ballard was a huge figure in the city, a business operator and philanthropist who put money into the football club and charitable institutions. The Ballard Institute for Boys that opened in May 1928 had a similar ethos to Fairbairn House where Jack Leslie had earned his football stripes as a youngster. Like Bob Jack, Archie seemed to have huge affection for Jack Leslie and at that dinner congratulated the club on having such an inspiring captain. Jack responded, promising that they wouldn't give up trying to win promotion. Here was a man of colour, accepted with open arms by Plymouth society. The same would almost certainly not have been the case for others who lacked Jack's sporting prowess.

As the team entered the last two months of the season, Plymouth Argyle were still in with a chance of reaching the top tier of English football. Although it never happened for the boys in green and hasn't been achieved in the entire history of the club, this campaign still stands alone. Argyle finished fourth in the Second Division. It was a remarkable achievement for a club out on a limb in the west, and for Jack Leslie, the captain. To date it's the highest league position a Plymouth Argyle team has ever reached. In 1953 they replicated that position with the same number of points, although Jack's team scored a stunning century of goals while conceding 66. Their 1953 counterparts' tally was 65 for and 60 against. On the way, Jack's Pilgrims beat Manchester United, Tottenham Hotspur, Nottingham Forest and Leeds United. Stats aside, the reports of Jack's exploits show what a talented and inspiring man he was. It's fair to say that, to this day, Jack Leslie is Plymouth Argyle's most successful skipper in history.

As the campaign drew to a close, Jack only saw the disappointment of missing out on promotion. Fading crowds at Home Park as the maths became impossible would dampen what, on reflection, was a successful season. In the disappointment of finishing fourth, he probably didn't realise how far the team had come. There had been many positives and he had also finally played and scored in Ireland. Argyle took a short trip on the steamship *Lady Leinster* late in April to Dublin, and on Tuesday, 26 April played a friendly against Bray Unknowns at Shelborne Park in the city. The match only attracted about 5,000 because there was an unfortunate clash with the state funeral of the mother of two men executed during the rebellion. It's remarkable that Argyle travelled to the Irish Free State, given that the English FA refused to play there. The team enjoyed the jaunt and won 3-1, with Jack on the scoresheet.

A Wednesday night benefit match for two Freds, Titmuss and McKenzie, on 4 May would have been another emotional occasion for Jack. Not just because it was against Arsenal but because Titmuss was his best friend among the players, and it was a farewell fixture as he was about to retire. Argyle closed out three days later with a thumping 4-0 win against Chesterfield, which took their goal tally to a century.

Jack Leslie's historic season shouldn't just be recognised for Argyle's league position. In becoming the first black captain of a Football League team, he had broken down a barrier. He continued to receive abuse from other players and sometimes his own fans. Jack's granddaughters believe that being skipper could, at times, have been an added burden: 'That was a feather in his cap, but it must have been quite difficult because I think there would have been elements who would have said, "I'm not having a black person tell me what to do."' As ever, Jack shouldered that without complaint, showing everyone that he should be judged by the content of his character, not the colour of his skin. He was warm and encouraging with his squad but was tough and had a physical presence too. If there was any dissent, his granddaughters imagine that he would have laid down the law. 'I'm the captain, this is my job and you've got to do as you're told!' is how they believe Jack would have responded. He showed the Plymouth Argyle fans just how strong he was, and it had been recognised across the land. Jack Leslie, captain of Plymouth Argyle, was a cool-headed general, an intelligent and utterly committed presence on the pitch who took his team to within a whisker of the highest tier in English football.

Chapter Sixteen

Laces Off

JACK LESLIE was fully aware that his sport could be cruelly unpredictable. Friends at Plymouth Argyle had come and gone. Some found fame, if not fortune, while others had to retire through injury or failed to find stability or regular first-team action. Jack may not have realised the significance of his becoming the first black captain in the Football League, but he was very aware of the spotlight on him in Plymouth and beyond when the team travelled. To say that Jack had become one of the leading figures in the game isn't an overstatement. From the time of that England selection onwards he garnered national attention and his talent was applauded. He had stopped asking the questions the press put in print: When would he and Sammy Black move to a First Division club? When would he get an England cap? By the summer of 1932 Jack knew his manager wouldn't let him go until he was no longer useful to the club's ambitions. As for England, reading any mention of that must have been frustrating and, although he would never show it, this hurt. It was something he immediately put to the back of his mind. Despite this, he would have felt there was still time to reach greater heights with Argyle. Sadly, in Jack's case, fortune didn't favour the brave.

In a repeat of the previous summer, after a relaxing break spent with family and playing cricket, Jack set off for a week at sea. On 21 July he cast off with goalkeeper Bill Harper aboard the steam trawler *Stormcock* for a bit of character-building and mildly perilous fishing. Harper was a tough 35-year-old Scot who had played in America for, among others, the New Bedford Whalers, so he should have had

178

his sea legs. Bill had only joined Argyle the previous December, yet pictures of the pair on the trawler and taking walks on Dartmoor show they quickly became friends. Harper stayed at Plymouth Argyle after his playing career as a trainer, groundsman and all-round helper, and would be a welcome sight when Jack returned to his old stomping ground in his later years.

There was a bit of a dampener leading up to Jack's 31st birthday. On 16 August 1932 he and Sammy Black were among the bearers at the funeral of Argyle director, William Olden. With Sammy in the party, the coffin's journey to the catafalque must have been a slightly lopsided affair. They played a practice match that evening, and the next day, Jack's birthday, took part in a bowls match against a 'Plymouth Hoe' team on The Hoe, the hill from which the beautiful oceanic panorama stretches. Jack and his manager Bob Jack were equal-top scorers in the match, but the Argyle team lost. Still, a day on sunny Plymouth Hoe was surely good for morale. A quick check of weather records suggest it was warm but rainy. Typical. Jack Leslie and Bob Jack could probably barely see the jack they were aiming at. 'It wasn't like this on the postcards you showed me,' our Jack might have said to his gaffer.

After a losing start at Oldham, the season kicked off well and Argyle were unbeaten for the next eight matches, winning six and scoring 24 goals. Things were looking good for promotion as they hovered around second and third. And home matches were brightened by Archie Ballard's innovative introduction of ball boys, eight lads decked out in green and black to fetch the ball and speed up play. This wasn't the only novel idea Ballard would come up with.

Plymouth's distance from, well, pretty much everywhere puts extra strain on the football club. The travel is an expense and takes its toll on the players. Just remember that 9-1 Everton debacle. With few other teams nearby and the weighting of the Football League towards the north, Plymouth was very much out on a limb, and until Argyle are purchased by a billionaire with a bottomless wallet and links to a dubious regime it remains a mighty hurdle on the track to success. The step up to the Second Division from Third Division

South exacerbated that. Archie Ballard's plan to ease the strain was simple. Argyle would fly.

The Football League Management Committee turned his idea down, but Ballard still decided to experiment with air travel. He and the club VIPs would take to the skies without the team for the Stoke City match on 15 October. The executives' outbound flight time was two and three-quarter hours due to a headwind, and just two hours, ten minutes home. The players had about eight hours each way on the train. The directors had a right old jolly-up. Argyle still lost 2-0, although a local reporter praised Jack and Sammy's talents and they had put up a good fight against the top-of-the-table team who would win the league. The *Football Herald*'s 'Special Representative' on the flight to Stoke gave a glorious review of this new-fangled transportation. It was 'A Trip to Enjoy But – What Would Leslie Say!' His pronouncement gives an insight into Jack's activities on away days: 'I can imagine Argyle players enjoying this trip, though I am not quite sure how Leslie, Black, and the other experts would arrange their little game of cards. The seating would present difficulties!' It's a lovely hint at the low-level gambling Jack enjoyed, although it's a habit that would get him into a spot of bother in his retirement.

But while most players missed out on this VIP experiment, club captain Jack Leslie was invited to join the return flight. It was his first time on board a plane, another milestone achieved through his talent and status. Remarkably, Bob Jack was a first-time flyer too. Seasoned air mile collector, 'Tamar', joyfully reported the thrill the pair experienced in a bumpy first ten minutes with the odd lurch and drop. But Jack brushed it off as the flight progressed, clearly experiencing bliss above the clouds compared to the weather in Stoke. 'I could go on forever like this,' said Jack, who was obviously loving it. 'I am sure there is not one Argyle player who would not hold up both hands for it if he could have just one experience such as this … I do not feel any worse than after a train journey and could play right away.'

Jack may have missed out on his card school with Sammy Black, and I'm sure the journey was far from the first-class luxury that elite footballers experience today, but air travel in the 1930s was definitely for the few. The concept was fraught with issues around the cost of flights and players' insurance. The weather might impact travel and there was a concern that this could affect fixtures. Archie Ballard was willing to pay for the team to fly but less than 24 hours after the plane carrying Jack Leslie and the Argyle VIPs touched down at Roborough Aerodrome, the Football League vetoed the idea. Argyle would fly no more. And that was true metaphorically as well as literally.

The influence of Archie Ballard on Plymouth and its football club was immense. He spread his wealth, and this definitely helped keep the players happy. Jack and Win's frustration after being refused a transfer was eased by Ballard's friendship and generosity, but it sometimes caused trouble with the authorities. Jack's granddaughter Lesley wears a beautiful gold ring on her finger, a treasured heirloom with a tale to tell. In an Edwardian setting sits a large central diamond surrounded by ten smaller stones. This fine piece of jewellery was once a tie pin, officially given to Win, but received in her absence by Jack at a dinner on 24 October 1932. The Football League obviously smelled a rat because such gifts to players weren't permitted, and a tie pin was clearly more useful to Jack than Win. Jack's wife had the last laugh when it had to go back to the jewellers to be converted into its current, more feminine form. The furore reached the *Daily Mail*, which reported on the League Management Committee's warning to Ballard that gifts to individual players were strictly forbidden. Archie's deft response: 'A gift to Mrs Leslie, wife of the captain of the team, was from the Supporters' Club.' He had also paid two players' income tax arrears 'to save the club from disgrace'. What a legend.

In the autumn of 1932 Plymouth, in third spot, looked like promotion contenders, but as their prospects faded, so did the crowds once again. Jack Leslie continued to win plaudits and Argyle battled hard, getting good results against eventual champions Stoke at home and sharing the spoils with promoted runners-up Spurs. But injuries mounted, goals dried up and lower gates affected finances. This led to the sale of young striker Ray Bowden to Arsenal in March. The transfer fee was speculated at £4,500 or £5,000, which was at the top end in the 1930s. Whatever the actual figure Plymouth received from the Gunners, the cash covered four new signings with a little spare to boost the club coffers. But the loss of a key partner up front must have been frustrating for club captain Jack Leslie and the now experienced crowd favourite, Sammy Black. These top senior players saw their ambitions hampered by financial concerns and the rigour of Second Division play, which had put several colleagues out for long periods. Jack himself missed nine matches in the crucial early months of 1933.

Plymouth Argyle ended the season with a flourish, beating West Ham United 4-1 at Home Park, but only 10,444 fans showed up now there was nothing but pride to play for. Jack Leslie felt his team had been unlucky, and he spent the summer of 1933 keeping himself fit, playing with Eve, who was now nearly six, and the usual round of cricket and bowls. Sadly, the only report of Jack in a charity cricket match on 9 August doesn't quite show his talent with the bat and ball. He was out for a duck.

Despite the fading hopes of 1932/33 and the loss of Ray Bowden, yet again there were hopes to progress in the season ahead. Bob Jack showed intent by signing some top players, including striker Jimmy Cookson, who had won the FA Cup and promotion to the First Division with West Bromwich Albion. Cookson looked like a great signing and would go on to score 28 goals in just 31 matches. What a difference it might have made had he been fit enough to play more often. What a difference it might have made had Jack been too. On Jack Leslie's 32nd birthday, 'Tamar' summed up a practice match, saying the skipper was 'splendidly fit'. He should have enjoyed a few more campaigns and, with this being a benefit year, Jack hoped for a little more success and some financial stability for his young family before he retired. Little did he know that this would, to all intents and purposes, be his last campaign for the Pilgrims.

When Jack's Plymouth Argyle thumped Manchester United at Home Park 4-0 on 26 August 1933, the Green Army would once again toss any logic aside and fill their hearts with hope. Around 25,000 fans turned up for this glorious opener and the thrilling 4-4 draw against West Ham that followed. Bob Jack and the Argyle selectors decided to experiment with Jack at centre-half, the crucial central midfield role or 'pivot' in the 2-3-5 formation, for the next home match against Brentford. It came after two defeats on the road and fans had been calling for the change. They could see how influential Jack was, and he was inspirational, nullifying Brentford attacks and turning them swiftly into Argyle opportunities. He scored in a 1-1 draw and saved his team from defeat according to spectators. But Bob Jack felt it wasn't worth breaking up the famous partnership with Sammy Black, and just before the next match at Burnley decided Jack Leslie should return to inside-left.

The Burnley match was a creditable 2-2 draw in which Jack scored and put in a captain's performance to secure a point. The match is notable not for the fulsome praise Jack received from the local press in the Lancashire town but for the reaction of Burnley fans to his skin colour. Two readers of the *Burnley Express and Advertiser* wrote in with apparently overheard conversations among the Turf Moor crowd. One reported a joke made about the Plymouth left-winger Black being white, while their inside-left was black. Another sent in this remarkable exchange (try to create an accurate Burnley accent in your head, not out loud):

Bill: 'By gum, Jack, this Plymouth Argyle just reminded me o' that there game o' snooker we had last neet.'
Jack: 'Heaw does ta mek that eawt?'
'Well,' remarked Bill, 'it seemed to depend so much on t' "black".'

Today's Argyle fans hate Burnley for historical reasons of footballing heartbreak, but this was decades earlier and these Lancashire fans were clearly impressed by Jack. But the way he's singled out is very different to how a white player would be spoken of. It's a bit like a jovial conversation with someone that you know that could turn nasty at any moment. Jack had to accept these kinds of jokes, because if he didn't people would see him as the problem. Jack's influence on that match was such that another reader had written in saying his team needs 'a Leslie or a Billy Walker'. Walker was the inside-left who played against Ireland in that England team of October 1925, of course. If Jack had played badly or reacted negatively to this kind of language, then the jokes would have turned sour and barracking from fans would have, no doubt, followed.

In October 1933 Jack and his Argyle team faced two long-distance away days that would be memorable for all the wrong reasons. 'Tamar' described heading to Grimsby as 'one of the most tedious of Argyle's long journeys'. A seafaring set of fans did their best to make Humberside feel like a home from home for Leslie's Argyle. Two hundred ratings from the Devonport cruiser, *Leander*, travelled from Hull with a traditional good-luck gift, a giant pasty draped in Argyle colours. It was presented to Jack ahead of the match and paraded around the ground, which the Mariners' fans found very amusing. They were laughing at the end of the match too. Jack Leslie worked his socks off but his efforts came to naught and Grimsby won 5-1. This was Bob Jack's 900th match in charge of Plymouth Argyle and Jack's 398th as a player. He would only play two more times for his beloved club.

Down the road from Humberside to Lincoln City on Saturday, 21 October, and a valuable away point for Jack and his weary Pilgrims. The match was seemingly drab according to 'Tamar', albeit with two accusations of handball, one by the beautifully named Eugene Melaniphy in scoring for Argyle, and another when a Lincoln outfield player made a terrific save. Neither was given. It ended 1-1. But the match is notable for what's absent from the match reports and only became apparent later. The effect of this incident proved devastating for both Jack Leslie and Plymouth Argyle and it doesn't even get a mention. In the blood and thunder matches of the 20s and 30s players would limp on unless they had either lost the use of their legs or died. So, it's no surprise that the injury Jack Leslie sustained that day went unreported and, whenever it happened in the match, Jack just carried on. Whether or not that worsened the impact, we'll never know.

What Jack's granddaughters tell me is a tale of terrible bad luck. A lace of the leather ball had come loose and, as it flew towards him in the air and Jack connected with it, as he had done on countless occasions, the stray material scraped his cornea. No one, least of all Jack, had any clue as to how serious this was. He brushed it off as a trifle and carried on. Jack was such a committed player with great vision who always kept himself fit, a player who always looked out for his team-mates. But he hadn't seen this one coming. It was not until months later that the extent of the injury came to light.

The following Tuesday, 'Tamar' wrote about Argyle team issues and the possibilities of selling players. The same writer in his guise as 'Pilgrim' had recently reported on more transfer rumours, with offers continuing to come in for players who Bob Jack refused to sell. He was presumably referring to Jack and Sammy Black, who had been the most consistent and lauded Argyle pairing for seven years now. Turns out Bob Jack should have probably accepted an offer. On the Thursday, 'Tamar' still thought Jack Leslie was in the team for the Bury home match, but next day the news was out and his appearance in doubt. Jack had 'developed eye trouble which has necessitated the attention of a local specialist and the protection of a shade'. It was confirmed the next day that he would have to sit this one out, but there was no sense of panic. 'Tamar' described the incident in the Lincoln match as 'a slight blow'. Wrong. It was a massive blow.

What was going through Jack's mind? He thought it a slight incident too and hadn't immediately got his peepers looked at, which probably made matters worse. Observers felt the injury would be a short-term issue and were sure Jack would be back soon to kick-start the push for First Division football. Jack felt the same, but as the weeks drew on it became increasingly concerning. There's a real sense of heartache and sympathy in the words of 'Pilgrim' and others. At the end of November, 'Pilgrim' gave eager fans an update. Jack was now a patient at Plymouth Eye Infirmary, but the club hoped it would be just two or three weeks before his return. Make that a year.

As 1933 drew to a close, Jack was frustrated and downright bored but still hopeful. He was discharged from the eye infirmary in mid-December and expected to start training soon. It was then that he used his time to pen his article, *Football and Fickle Fortune*. In the same unassuming way that he reflected on others' bad luck in missing out on international caps, so he mentions the ill fortune affecting fellow wounded Argyle players while making no complaint about his own unlucky strike. And he would have been gutted to miss a festive away day at Old Trafford where his team-mates bagged two points against Manchester United in a stunning 3-0 win. After another 3-0 victory, at home to Bolton on 6 January 1934, Argyle were seventh in the table and only a point behind the second place that would secure promotion. Jack Leslie was a mere spectator at Home Park when he could attend and was still wearing a pad over his injured eye. But he would be overjoyed that his team were doing well.

An FA Cup third-round tie brought Huddersfield Town, then a major force in First Division football, to Home Park on 13 January. Jack joined what was then a record crowd of more than 43,000 fans at Home Park in a thunderous cheer as his team went ahead after 20 minutes. The excited, nervous Janners were hopeful of a massive upset as the clock ticked by. They went silent when Town equalised with 90 seconds to go. Agony for the club captain forced to watch in the grandstand with the Argyle suits. Huddersfield won the replay and the league results that followed weren't pretty.

'Pilgrim' felt that Jack's long-term injury was hampering Argyle's campaign. It certainly can't have helped. By the end of March 1934, he was yet to train, and while he was still being paid, his lack of action meant no win bonuses, and what of his benefit year? This was additional income Jack expected to receive, and as the season came to an end he and Win were worried about the future. A month later and Argyle were in mid-table obscurity while Jack faced the end of his professional football career. When Bob Jack issued his retained list, published by the *Western Morning News* on 18 April, Jack's name was absent. But he wasn't on the 'open to transfer' list either. On the one hand this seems rather cold-hearted, but given how long he had been sidelined, the 'special consideration' the manager and directors were giving him shows how much he was valued. They badly wanted a fit Jack Leslie in the Plymouth Argyle team.

Bob Jack awaited a specialist report before deciding. 'Pilgrim' told anxious readers that Jack's damaged eye was improving but the other had also been affected and they were hoping it would clear up over summer. It must have become infected during the procedures, compounding the distress for Jack and Win, and there were times when it was feared he would lose his sight. No doubt he was talking to friends who had faced the fading of their football journey and taking comfort from their advice. Fred Titmuss was now running a pub in Cornwall. There's an idea.

Just before the season end, Jack's benefit match took place against Bristol Rovers. He didn't play, of course, and amid the despondency that league mediocrity brings, only 1,000 fans turned out. On 10 May Jack attended the annual supper and social for the Plymouth Argyle Supporters' Club Ladies Auxiliary Committee. At this glamour affair, he was presented a cheque for £10 to augment whatever takings he was due from the match, which can't have been much. I'm sure he was as gracious as ever but would have been hoping for upwards of £100 in his benefit year given his service to Argyle. This is not to say he wasn't appreciated by the club or fans. He truly was loved and the adventures he had been on and the many gifts he had received over the years, all within Football League rules, of course, were a testament to that.

A summer of uncertainty was finally put to bed on 19 June 1934 when he was re-signed for Plymouth Argyle. The optimistic report from his specialist suggested he would be able to start the season and the good news made the papers across the country, such was Jack's reputation in the game. Top players like him attracted crowds. Argyle's visits often boosted gates and his absence was noted in local papers across the country. It was different at Home Park, of course. Like any long-term relationship, Jack's skills were sometimes taken for granted but were sorely missed when they were gone. Jack Hodge, editor of the *Football Herald*, wrote in the 1934/35 Argyle *Hand Book*: 'The prolonged absence of Jack Leslie was a big handicap; his recovery from eye injuries is good news and should greatly enhance the club's prospects.'

However, despite his specialist's optimism, Jack wasn't ready to play in August 1934. It wasn't until November, more than a year since the injury, that 'Pilgrim' saw Jack Leslie in action at the weekly Tuesday practice match. 'It is a long time since he was in the old knicks and jersey,' wrote 'Pilgrim', with a lump in his throat and hope in his heart. He thought Jack would be back soon. On 15 December he finally graced Home Park once again. As he led the Argyle reserves on to the pitch a rousing cheer echoed throughout the ground as 3,000 fans had turned out to show their appreciation. A caricature of Jack with the ball at his feet and the caption 'An Old Favourite Makes a Welcome Reappearance' is a moving tribute.

Jack was 33, and 'Pilgrim' wrote that their star was in good shape: 'One thing that struck followers was that quite obviously Leslie has been carefully looking after himself during his long break.' Fitness was always a key part of his game, and this just shows that, for the time, he was a model professional. Sure, there was no data-driven dieting and Jack enjoyed a beer and a smoke, but he was focused on making a first-team comeback. There were surely struggles during this year-long hiatus and discussions about the future with Win, but he demonstrated the fortitude he was known for.

On Saturday, 29 December 1934 Jack returned to lead Plymouth Argyle's attack as centre-forward against Fulham at Home Park. Why he was chosen in that position isn't clear. Perhaps Bob Jack felt it would be less exposing and taxing than the inside-left spot he usually occupied. Jack played well in this new role and scored an incredible goal. He launched into a diving header that gave no thought to what he had been through over the past 15 months, throwing himself at a low cross. 'It was a splendid do-or-die effort on Leslie's part, in which he seemed to have been badly shaken. The crowd gave him a wonderful ovation.' Classic Jack. Argyle won 3-1.

Famous player turned journalist, Charles Buchan, wrote in his *Daily News* column of his delight at Jack's wonderful recovery. The news was welcomed not just in the West Country, but across the football fraternity. His goal against Fulham had come in the 37th minute. He might have been shaken but his performance after the restart included an assist and gave no indication that this was the end. But, sadly, Jack Leslie wouldn't add to his tally of 137 goals, and his 400th appearance for Plymouth Argyle was his last.

Jack was selected to play in the next match at Bradford Park Avenue, but on Friday, 4 January 1935 he received the terrible news that his mother, Annie, had passed away. She was 73. He was allowed to return to his family in London and grieve with his sister, Letty, and father, John, who was a year younger than Annie and would live for a few more. This devastating blow and the state of his football career would make this a time to reflect. It also gave Jack the opportunity to talk to family, particularly his father. His parents had been supportive of his sporting dream and were proud as punch at what he had achieved.

It's a sad and premature postscript. A freak injury followed by the loss of his mother is no way to end such a glorious career. He would otherwise have played for at least two or three more seasons in the first team, possibly more given his fitness levels, and be competing with his mate Sammy Black to be Argyle's all-time top scorer. The grace Plymouth Argyle gave Jack Leslie in keeping him on the books until 1935, which was the very least he deserved, gave him time to grieve for his mother and think about the future for himself and his family. Jack was still being considered for the first team, but it was clear he was no longer the same player. He would regularly turn out for the reserves and scored a few times for them too, including the odd one with his head. Jack's granddaughters feel that if he knew he could no longer give his best to the game then he would rather step back than, say, move to a lesser club. Incredibly, he wasn't the only player to have his career ended this way and one paper reports eye injuries caused by laces happening to three players, including Jack. Can you imagine the uproar now?[23] There would be an immediate campaign to redesign the ball, but the 1930s were simpler times.

By the end of April, Jack Leslie knew he was on his way, having been given a free transfer. His final match in green was on 4 May for Argyle reserves against Bristol Rovers reserves. It was in Bristol and had a distinct lackadaisical end-of-season feel. Far more enjoyable would have been a charity match the week before in East London. It was 29 April and a Monday night reunion with other successful old boys from Fairbairn House against West Ham United at the Boleyn Ground. The Old Boys won 3-2 in front of 3,000 spectators and Jack showed his class by creating two goals, according to the *Daily News*. Among his team-mates was Albert Barrett, a Fulham legend who won an England cap, while the West London team were still in the Third Division South in 1929. Jack enjoyed a few pints with his boyhood comrades and compared stories. He had a tale to tell from his 14 years by the sea.

The Argyle *Hand Book* for the next season rightfully paid tribute to a club legend:

> First and foremost the name of Jack Leslie, one of the most popular players who has ever donned the Argyle colours, comes to mind. An eye injury ... has cut Jack's League career short, and has also broken a long and brilliant partnership with Sammy Black – a distinct loss to Argyle and football generally.

Jack's granddaughters sum up the hole he left at Plymouth Argyle with a wry chuckle: 'He was the best player so his absence would be felt until they could fill his boots, and they were big boots to fill.' But once a Pilgrim, always a Pilgrim, and Jack Leslie's bond with the club that embraced him continued until the end of his life and beyond.

* * *

The end of Jack Leslie's football career was sad, poignant and, like many of Plymouth Argyle's campaigns in his time, desperately unlucky. But luck played no part in how he had been treated by the FA. Richard Amofa reflected on how this great player might have felt and how his story fits into the chequered history of what football and society expects from black players and how it treats them ...

> As Jack Leslie bore down on goal during Plymouth Argyle's match against Bournemouth and Boscombe Athletic, one can only imagine what was going through his mind. It was a position he'd been in many times before, but this particular goal, his first of a brace during a 7-2 win on 24 October 1925, was particularly poignant. It was the date that Leslie could have made his England debut, but after being deselected from the squad, he wore the green of Argyle on the same day. As England toiled against Ireland in a 0-0 draw, Leslie responded to his omission in perfect style.

It's interesting to look at the context of that period, when black people were described as 'aliens', areas with significant black populations were ambushed and rioted in, and many were discouraged from enlisting in the army, among other things. It made Jack's selection for England even more incredible, but it also touches on a topic that remains pertinent today.

Children of immigrant parents, especially in the African and Caribbean community, will be familiar with the following: 'You have to be twice as good and work twice as hard to be accepted.' Nowadays, we see this in the workplace. Back in 1925, it was black people being accepted into the army based on discretion rather than meritocracy. This applied to wider society, too. In a backdrop of riots and racism, Leslie was adored by Argyle supporters because of his exceptional ability and the goals he scored. Away from the pitch, he mixed with the upper echelons of society and was even invited to become a Freemason. It must have been a strange juxtaposition for his wife, a white woman, who was regularly abused for being in an interracial relationship, despite her husband's elevated status.

But even for Leslie, when it came to gaining the biggest honour an English player could achieve, meritocracy wasn't enough. He was loved locally for *who* he was, but not on a national stage for *what* he was. Even in the crowded rooms of the parties he attended and the functions he appeared at, he was completely alone. Were those who enjoyed his company aware of the potential trauma he was internalising? The local press alluded to the fact that his race was the determining factor in his deselection and this may have brought an element of consolation.

The sheer irony here is that while England were not at the 1930 World Cup in Uruguay having resigned from FIFA, world football's governing body, those in South America were already aware of Jack's talents, having excelled on a tour of Uruguay and Argentina in 1924. His name reverberated internationally but he was unable to showcase his talents on an international stage.

Leslie was already a history maker having been the only black professional footballer at the time. On 10 March 1928 he became the first ever 'gentleman of colour' to captain a Football League team. That he was denied the triumvirate of becoming England's first black footballer and then having the incident airbrushed from history makes it a difficult pill to swallow.

The boy from Barking made the FA look pretty barking mad; their eagerness to have an all-white team rather than putting out the best XI possible to succeed is a concept difficult to fathom. But, alas, 100 or so years later, while the benefits of a diverse workforce are plain to see, there are still barriers to success. It's why that message of 'having to work twice as hard' continues to be repeated through generations.

In 2017, the McGregor-Smith Review, which studied race in the workplace, revealed that all black and minority ethnic groups are more likely to be overqualified than white ethnic groups but white employees are more likely to be promoted than all other groups. In Leslie's era, the Manual of Military Law of 1914 prohibited black people's 'promotion to commissioned rank'. Further, a report from McKinsey identified in 2015 that companies in the top quartile for racial and ethnic diversity are 35 per cent more likely to have financial returns above their respective national industry medians. The benefits of diversity are plain to see, yet glass ceilings continue to be built. Jack Leslie found this out in 1925; then, the ceiling was very much made of stone.

When Jack worked at West Ham, his deep, soothing voice would rebound off the walls inside Upton Park. It was the reassuring tone of a man who prepared the tools (the boots in this case) for West Ham's players. He was a

Argyle trainer Tommy Haynes plays dress up to encourage the lads towards promotion in the 1926/27 campaign. They had finished runners-up and missed out five years in a row. It didn't help – they came second that season too.

Win with baby Evelyn and Jack's mother, Annie, in London. She often stayed in London with her family and in-laws while Jack was away playing football.

This beautiful picture of Evelyn featured on the front page of Plymouth's Western Evening Herald.

Finally! Jack and his Argyle team-mates win promotion to the Second Division in 1930 after a decade of near misses.

Pre-season training, Plymouth style. Jack and keeper, Bill Harper, spent a week on a trawler ahead of the 1932/33 season. The jaunty angle suggests it wasn't plain sailing.

Jack was the first black captain of a Football League club. He shakes hands with Arsenal's Tom Parker, but there would be no smiles after this fourth-round FA Cup tie in 1932.

Ahead of the Arsenal match, Jack sits with no ball at his feet, but the traditional good luck charm ... a giant pasty. Had it been stuffed with meat and potato rather than cigarettes, Argyle might have fared better.

Plymouth VIPs experiment with air travel to ease the tedious journeys to away games. Captain Jack is the only player to fly on the return from Stoke. The Football League veto the idea shortly after.

Jack with a club director and, on the left, Pat Twyford who wrote for local papers as 'Pilgrim' and 'Tamar'. Twyford was the journalist banned from telling the truth about the England selection.

Despite more than a year out with an eye injury which almost cost him his sight, Jack launches himself at the ball and scores with a diving header. It's his 137th and final goal for Plymouth Argyle on 29 December 1934.

The famous Jack Leslie welcomes you to The Swan Hotel in Truro. His bonhomie was such that customers got free booze and sometimes one of his football medals. After a few years Win decided they should stop giving away their hard-earned cash and move back to London.

This medal belonged to Jack's Barking, Essex and Argyle comrade, Frank Richardson. Win was furious when Jack gave his away to a punter in *The Swan Hotel*.

Jack was moved to tears when he got a standing ovation from the Plymouth crowd in 1965. Here he's having a laugh with old mates, Bill Harper, Sammy Black and Frank Sloan.

In the West Ham United boot room aged 77. Jack tended the boots of World Cup winners and club legends for 15 years.

The bronze statue of Jack Leslie at Home Park, Plymouth Argyle's stadium.

Gill, Lesley and Lyn unveil the statue of their grandfather on 7 October 2022.

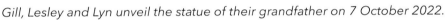

Viv Anderson MBE and Debbie Hewitt, chair of the FA, present Gill and Lyn with Jack's posthumous honorary cap at Wembley on 26 March 2023.

Lesley and club legend, Ronnie Mauge, present the cap to Plymouth Argyle fans at Wembley on 2 April 2023

calm individual, even in the face of overt racism. Yes, he was aggressive on the pitch, he had no other option, but he remained calm and focused even if he was struggling to come to terms with his unjust England omission. He knew he couldn't react as condemnation wouldn't be far away. In fact, Leslie never faced a suspension during his career.

It brings us on to another line that black people have often heard through the generations: 'Turn the other cheek. Be the bigger person.' It's a familiar line, even for those not familiar with Matthew 5: 38–48, but through history, those in minority groups are often praised for doing this, even when receiving the gut-punch of racist remarks.

Leslie's way of responding was by scoring goals. Who knows whether the catharsis of the ball hitting the back of the net was enough to outweigh the emotional trauma of missing out on the biggest accolade for an English footballer, amid everything else that was happening to black people at the time.

In 2022 broadcaster Sangita Myska was praised universally for her stoic reaction to a racist caller during a radio show on LBC. She absorbed 'Jerry from Lowestoft's' blows before calmly dissecting him and his abhorrent views. They say an action causes a reaction but this was not proportionate. Even when being abused, black people have been trained, maybe conditioned, to consider the feelings of the abuser. Externally one can look gracious, but the inner turmoil remains unseen.

And what if you do react to such treatment; if the capacity for calmness has reached its limit and can't be diluted into a reaction that's deemed acceptable. During Inter Milan's 2023 fixture against Juventus, striker Romelu Lukaku was subjected to racist abuse throughout. When referee Luca Marelli pointed to the spot in injury time, it provided Lukaku with the perfect opportunity to respond. Indeed, he scored, and followed up the goal with a harmless celebration: a salute and a finger to the lips.

Inexplicably, he was shown a second yellow card and was sent off for 'over-celebrating'. A decision that was upheld by Serie A after an appeal but was later rescinded after widespread condemnation.

The year before, Barnet captain Jamie Turley was suspended by his club after sticking up for an opposition player, from Stockport County, who was racially abused by a member of Barnet's backroom staff. You probably have to read that sentence twice and even then it's a scenario difficult to fathom. 'Know your place,' these situations scream. It's humiliating.

Lukaku and Turley both have ample role models to learn from. Those who, before them, paved the way to even allow for black voices to be heard. Rewind 100 years and Jack Leslie, as the only black professional footballer in England, had no one. Walter Tull, perhaps, who was a professional footballer and a British Army officer before he died during the First World War. But Leslie was learning the ropes all by himself.

He achieved greatness, which got him accepted, but when he was marginalised, he had to carefully manage his reactions. The only thing he did wrong was being born black. It meant he was English, but not English enough.

Chapter Seventeen

Swanning About

RUNNING A pub or guest house in Cornwall is an idyllic dream for many today. Back in the 1930s the prospect was like an otherworldly adventure to Jack and Win Leslie, a working-class couple from the big smoke. They had seen other Plymouth Argyle players, including Moses Russell and Jack's good friend, Fred Titmuss, go into the trade, and football writers loved to refer to former players as 'Mine Host' at a particular establishment. It was probably Fred who sold the upsides of the trade to Jack as he had taken over a Cornish inn a few years earlier. The attractions for someone with a certain amount of cachet are obvious.

Being a famous footballer would bring in trade, and a London reporter for the *Weekly Dispatch* stayed at Titmuss's hostelry when in St Austell and said, 'Another Argyle hero we met was Jack Leslie, who has just thrown open hostelric doors in Truro.' When he took over The Swan Hotel, Jack's name not only stood proud above the doorway as the licensee, but also on the sign hanging from the wall outside. Every potential customer passing along Kenwyn Street in Cornwall's capital would see his name and know the man who would welcome them, Plymouth Argyle legend, Jack Leslie. It was a shrewd move from a man who had been a master tactician on the football pitch. If only Jack had been as skilful in the actual running of a business.

Taking on a pub and hotel is all-consuming. Jack and Win were still young, in their mid-30s and full of energy. Eve was nearly eight and, when not at school, could help out. The Swan would be a family affair, and one of Win's nieces came down from London to work with them too. But running a bar and a guest house isn't just hard work; it ties you to the business and it's also your home. My parents took over a B&B in Plymouth when my dad left the army and we later moved to a small hotel with a bar and restaurant. A bustling home with interesting people, and the odd tedious one, passing through is exciting and stimulating for a child. But there was always a job to be done and you have to be on top form, or at least pretend to be, whether you're dealing with friendly guests or customers from hell. On top of that, it's taxing keeping on top of the paperwork and you're tied to the building from morning 'til night. It's often intense. It doesn't suit everyone, and, in the end, it didn't suit Jack.

He loved the social side of The Swan. Jack Leslie was a charismatic, genial host, and while he wasn't someone who boasted about his career, he enjoyed chatting to people about football. And they loved talking football with him. What a privilege for any Argyle fan, or any fan of the sport, to be able to chat at the bar to a player who had done so much in the game. Win, on the other hand, was a much more reserved person unless she'd had a couple of drinks, when she would let her hair down a little. Not that she was a big drinker. Jack, on the other hand, did enjoy a tipple, and while this didn't become a serious problem during his life, it was at times an issue, and now he had his very own bar.

It makes you wonder how the couple coped. Until very recently, Jack had frequently been absent and they barely spent a Christmas together. Now they were living and working under the same roof, trying to make ends meet running a business in which they had no experience. And there was young Eve to look after too. Win also liked to take in all manner of injured or sick animals and care for them, something her daughter loved. The Swan Hotel was a menagerie of humanity and other creatures. It sounds brilliantly chaotic.

Being nearby in Cornwall, Jack was able to follow the fortunes of Plymouth Argyle, the players and former colleagues who had stayed in the area. The Swan was handily placed near Truro Bowls Club, and pictures of a sun-drenched green with Jack, Fred Titmuss,

Norman Mackay and a host of other friends during a game suggests these were halcyon days. Jack turned out for Truro City FC a few times at centre-half too, including matches in Plymouth. And he would go to sporting events with mates such as Titmuss. Their presence at a big boxing match in the city attracted comment in the national press, which shows how long his reputation lingered in the public consciousness.

While Jack continued to enjoy a good social life, Win was less happy. It was great to be together with her husband and daughter as they began to live something approaching a normal life, but the beauty of Cornwall was tempered by being even further away from her extended family back in London. Jack's granddaughters remember their nan telling them that running The Swan was damned hard work. It was a good business and the owner's name and reputation brought customers in; it's just that Jack was happily pouring the takings into their grateful gullets. Lesley laughs as she recalled: 'Nan said it was a successful business if Granddad had only been a bit more savvy and not given away most of the profits. They'd only have to come in and start talking about Plymouth Argyle and he'd say, "Have a drink on me mate!"' Maybe people assumed that he was well off, and compared to the average working man he was. But it wasn't a bottomless coffer.

And it wasn't just pints that were on the house with Jack. He didn't seem to care for all the medals and memorabilia he had acquired from his football career. Imagine a famous player just handing over such collectibles now. This is something the family now struggle to understand but it's, yet again, a reflection of how Jack saw himself. His career was over and, while it was nice to remember those times, he didn't think the physical mementoes he had accrued were a big deal. According to his granddaughters he had a classic old-school, male attitude in thinking that girls weren't interested in football, so he didn't think Eve would want any of that stuff. Win talked about one piece she particularly loved, a gold medal enamelled with a crest. Frank Richardson's collection includes several that fit the description, including his 1920/21 London League Championship-winning medal with Barking Town. It's stunning, and one of these with his name engraved on it had been hung around Jack Leslie's neck too. Win was absolutely devastated when he gave it away without a thought. Fortunately, a few mementoes survived Jack's big giveaway, and Lesley, Lyn and Gill always wear one of his surviving medals as a pendant on special occasions.

After a couple of years the pressure of running the business got too much. They had even had a run-in with the law when Jack and Win were accused of 'suffering gaming to be carried on' in October 1936. Court proceedings turned into a farce as this wasn't a terribly serious charge. Jack, Win and some guests were having a late-night game of cards for money, something Jack had enjoyed with Sammy Black on their long train journeys. Local police spotted a light on at The Swan and, on investigating, claimed they heard a woman say, 'I shall have to pay you half a dollar,' and 'Every time I play against you, you seem to get the king.' Sounds like Win might have had a tipple and was finally letting her hair down. She earned that drink. It was about half one in the morning.

One copper lifted another on to the sill, opened the window and pulled back the curtains. Although this isn't reported, he presumably said, 'What's going on 'ere then?' But in a Cornish not cockney accent. The players quickly but ineffectively tried to cover up any coins on the table. Jack employed the kind of time-wasting tactics a goalkeeper whose team is one up in injury time would be proud of. Eventually he let the police in to survey the crime scene. In court, the defendants' lawyer asked the constable whether the card game was rummy. 'It was a rummy affair,' he replied, before being told by the advocate to take the case seriously. The midnight gamblers were found guilty, and Jack was fined £2. Win and the others had to cough up £1. Slightly embarrassing but hardly immoral compared to, say, taking a multi-million-pound shirt sponsorship deal from a betting company.

It's incredible that there's no mention of Jack's status as a local footballing legend. Newspapers were so much more polite back then. Today, the story would be splashed across the tabloids or at least Plymouth Live's website and social media accounts, with the inevitable heart-sinking comments below.

There are a couple of other minor misdemeanours on record too. In 1936, Jack and two other former Argyle players had failed to pay their income tax on time, something that was a common problem it seems, given Archie Ballard's intervention in paying two Argyle players' arrears a few years previously. The most telling of Jack's encounters with the law was in February 1938 when he appeared at Plymouth Police Court on a charge of being drunk and disorderly on Union Street. If you're not from the city, by way of explanation, Union Street was once the most notorious den of iniquity in the West Country, a long boulevard of pubs, nightclubs and takeaways. In Jack's time it was a bustling mix of hostelries, shops and the now sadly dilapidated Palace Theatre. Trams and cars would travel along the strip, and it looked like a great and comparatively civilised area for an evening's entertainment. Nightspots such as Sergeant Pepper's Fun Pub (neither a pub, nor fun), and Boobs Disco, were yet to be established.

Those charges were dismissed, although Jack had to pay four shillings costs, but this incident came in his final year at The Swan and was a tipping point. Win told her husband in no uncertain terms that it was closing time. It could have been a good living for them but Jack's more carefree attitude to paperwork and taking customers' money meant The Swan became a struggle. And a fully stocked bar in your home is a temptation. They may not have been great businesspeople, but they were no fools and knew when it was sensible to call it a day. Win wanted to live on a more even keel as well as return to her roots. In later interviews Jack says he was keen to get back to London too, and once they made the decision to leave they were able to buy a property outright – Wakefield Street was in a nice area of East Ham and would provide a happy home for most of the rest of their lives.

When the family made their way back to London, it must have felt like the time was right. Jack Leslie had left the capital shortly after the First World War. It was now 1938. What a perfect year to set up home back near the docklands, where Jack would return to his old trade.

Chapter Eighteen

Boiling Point

IN 1938 Jack Leslie picked up the tools he had last used 17 years earlier. Little did he know that his country's need for those skills would soon be just as vital as they were when he served his apprenticeship. Jack found work as a boilermaker, riveter and plater at the East India Docks, where he would remain until his retirement. But he never severed ties with football and the clubs where he had made his name. In August he was back at Barking Town, having been appointed as trainer. The club secretary told the *Western Morning News* down in Devon that Jack 'would be warmly welcomed, as he was very popular in the district'. Readers were reminded that 'Leslie was one of the finest players ever to wear an Argyle jersey. He played at inside-left and was a tactician of outstanding quality.' Jack's new role was reported nationally too. Barking was an amateur club, of course, and while Jack never had serious designs on this as a career, he still wanted to be involved. That soon had to be put aside.

The Swan Hotel might not have been the success the couple imagined but with savings from Jack's football career they bought the Wakefield Street house. East Ham was a step up from Canning Town and it would remain the family home for more than 40 years. It was a short walk from a prosperous, bustling high street that was one of the nicest areas in East London at the time. And it was a desirable semi-detached property, because it had a gap of a few inches between them and one of their neighbours. The couple still had to work to provide for their daughter Eve, who was only ten when they moved, and the extended family that came along over the years became their focus. Their new home gave them stability, and this, along with the love and companionship that thrived there, would see the Leslies through the good and bad times to come.

When Jack and Win heard Neville Chamberlain's declaration of war in September 1939, they knew what was coming. Memories of bombs falling near their childhood homes during the First World War were still raw and they were back living and working in the same area that the Germans had targeted back then. This time it was sure to be even worse and now they had a daughter to worry about. Evacuation began in autumn 1939 and Eve reluctantly went to a farm with another girl. It would have been a wrench, particularly for Win, but for Jack too. When Eve wrote a letter saying she and her friend weren't being well treated, it was heart-breaking. The farmhouse was cold, there wasn't much food, and a vicious dog was terrorising them and had even bitten through her foot. Jack and Win knew they had to do something, and as the bombs that had been predicted were yet to arrive, many parents brought their children home against government advice. Win decided she had to get Eve away from the farmhouse from hell, but the Nissen hut in the garden was the only protection from air raids. Jack was adamant that there was no way Eve could stay in Wakefield Street. It was too dangerous.

Had they remained in Cornwall, it would have been a more peaceful existence, but despite the danger, the couple were glad to have a support network nearby. This was a time to pull together, and they were a close-knit family, particularly Win with her many siblings. They joined forces to rent two cottages in Oxford where the mothers took turns to care for around six children, including Eve. Win split her time between there and East Ham, where Jack remained working, and his job was now essential to Great Britain's war effort. The register of 1939, taken just after hostilities began, shows that Win was working as a cardboard box maker, a job she did near the docks when in London.

The bombs began to fall in the summer of 1940, but it was Black Saturday, 7 September that marked the beginning of devastating air attacks. Some 348 German bombers attacked London, targeting the docks, surrounding factories and infrastructure, including the site where Jack learned his trade, Beckton Gas Works. There were 146 people killed in East and West Ham that night alone. This was a terrifying beginning to 56 consecutive raids and the incendiary bombs kept fires in these highly flammable industrial areas burning for hours. The onslaught continued until the summer of 1941, and the sights Jack would have seen must have been dreadful. Jack and Win missed Eve but were glad she was nowhere near East London.

The stories passed down through the family tell a wartime tale of hard work, spirit and the kind of good fortune that rarely favoured Plymouth Argyle. The granddaughters remember Jack facing an incredible, heart-stopping brush with death in the docks. Jack himself wasn't sure exactly what had happened or how on earth he survived but the story goes like this. He was working high up, with a drop below that would certainly kill you should you fall. Jack told Win how an explosion blew him off the platform he was standing on but, somehow, he was able to fling himself to the other side of the structure, grab hold and pull himself up. It conjures up images of a disaster movie, and Jack told Win that when he looked back he had no idea how the hell he had managed to make it so far. It was a distance he was sure he would never have been able to jump. But he did make it and he did survive. Maybe bankruptcy in Cornwall would have been better than bombs in London but they had made their choice and got on with it, just like they always had.

It took about an hour for Jack to walk from Wakefield Street to work. That journey could be as perilous as his occupation during the Blitz. One evening Jack was on his way home when he heard the air raid siren and immediately looked for shelter. A pub was his only option, so he ran in and threw himself under a table. The bombs brought the roof down and, although he had to be dug out, that sturdy pub furniture saved his life. 'Knowing granddad, he'd have grabbed a pint before ducking under it to calm his nerves!' jokes Lyn. There was another near miss that shook the family home so hard it left a crack in a wardrobe. Wakefield Street and the wardrobe were left a little shaken but made it through the war. Eve loved that heirloom so much that she kept it until she moved in with Lesley a couple of years before she passed away. Eve finally had to say farewell to that furniture. It was just too big.

Like most who went through those horrendous times, Jack was happy to do his bit. Had he been in Plymouth, he would have been in just as much danger. His old partner Sammy Black had continued playing for Argyle until 1938 and is still to this day the club's leading goalscorer. He had a brief stint playing at QPR before returning to the city he had made his home and found work in the Royal Naval Armaments Depot. Sammy would have faced similar threats to Jack on his commute and in the workplace, possibly more given he was handling explosives. As a military city with a naval port and dockyard, Plymouth was a key target that was levelled by the Luftwaffe, with 1,172 civilians killed, only 484 fewer than in East London. Fortunately, Jack and Sammy would meet again, but the city and football club they loved would be unrecognisable. In April 1941 the grandstand that had been built after they won promotion with Argyle in 1930 was hit by incendiary bombs. Home Park had been considered a safe enough distance from enemy targets to store more than 100 tons of furniture, including more than 50 pianos, adding a cacophony of fuel to the fire. Only twisted metal and concrete remained once the flames had subsided.

As the war approached its end, Jack and his wife saw their daughter, Eve, blossom into a fine young woman. She would carry the torch and her father's story with the same dignity and integrity that her parents held dear, but she had a fire and anger at his treatment that her father never had. Family was the cornerstone, and Jack's granddaughters remember how Eve was pursued by an American serviceman posted to England ahead of D-Day. He took gifts to the Oxford cottage in a bid to win her heart. The 17-year-old was swept off her feet, but when he asked for her hand in marriage and to join him in the USA, she just couldn't do it. There was no way she would leave her parents, particularly her mum.

Jack hadn't been around much during her early life and war had separated them again, but when peace returned so did Eve. Father and daughter got to know each other at last and their relationship became almost as strong as the maternal bond. Eve adored her dad.

Jack may have had traditional views but he wasn't overprotective, and Eve would go to pubs and out dancing with friends. She met her future husband, Reginald Baxter, or Gerry as he was known, in The Burnell Arms in East Ham. He had served in the Royal Navy and was now a merchant seaman on shore leave. Eve wasn't short of suitors, she had her parents' good looks and father's charisma, but this tall sailor was persistent. He would call round at Wakefield Street but always waited for his sweetheart to come out. One day Jack was coming home, spotted Gerry outside and said hello, before going in to quiz his daughter. He told her that the fella patiently sitting on the wall seemed like a nice young man and she should invite him in. Eve married Reginald Arthur Hoffman Baxter in July 1950. He was given the nickname Gerry because of his Teutonic third name, and it stuck.

This post-war period was one of stability and togetherness. The heady days of Jack's Plymouth Argyle career and the struggle of separation and danger from 1939–45 were done. The family mucked in through the lean times of the late 40s and early 50s. Gerry didn't have much money, so Win even gave him the ring to propose to her daughter. The newly-weds moved into Wakefield Street and that's where they stayed for the next 30 years and where their children, Lesley, Lyn and Gill, grew up. It shows how important it was for Jack and Win to support their family.

Jack was never forgotten in Plymouth, and Argyle never left his heart. Bob Jack had passed away in 1943, his ashes appropriately scattered on the Home Park turf. Jack could raise a glass to the gaffer with some old friends when Argyle visited the capital in 1946. The club's new manager was a former Barking and West Ham United player, Jack Tresadern, who won two England caps in 1923. He had probably met Jack already but would certainly be aware that the aura of Plymouth's pre-war team still hung above Home Park. The match was a 2-1 loss to Spurs but Jack told the papers with no hint of sarcasm: 'They are as good as ever.'

Jack did make occasional trips to the West Country. His older sister Letty had settled in Exeter after the war and those Plymouth team-mates who had become good friends, Fred Titmuss, Bill

Harper and Sammy Black, all lived locally. Like many men, Jack didn't write letters, but he did keep in touch with his old partner. On his trips to the city after the war, he visited Sammy. His daughter, Gloria, remembers Jack coming to their home in Devonport a few times when she was very young. It warms the heart to know that this pair who were so loved as a partnership on the pitch remained close off it.

The modesty Jack maintained throughout his life is no more clearly seen than in a remarkable rescue at sea during one of his West Country visits. It was 1948 and a pleasure boat recklessly careered towards the *Pride of Devon*, a paddle steamer Jack was aboard, near Brixham Harbour. The steamer took evasive action, which lessened the impact, but the pleasure boat passengers were forced to jump into the water and two women in their 60s sadly drowned. It's reported that Jack was crew on the *Pride*, so he must have been reliving one of those pre-season seafaring trips he used to take. Jack told the inquest he heard a bang, then saw people in the water and immediately dived in to rescue two women. His strong swimming skills saved lives that day and he and other crew members were commended for their actions.

As Plymouth Argyle searched for talent in the 1950s, a potential London spy sprung to mind. The club engaged Jack Leslie as a scout. From 1954 he ground-hopped the capital, visiting many pitches he had played on as a youngster for Barking. Jack may have given away valuable medals, but his neat, hand-written scouting notes have been kept in the family and have a unique beauty to them. His record of the conditions, style of play and any standout talent were set out in a clear and concise manner for the Argyle management. Jack also listed his expenses for each match, which included fares, food, entrance fee and, occasionally, 'incidentals', which I'm guessing covered vital refreshments needed for a hard afternoon's scouting.

In April 1955, Argyle director Archie Cload, who had been the Supporters' Club chair in Jack's time, asked to meet him at the Charing Cross Hotel the next day. It was a hand-written note on Cload's business headed paper. He was a fish merchant but he hadn't journeyed all that way to give Jack some free mackerel. Archie was keen to ensure Jack attended a promotion reunion planned for the next weekend. On 30 April 1955, Jack travelled on the night train to Plymouth for a celebratory lunch with Sammy, Fred, Bill and other 'Class of '30' heroes, dignitaries and his old friend from the press, 'Pilgrim' Pat Twyford. After lunch they headed to the ground, where Jack was surrounded by old admirers who remembered him fondly. They hoped his presence would bring them good fortune as this final match was a relegation nail-biter. Amazingly, Argyle won that day and stayed up. They went down the following year.

Ten years later Jack was once again invited to return as a legend to Home Park. He was now approaching his retirement as a boilermaker at East India Docks and had been living a straightforward, if hectic, family life. It had become a much busier home than he had been used to as Eve and Gerry remained with them at Wakefield Street. They were joined by Lesley in 1952 and Lyn the following year. Gill came along later, in 1963. The new, larger extended family was water off a duck's back for Win, with her big clan. Two years after the youngest grandchild arrived, Jack said farewell and made the long journey to Plymouth. He hooked up with Sammy Black once more as the old partners were guests of honour when Argyle took on Middlesbrough on 25 September 1965.

Jack's beloved Argyle had been yo-yoing between the second and third tiers since his retirement. When he visited, they were in the Second Division and Jack watched some great players, such as Mike Trebilcock. The Cornishman was signed by Everton a few months later and went on to become the first player of colour to score in an FA Cup Final, which his team won. Mike is a fantastic character who lives near Plymouth and attended the Jack Leslie statue unveiling. When Jack was welcomed on to the pitch before the match, he wasn't expecting much of a reaction, but the ovation he and Sammy received that day moved him deeply. When he returned to East Ham, Lesley and Lyn recall how proud and special that moment was: 'I can remember so clearly him coming home and talking to Mum about it and he didn't cry but you saw his eyes well up. He said, "I couldn't believe that people would still know me after all this time." He was blown away.'

Now in his mid-60s, Jack Leslie thought his working life was nearly done. As he travelled to his beloved Home Park where he had made such a deep and lasting impression, Jack felt this would be his farewell to football. But there was to be one final hurrah for Jack, and it would last even longer than his professional playing career.

Chapter Nineteen

The 66-Year-Old Boot Boy

JACK LESLIE ended his working life cleaning the boots of the country's World Cup winners Geoff Hurst, Martin Peters and Bobby Moore at West Ham United. This is a fact that's now widely known, and this simple framing – the man denied his England chance spending his later years doing a menial job for these national treasures – gives the story an elegant, bittersweet poignancy.

Jack deserved more and should have been celebrated in his lifetime. But there's a danger of seeing it as demeaning to Jack and that doesn't reflect what the job did for him, the pride he took in it and the love and respect he clearly enjoyed from the players and staff. Jack's return to the East End club he nearly signed for in the 1920s gave him a new lease of life. One year after that historic England victory against West Germany, 66-year-old Jack Leslie stepped back into football and went on to enjoy 15 happy years with the Hammers.

They were some of the best times of his life and he loved it. Jack would see black players come through the ranks in numbers. Doors were opening, particularly at his new club, but opportunities came with a price: abhorrent abuse from the terraces, opponents on the pitch and dressing room 'banter' that black players had to brush off lest they be seen as troublemakers, 'difficult' or 'not one of the lads'.

It didn't begin or end in football. The tone of Jack's granddaughters' skin varied and, sadly yet unsurprisingly, Lyn, who had the darkest complexion, would face discrimination as a young girl:

I was told to go back to my own county. I used to come home from school in tears. Mum told me not to react and show them they couldn't hurt me. I would pass that on to other girls who were getting the same abuse and save the tears 'til I got home. I told Granddad and he started to cross to the other side of the road if we saw him, so people wouldn't think we were related but I wouldn't have that. I was proud of my granddad.

This is how many people of colour have found to be the only way to deal with abuse. Just as Jack Leslie couldn't react and say anything about what happened to him, so his granddaughter had to steel herself to get through the school day. And how sad to think that the only way Jack felt he could make things better for Lyn was by pretending not to know her.

In football there are connections everywhere but Jack Leslie's bond with West Ham United was as strong as you could get without playing for them. He grew up on their doorstep, and Fairbairn House channelled promising players towards Upton Park, often via non-league clubs such as Barking Town. West Ham United wanted to sign Jack in 1921 but he only ever played against them, including one of his final outings for Fairbairn Old Boys in that 1935 charity match. He knew many fans through work and the community, and through players such as Jack Tresadern, whose career at Barking and West Ham in the 1920s preceded his taking the management reins at Plymouth Argyle. And when Jack turned up at the Boleyn Ground in 1967, he would be greeted by a familiar face. Albert Walker was a West Ham defender who faced Jack three times in 1932 and 1933 – the honours were even with a win apiece and a draw. Albert had been a coach with the Irons and was the kit man when Jack joined.

It all happened because of Eve. Jack retired when he hit 65 and soon became restless, not knowing what to do with himself. It was a lively household with Lesley and Lyn now teenagers and young Gill aged just three. Jack was getting under their feet and his daughter could see he needed a purpose, so she sent her dad to West Ham and told him to ask whether there were any part-time jobs going. Manager Ron Greenwood had not only brought through those World Cup stars but also John Charles, who was the first black player to represent England at under-18 level. After selecting Viv Anderson for England in 1978, Greenwood said, 'Yellow, purple or black – if they're good enough, I'll pick them.' He became England manager after a legacy of bringing many black players into the West Ham team and thankfully was only too happy to take on the sexagenarian wunderkind, Jack Leslie. With the current boot room manager 'getting on a bit', in Jack's words, Ron would soon need a spritely replacement. Greenwood was old enough to know of Jack's achievements as a player and welcomed the old pro into the fold.

Jack served his apprenticeship sweeping the terraces on a Sunday and soon took over responsibility for the boots of around 30 professional West Ham United players. He could keep his own hours as long as the boots were in good order in good time, and they always were. Jack was in the boot room most days, taking the job very seriously, and the granddaughters are sure the club had the best-kept boots in the country. Ron Greenwood told Jack he was the greatest in the game too.

Geoff Pike won the FA Cup with the Hammers in 1980 but began as an apprentice. He had to collect boots after training and matchdays and deliver them to Jack: 'To me he was someone I didn't want to let down and I made sure I got the boots to him. He had a quiet way of letting you know if those boots hadn't arrived on time!' Everald Laronde captained the FA Youth Cup-winning team of 1981 and once asked Jack how long it took him to clean all those boots. Jack's reply has always stayed with him: 'Everald, if you ever get to my age, you will realise that it is not the time it takes to clean the boots, it is the privilege you feel and the pleasure you receive from doing it.'[24] Jack Leslie not only cared for the lads' boots, but also knew what it was like for a young player trying to make it in the game and was a friendly soul they could talk to.

It was lucky that Jack's house was only a ten-minute walk from West Ham's Boleyn Ground. Like most ex-pros, his knees were knackered and he suffered what he stoically called 'Arthur-itis', rubbing pain-relief cream on them every day to help him through. He may not have had the diet of a modern athlete and continued to smoke Player's throughout his life, but Jack did always follow his hot bath with a cold one to close the pores. He never complained about his ailments, just got himself up and dressed, always smartly, and off to work.

These were heady times in football. Players weren't earning the millions they do now, but the game was becoming bigger business. Jack was a football celebrity in his day, but stars such as Bobby Moore had money and status that was on a different level. Jack understood that times had changed as more black players came on the scene. He also saw what they had to deal with. West Ham was in one of the most diverse areas of the country, just as it had been in Jack's time, and the black population had increased sharply in the last two decades. The club was the first to field three black players, in a 2-0 victory over Spurs at Upton Park on 1 April 1972 – Ade Coker, Clive Charles and Clyde Best. Best, the charismatic Bermudian striker, remembers Jack with great fondness:

> He was not only a great person at the club but also a great friend. He would give me information about doing things the right way and he was a tremendous help to me. We had many a chat on a Friday because I would change my boots every Friday because I had a contract with Puma, and he would make sure that my studs were the correct size and everything. He really looked after me. I will never forget it. He was the type of person who was more interested in helping people. Playing at the time that I played it was tough, but after finding out what Jack had to go through, I'm sure it was a lot harder. He would have been by himself just like I was by myself, and it makes you a different individual when you have to face up to stuff like that.
>
> I was fortunate because my dad was from Barbados, he was in the British Navy and ended up in the prison service in Bermuda. He taught me at an early age to respect people, treat them decently just like you wanted to be treated and remember when you achieve things you are not doing it for yourself, you are doing it for people who come after you. It's just like what Jack has done. When I

see all the kids that are playing now, especially other kids of colour I know Jack and myself had something to do with that. That's what makes me happy.

While West Ham United were progressive in developing and fielding talented black players such as Clyde, when rivals came to play at Upton Park it was one of the most hostile of them all. The National Front used football as a recruiting ground and those black football pioneers of the 60s and 70s had to show courage, resilience and, like Jack, bury any resentment or trauma. There were writers, fans and officials who wanted Jack Leslie in the England team, and similarly in the 70s the idea of a black player winning a cap started to gain momentum and was talked about in the press; there was too much black English talent to ignore. But the same reasoning behind Jack's deselection, that he was considered foreign, was trotted out by racist fans whose faces creased with anger and rage at the very thought that this could ever happen. And the racial stereotypes in articles such as Bernard Joy's (see Chapter Two) gave succour to them.

Viv Anderson has secured his place in history. When he walked on to the Wembley pitch on 29 November 1978 as England's right-back to play Czechoslovakia it was a huge moment for him and for the country. It also had a massive impact on Jack Leslie. For those old enough to remember the famous Plymouth Argyle inside-left, the attention on Viv's selection stirred up thoughts of 1925. The granddaughters remember that it was a woman from Devon who wrote to the *Daily Mail* to tell them that the Nottingham Forest full-back might be the first black man to play for England, but Argyle's Jack Leslie was the first black player to be selected. It was easy to track him down at West Ham, and when Brian James asked to interview him, Jack agreed. He never hid what happened; he just never shouted about it.

Albert Walker, the West Ham legend who still worked with Jack, knew his story. He told some players about that 1925 selection, including Pat Holland, a 1975 FA Cup winner. Holland says:

Being a winger, I had struck up a good rapport with Jack. He would pay me particular interest. 'Patsy,' he would say, 'show them your heels.' On the way back to the changing room after a game, if I'd had an off day, I was usually greeted by Jack saying: 'Patsy, you haven't shown them your heels.'[25]

The conversations that would accompany Anderson's selection brought it all back for Jack. We can only imagine how reflecting on what might have been in 1925 felt for him now. Trevor Brooking loved spending time in the boot room chatting to Jack and believes it would have been harder as he grew older and more players of colour emerged:

> When it happened, I'd like to think it made Jack more determined to become the success he was. I mean, to play 14 seasons, scoring those goals, and play 400 times for a club like that was a massive, massive achievement. And it's something he must have looked back on when he retired with pride. But later in his life, when one or two black players come along people would say, 'You were better than him Jack,' and 'Why didn't you get a cap?' and then it becomes a discussion point. That is when it becomes tough.

When the *Daily Mail*'s Brian James came to Upton Park, he saw Jack Leslie tending the boots of stars such as Brooking and the young hopefuls: 'Each pair get the same careful attention ... laces levelled, studs tightened. At 77, Jack Leslie brings a craftsman's dignity and an old man's patience to his work.'

Jack couldn't believe James wanted to interview him, 'You really interested? All that way back?' This brought one of the few records we have of Jack telling the story just like it was. He was delighted that Viv Anderson got the chance he was denied. Of course, he was. And he would be proud to see how things have progressed today, while being saddened that black players still face abuse and discrimination. Yet, when James described the selectors as 'those long-dead bigots' and asked Jack whether he held any resentment towards them, his reply was remarkable: 'Lord, no. They was only doing what seemed right to them. In them times. They found out I was a darkie, and I suppose they thought that was like finding out I was foreign. I wasn't eligible for England. I am just glad for young Anderson that times have changed.' The ruling to say Jack wasn't eligible was entirely unwritten, of course. And unjustified.

We have a lot to thank Viv Anderson for. As a pioneer himself this was a breakthrough moment, but it also gave Jack the chance to tell a story that had begun to fade into history. For those Plymouth Argyle fans who were around in 1925, Jack's treatment was still something that brought resentment in the way football injustices can stick in the craw. They and we can't understand what impact it had on Jack, but they felt that one of their own had been badly let down.

Brian James mentioned that radio and TV personality, Leslie Welch, a walking sporting encyclopaedia known as the 'Memory Man', had talked about Jack on a radio show in the West Country that week. When Welch said Jack was 'part of the best left-wing I ever saw. He'd have played for England scores of times but for his colour,' it brought bursts of applause from the live audience. Those Argyle fans knew what had happened to their hero in 1925. They had talked about it on the terraces and in the pubs at the time and for decades to come.

Lesley and Lyn were young women when the interview took place, and they remember the impact it had on the family. Jack's story was known, particularly among Argyle fans, ex-players and staff, but he never spoke about it to any great degree. He didn't want to make a big thing of it within the family, but now it was in print, clear as day, and they've carried it with them ever since. 'He never blew his own trumpet; it was only after reading that article that we became fully aware of just how great a footballer our granddad was. It was a revelation; our wonderful granddad was a bit of a hero.' But sadly, when they tried to spread the word back then, they hit a brick wall. 'It was then that you went out and tried talking to people about it and you soon learned that people just didn't want to know, they didn't believe it.'

The media spotlight that briefly shone on Jack once again panned away to the next person. He got on with his day job and family life. It wasn't always easy for Eve and Gerry living with Jack and Win. Imagine living your whole life with your parents or in-laws, but the support they gave in bringing up Lesley, Lyn and Gill was invaluable. Gerry might have recommended that his daughters should avoid such a living arrangement if they could, but it was a testament to the strength of their bonds that they would even spend their leisure time together.

All seven would take camping and caravan trips to Dorset, sometimes with other family members too. They had a few mishaps along the way. One time, the caravan, with several people inside, came unhooked from the Land Rover that Gerry was driving and went into a bush at the side of the road. Whenever disaster struck, Jack would be on it sharpish, dodgy knees be damned, doing what he could to sort it out. A farmer came running down, demanding compensation for the damage to his bush, but at least there was no serious injury. Lesley, Lyn and Gill were fine, but Aunt Lil came away with a couple of cracked ribs by all accounts.

Holidays and family Christmases were big-hearted affairs as this close-knit bunch shared laughter and tears. Jack and Win faced many a trial and tribulation throughout their lives and were now on hand to help their daughter and granddaughters with theirs. The way Jack is spoken of in terms of the love, support and practical help he gave during trying and tragic times speaks volumes. Lesley lost her husband Gordon when he was just 23, after he was hit by a vehicle. It was an awful, shocking loss and she had a baby and a toddler to care for amid the grief. Jack comforted her and told Lesley that he wished it had been him instead of Gordon. He and Win welcomed Lesley and her two children back to Wakefield Street. There wasn't enough space to stay long term, but when she did find a new place, leaving them was a terrible wrench. They all came together to help Lesley through this awful, physically and emotionally exhausting time.

Lyn lost two husbands in very different circumstances. She had enough of them. When her second marriage ended, Lyn had to take on sole responsibility for the house they had bought, also in East Ham. She did the maths and realised she couldn't quite make ends meet, so Jack stepped in to meet the small shortfall. He may have had old-fashioned views, but Jack never judged his young granddaughters. Lyn says she wouldn't stand for any nonsense from her partners and her granddad would joke, 'She's blown the whistle again!', a reference to the 60s sitcom, *The Rag Trade*, and the signal the militant shop steward made before shouting, 'Everybody out!' But Jack also had warm words of support, telling Lyn at that time, 'I admire you for not giving up.'

Meanwhile, Jack and Win continued to live in Wakefield Street, although they had sold the house to their daughter. Eve, Gerry and Gill moved to Essex, where they opened a car parts and bicycle repair shop. Unfortunately, that became even more financially draining than The Swan Hotel, and Wakefield Street was collateral. Jack was upset but understood the situation and the need to sell the family home of 40 years. Lyn stepped in to provide her grandparents with a home that was still within walking distance of Upton Park. This potted family history shows what a connection they had and the support they gave each other. Family was the most important thing for Jack and Win, and what a positive impact this humble ex-footballer and his wife had on their nearest and dearest.

One of Jack's finest hours in the Boleyn boot room came in 1980. West Ham would take on North London rivals Arsenal in the FA Cup Final. The highlighting of his story a couple of years previously meant Jack, now in his late 70s, was getting attention again in the pre-match coverage. Superstitious striker (aren't they all?) David Cross had scored 18 goals that season with the same beaten-up pair of boots. As the final approached, they were in a parlous state and Cross feared he would have to wear a fresh pair lacking in that fairy dust of fortune:

> Jack knew this and unbeknown to me he somehow managed to get my existing pair mended. The timing was tight, and I awoke on FA Cup Final day resigned to wearing new boots. However, when I entered the Wembley dressing room my old boots were there waiting for me!

Jack had arranged for them to be sent to Wembley on the morning of the match. You can imagine the lift that gave me. Everything felt just right as I took my place on the Wembley pitch.[26]

Cross didn't score that day, but the boots did their job. West Ham won with a single goal from Trevor Brooking.

As Jack Leslie entered his ninth decade his time in the boot room was coming to an end but, like his football career, it wasn't planned. Thankfully there was no career-ending injury, although he did lose a fingertip by trapping it in an Upton Park turnstile. Eve and Gerry had a rural retreat in the tiny Kent village of Meopham, where the family would spend weekends and holidays. When Wakefield Street had to be sold, Lyn suggested that she move to Meopham with her boyfriend, son Michael and Jack and Win. The grandparents loved it there and agreed. But it would mean there was no way Jack could continue working at West Ham. To be fair, it probably was time for him to retire. He was still active but his old knees were starting to make even the walk to Upton Park a struggle.

On 30 October 1982, dressed in his usual shirt and tie, with a smart pullover to keep out the chill, 81-year-old Jack Leslie tightened the studs in the Boleyn Ground boot room for the last time. He was preparing boots for the likes of Billy Bonds, Frank Lampard and Geoff Pike, who he had seen come through as an apprentice, ahead of Manchester United's visit. ITV's *The Big Match* showcased the game, but before the highlights kicked off, Brian Moore told viewers there had been a 'touching little ceremony' as Jack Leslie 'put out the West Ham boots for the last time'. The feature feels uncomfortable to us watching now, particularly when manager John Lyall thanks Jack and then tells him to go and get the boots out so they can have a game. It's only fair to say that Jack worked with Lyall for many years and spoke highly of the manager.

Jack's granddaughters tell me the cameras came as a surprise that day and their granddad was uncomfortable with the attention. As Jack quietly chats to Lyall, his hand comes to the side of his face, a sign of his unease, they say. That was what Jack was like. He didn't want a fuss. He was proud that the players appreciated him. As Moore said, he was well liked, and they showed that with a 'pretty healthy whip round' and a card presented in the dressing room, with all the players sat just in their towels. It really was a simpler time, but for former Argyle player, Ronnie Mauge, that clip shows how tough it was for Jack: 'Being a black man, I know how that feels. You feel intimidated and as if it's a privilege to be there. We felt that we weren't good enough to be in the same arena as our white peers.'

As Jack Leslie entered what he knew would be the final stage of his life, he could reflect on a happy 15-year second career in the sport he loved. 'I don't know if he would have lived as long had he not had the job. He needed a purpose, and this gave it to him. He absolutely loved it. They were really happy days,' say Jack's granddaughters.

Moving to Kent brought a welcome slower pace of life that Jack and Win appreciated. They and Lyn lived in two connected mobile homes and, although they were far less mobile themselves by now, the couple still enjoyed each other's company, having a laugh with their frequent playful bickering. They would while away the hours watching the birds and squirrels come and go, but restless Jack still needed something to do. Lyn gave him the job of chopping wood for the fire, and like everything he had done in life, Jack committed to the task. Rain, shine or snow, he would get it done. Even if he was told they had enough, he would say, 'No, I'm going to get some more. You never know!'

There was still time for one last dramatic episode. When Jack and Win settled into their beds on 15 October 1987, they were reassured by the words of the BBC's Michael Fish as he responded to concerns of an impending hurricane: 'Don't worry, there isn't.' Gill was there at the time and tells a shocking story of an escape as narrow as Jack's in the docks during the Second World War. It was early morning, and she was with her ex-partner:

> My dad had gone out the front door with a torch; my nephew, Michael, was sitting in the chair in the front room eating a bowl of cereal. For whatever reason, they came out of the front room and went into the kitchen.

That second, the tree came down and the front room was just squashed.

Their thoughts immediately turned to Jack and Win, who were still asleep. Well, they were until the tree came crashing down, but they had been saved by the large, sturdy wooden headboard of Win's bed. They had no idea what happened at first and thought maybe the ceiling had just collapsed. But photos show their home was obliterated. Jack said, 'I wondered why I got a draught up my back!' The other family members struggled to get the elderly couple out and they then had to struggle to stop Jack going back in to get his cigarettes and his trousers.

Jack dealt with the disaster in his customary stoic, funny manner but it made Win's final days very hard. She had recovered from cancer once before, but while they were in temporary accommodation she was to be diagnosed again. At the age of 88, Win didn't want to go through any more medical procedures and in April 1988 she passed away. Knowing Win was facing the end of her life affected Jack deeply, and he joined his wife just seven months later. On 25 November, with his daughter by his side, Jack Leslie's remarkable life came to an end.

Young children often ask how Jack died and the answer his granddaughters give seems the best. It was a broken heart. He and Win had lived a life together that saw them through everything a couple commit to in their wedding vows. Eve remembered how Jack had so much emotion in his voice that when he sang 'Danny Boy' it would make her cry. And when Jack and Win were at home, they would do a duet from the 1930s black-and-white musical, *Rose Marie*. 'When I'm calling you,' Win's voice would echo through their home. Jack would always tunefully reply, 'Will you answer too.' They answered each other's call until the very end.

On his death certificate Jack's occupation is noted as 'Boiler Maker (Retired)'. That was his trade, and he would have no issue with it being listed as such. What a typically modest and unsung ending to the life of a hero who deserved to be noted and feted throughout his life, not just in the years he made the crowds at Home Park jump for joy.

Chapter Twenty

Jack's Legacy

THE STORY of Jack Leslie, the lion who was never given the chance to roar for his country is at once significant, tragic, moving and inspirational. It has an immediate resonance and that prompted the campaign to create a lasting monument to him. Our collective failure to tell the rich variety of human experience within our shared history is being addressed and there are tangible benefits for us all. Jack Leslie's place in our national game is finally being recognised alongside many other previously forgotten heroes. There are more to come, I'm sure. I hope the story of his whole life inspires you to talk about Jack and other figures who have contributed so much. That's why a statue now stands outside Home Park in Plymouth, the ground where he *was* given a chance to roar for Argyle like the lion he was.

My journey alongside fellow campaigners began in 2019 and we naturally contacted Plymouth Argyle. We were delighted to discover the new owner, Simon Hallett, was already keen to recognise Jack Leslie and send out a clear anti-racist message. In December the boardroom in the new Mayflower grandstand was unveiled in Jack's honour, while we began forging our plans. The campaign itself was in the public domain early in 2020 as we set up a website and quietly began fundraising. The big launch was due to kick off in April at Argyle's home fixture against Forest Green Rovers, with Jack's family in attendance. That match was the first to be cancelled due to Covid-19. We thought it best to put everything on ice. That ice began to crack in the summer of 2020, and we had no choice but to crack on …

When George Floyd was murdered by a white police officer in Minneapolis in May that year, it set off a chain of global protest. Here in the UK, the Black Lives Matter marches to highlight contemporary and historical injustices culminated in the toppling of slave trader Edward Colston's statue into Bristol Harbour. The febrile atmosphere cultivated during the strangest of social climates polarised views on statues and street names and took post-Brexit divisiveness to another level. As the population took its solitary and, for many, tragic march through lockdown after lockdown, there was a hunger for something positive. The idea of putting up a statue to a figure who deserved it caught the public's attention.

The pandemic and postponement of the football season meant our launch was strange, to say the least, but it snowballed, gaining national and international attention. Like the excitement of a Jack Leslie and Sammy Black attack of the 1920s and 30s, we sensed the crowd behind us, even if that was only on social media and video calls. Like a footballer spurred on to success by the taunts of opposition fans at an away fixture, any negativity only served to energise us. The appeal of Jack's story and an understanding that a wrong needed to be righted helped us raise more than £100,000 in six weeks in the summer of 2020. The backing of Argyle as well as other Devon clubs and those two so closely associated with Jack, Barking FC and West Ham United, ensured we got over the line without having to rely on Fergie time.

The challenge then was to deliver something lasting and meaningful. After an exhaustive pitching process involving campaigners and Jack's granddaughters, we chose Andy Edwards as our sculptor. If you've visited the monument, you'll see that was a great decision. He bought into what we were aiming to achieve and worked with us and Jack's granddaughters to create both the work and the storytelling that surrounds it on the plinth.

When Lesley, Lyn and Gill visited Andy's workshop, it was a special moment, he said:

> Statues have to stand in for their subject, so we have to get everything right. Not just the detail, but the character has to come over too. For fans, they will never have been

able to walk around an image of Jack before, but for his family, I know this is very emotional. It was emotional for me too, and I don't know which of us was more, but the first thing they said was, 'We want to hug him.' All three girls carry their granddad's likeness here and there, and I added refinements and detail directly from their faces. I just hope we've done him proud, but as the saying goes, we've left nothing on the pitch in terms of effort.

When Lesley, Lyn and Gill unveiled the statue on 7 October 2022, crowds were able to return and they came along with the nation's press. The attention they received was joyous and overwhelming. Jack, as mischievous in bronze as he was in life, wanted to play his own joke on us. The rain abated, the clouds broke and the sun shone through, but the wind was still high. Better conditions than for many of Jack's home matches but a gust blew the green drape over his outstretched arm, and he briefly revealed himself too soon. As campaigners pulled the material back into place, we reminded supporters that Jack was a man of action, not words, who was always keen to make his presence felt on the pitch.

It was a remarkable day that reminded us of the importance of Jack's legacy. His story is a piece of our nation's history that tells us much about our past and how to confront our present to create a better future. That's easier said than done but the presence of school children at the unveiling, many of whom had been learning about Jack's story, is what will help prevent the social media abuse faced by today's England stars. Just ask Jadon Sancho, Bukayo Saka and Marcus Rashford whether everything is fine now. Talking about Jack helps create a connection with the past and gives at least some understanding of what people of colour have faced. The campaign continues to talk to schools, football clubs and other organisations, hoping that Jack's story inspires and motivates understanding and change.

On the day of the unveiling the most significant recognition of Jack Leslie to date was announced. For almost 100 years the FA denied that Jack had been selected despite the evidence to the contrary.

Greg and I had contacted the FA at the very start of our campaign, and staff were gracious and supported us with a donation, which we appreciated greatly. But while there was an acknowledgement, the idea of any official recognition seemed highly unlikely. More than two years after we had hit our fundraising target and with the unveiling approaching, something changed. It takes people willing to engage, take the time to look at a case in detail, ask the hard questions and at times ruffle feathers to make a difference. Debbie Hewitt, FA chair and now vice-president of FIFA, did just that ...

> I hadn't heard of Jack Leslie until a few weeks before the England v Germany Nations League game on 26 September 2022. It was Paul Elliott, the former chair of the FA's Inclusion Advisory Board, who explained Jack's story to me. Paul is a remarkable driving force for equality across football who continuously challenges our approach to inclusion. He provides good counsel to me – pointing out uncomfortable truths, with a sense of perspective.
>
> He came up with the idea to celebrate Black Lives Matter by inviting several football legends – and families representing these legends – to the England game at Wembley, and added a number of interesting people to the list, including Lesley, Jack's granddaughter.
>
> I met Lesley that evening when she attended the game with Matt. I mentioned Jack in my pre-game speech and Lesley told me what a proud and significant moment it was for her to hear such public recognition of Jack by the FA. I was particularly struck by Lesley's determination and resilience as she described her quest to get Jack's contribution recognised as part of the history of English football, as the first black player to be called up to play for England, though not allowed to play due to the colour of his skin.
>
> I left Wembley hopeful that the night had been a good experience for Lesley and thoughtful about the mixed emotions she must have felt about the FA and what happened many decades ago.

The very next day, Matt reached out to say thank you, giving me more information on the recent history of the Jack Leslie Campaign, the contribution that the FA had made to researching Jack's story and his appreciation for quotes we'd given acknowledging the story. He also directly addressed the issue of what Jack had missed out on – an England cap. And he raised the idea of awarding Jack an honorary cap.

Matt sent me a link to the campaign website, and it was compelling reading. I spent over an hour reading the copy and learned many more details of Jack's story. I learned of the *Daily Mail* interview with Jack in 1978, which I found deeply moving, and the determined battle that Lesley and her sisters Lyn and Gill had fought on Jack's behalf. It was clear to me that we needed to right a historical wrong.

Matt forwarded to me several emails he had received from the FA over the years, all of which were sincerely respectful and genuinely sorry for Jack's experience, positively supporting the campaign. But the ultimate recognition of a posthumous honorary cap had not been forthcoming. There were many sensible, genuine and practical reasons why an honorary cap could not be awarded, not least because he had not played for England, but no one could deny that the reasons he hadn't played were wrong.

We talked about this internally, and increasingly the case for awarding an honorary cap was undeniable. I give credit to our CEO Mark Bullingham and our communications director Joanna Manning-Cooper, who both significantly influenced the debate.

We decided to award Jack a posthumous honorary cap – the first time the FA has ever awarded one.

I remember calling Matt to give him the news. Coincidentally, it was the week of the unveiling of Jack's statue at Plymouth. I explained that we would work out the best timing to award the cap – on the basis that they would be focused on the statue on Friday – and that there would be another opportunity for them to celebrate his achievement.

My most significant memory of that day was calling Lesley to tell her the good news. The silence at the other end of the line was deafening. For 20 seconds or so it crossed my mind that, somehow, we had misjudged this. That it was all too late. Then I heard a mixture of joy, disbelief and elation. Relief too, that at last Jack's battle for recognition had been won.

We thought hard about how we communicated the decision to award our first-ever honorary cap. It was so important to us to send a very clear message about the injustice Jack endured. We said, 'Jack Leslie is a true football legend who, through his own adversity, has positively shaped attitudes and behaviours to identify and remove discrimination from football. The FA is awarding Jack a posthumous honorary cap, to recognise his unique contribution and set of circumstances – and to right the historical wrong.'

Sadly, Lesley was unable to attend the capping ceremony at Wembley as she was unwell. It was a wonderful and moving occasion pitchside at Wembley before England played Ukraine in March. England legend Viv Anderson joined me to present the award to other members of Jack's family, including granddaughters Gill and Lyn, and did a tremendous job in capturing the emotion of the moment. The warm response of the Wembley crowd was a poignant moment for us all.

The very next weekend, Plymouth Argyle played at Wembley in the Papa John's Trophy Final against Bolton Wanderers, and Lesley was able to attend. She presented the cap to Plymouth in front of thousands of their fans. I'm so pleased that Lesley, Gill and Lyn were involved in those presentations – their resilience and determination to honour their grandfather and ensure he was rightly recognised has been incredible.

It's been a real privilege to have been involved in recognising Jack's unique contribution and set of circumstances at the home of English football and to know that we have righted the historical wrong. As I reflect on the significance and impact of that decision, my sense is that Jack's legacy has become so much more than being the first black player to be called up to play for England. His campaign has been a catalyst for a change in how football understands our history and how, by understanding our history, we can make the future a more inclusive game for all.

On that day in October 2022 when the statue of their grandfather was revealed to the world, Lesley, Lyn and Gill sat on the podium as I was able to announce the awarding of that posthumous honorary cap. Turning to look at them while I did so was a bad idea because it was suddenly very tough to get to the end of the speech. Something in my eye, something in my throat. Fortunately, the heartfelt reception from the crowd outside the popular corner of Home Park where Jack now stands gave me enough time to gather my composure.

If you believe these 'gestures' are pointless and we should all just move on, well, you've probably not got to the end of this book. But if you or any of your friends or family aren't sure, then I suggest you or they talk to the people who have experienced the discrimination Jack faced, and their families. I can tell you it means a hell of a lot to have their ancestor recognised and honoured. Only Jack and his descendants have carried the weight of his denial. His story being released into the world doesn't change what happened, but it does share the truth and lift that weight just a little.

I began by stating that Jack would probably wonder what all this fuss was about and claim he didn't deserve all this praise and recognition. He was a charismatic leader on the pitch and charming company off it, but he didn't like public attention. His granddaughters do, however, believe that he would be incredibly proud that his story is being used to talk about racism and show what effect it can have.

After Marcus Rashford's heartbreak of a missed penalty in the European Championship Final against Italy on 11 July 2021, the abuse that followed was countered by the support of his local community. He was moved to write:

> I've grown into a sport where I expect to read things written about myself. Whether it be the colour of my skin, where I grew up, or, most recently, how I decide to spend my time off the pitch. I can take critique of my performance all day long, my penalty was not good enough, it should have gone in but I will never apologise for who I am and where I came from. I felt no prouder moment than wearing those three lions on my chest ... I've dreamt of days like this ... I'm Marcus Rashford, 23 year old black man from Withington and Wythenshawe South Manchester if I have nothing else I have that.

There's a defiance in Rashford's words that Jack Leslie never felt able to express but he was still put in a position where he had to. Football may have edged forward but the lack of black managers and representation at a senior level in the game has failed to progress. The words of Ronnie Mauge hit home: 'In the last one hundred years since Jack's time have things changed that drastically? I would have to say not. I would have to say not. You just have these stigmas in different forms and shapes now.'

Just before retiring from the West Ham boot room, Jack spoke to Brian Woolnough about black football pioneers of the 70s and early 80s. Viv Anderson had been followed by Laurie Cunningham, Cyrille Regis, Ricky Hill and Luther Blissett in winning England caps. It was 1982. There was still a long, long way to go and there still is. This is what Jack Leslie said:

> They are getting us some recognition. People should realise there is good and bad amongst us all. In society there will always be people who spoil it for others. I am just happy to see blacks and whites moving closer together. There is at last real hope for the coloured kids today.

Endnotes

1. Jonathan Wilson's *Inverting the Pyramid* is a modern classic on the subject of football tactics.
2. *Newcastle Evening Chronicle*, 24 February 1975.
3. The West Ham Years newsletter author Tim Crane produced a special edition featuring player and staff memories of Jack in October 2022 (tcrane183@gmail.com).
4. Celestine Edwards's story is told in Peter Fryer's *Staying Power: The History of Black People in Britain*.
5. Fiona Rule, *London's Docklands – A History of the Lost Quarter*.
6. Morley wrote the article 'Londoners over the Border' in 1857 for Charles Dickens' *Household Words*, Volume XVI, Magazine No. 390.
7. Quoted in Stephen Bourne's *Black Poppies*.
8. *East End News and London Shipping Chronicle*, 13 April 1913 and 1 October 1918.
9. Carr R.J.M. (ed.), *Dockland: An Illustrated Historical Survey of Life and Work in East London*, NELP/GLC, 1986.
10. See Alexander Jackson's *Football's Great War* for a thorough examination of the national sport through the First World War.
11. F. Shyllon, 'The Black Presence and Experience in Britain – Paper Presented to the International Conference on the History of Blacks in Britain, London', 28–30 September 1981 cited in Peter Fryer's *Staying Power: The History of Black People in Britain*.
12. See the letter of 29 May 1919 from a black seaman called William Samuel to the Colonial Secretary. 'We beg to remind you, as at least, inform you we are boycotted in this country …

the same people whom less than a year ago our blood was shed on the battlefield for your safety. Laying that aside we were brutally and most barbarously attacked two nights during this week without reasonable occasion. All we want is to ask Great Britain to allow us to get out of here to Japan or other countries where we have friends for England is our enemy not our friend. We beg to remind you a sergeant of police said to us last night ... "we want you n****** to get out of our country, this is a white man's country and not yours.'"

13. Jacqueline Jenkinson, *Black 1919: Riots, Racism and Resistance in Imperial Britain*.

14. Jacqueline Jenkinson, *Black 1919: Riots, Racism and Resistance in Imperial Britain*.

15. See Alexander Jackson's *Football's Great War*.

16. British Pathe archive: www.youtube.com/watch?v=mOXxSH-QIIwY

17. *The Great Game* released in 1931 can be found on BFI Player.

18. *Athletic News Football Annual* 1933/34.

19. Foreword to Harley Lawer's *Argyle Classics*.

20. *The Football Association International Selection Committee Minutes*, 21 September 1925.

21. Sir Frederick Wall, *50 Years of Football 188--1934*.

22. PRO CO 318/333/50043 'West Indian Contingent' Min. by Gilbert Grindle, 21 December 1914 (as quoted in Stephen Bourne, *Black Poppies*).

23. *Halifax Daily Courier and Guardian*, 16 January 1937.

24. From The West Ham Years Newsletter Tribute to Jack Leslie 2022.

25. From The West Ham Years Newsletter Tribute to Jack Leslie 2022.

26. From The West Ham Years Newsletter Tribute to Jack Leslie 2022.

Bibliography

Banton, Michael, *White and Coloured: The Behaviour of British People Towards Coloured Immigrants* (Jonathan Cape, 1959).

Bourne, Stephen, *Black Poppies: Britain's Black Community and the Great War* (The History Press, 2014).

Bourne, Stephen, *Under Fire: Black Britain in Wartime 1939–45* (The History Press, 2020).

Buchan, Charles, *A Lifetime in Football* (Phoenix House, 1955).

Butler, Bryon: *The Official History of the Football Association* (Queen Anne Press, 1991).

Carr, R.J.M. (ed), *Dockland: An Illustrated Historical Survey of Life and Work in East London*, (NELP/GLC, 1986).

Close, Marvin, *1923: Life in Football One Hundred Years Ago* (Pitch Publishing, 2022).

Cowdery, Rick, *Plymouth Argyle on this Day* (Pitch Publishing, 2008).

Fabian, A.H, & Green, Geoffrey (ed.), *Association Football Volume 1* (Caxton, 1960).

Fishman, William J., (photos by Nicholas Breach), *The Streets of East London* (Gerald Duckworth & Co, 1979).

Fryer, Peter, *Staying Power: The History of Black People in Britain* (Pluto Press, 3rd Edition, 2018).

Girling, Brian, *East End Neighbourhoods* (The History Press, 2005).

Green, Geoffrey, *The History of the Football Association 1863–1953* (Nadrett Press, 1953).

Hayward, Paul, *England Football: The Biography 1872–2022* (Simon & Schuster, 2022).

Hern, Bill & Gleave, David, *Football's Black Pioneers* (Conker Editions, 2020).

Inglis, Simon, *League Football: The Official Centenary History of the Football League 1888–1988* (Harper Collins, 1988).

Jack, David, *Soccer* (Putnam, 1934).

Jackson, Alexander, *Football's Great War: Association Football on the English Home Front* (Pen & Sword Military, 2021).

Jenkinson, Jacqueline, *Black 1919: Riots, Racism and Resistance in Imperial Britain* (Liverpool University Press, 2019).

Johnes, Martin, 'Race, Archival Silences, and a Black Footballer Between the Wars', in *Twentieth Century British History*, Volume 31, Issue 4 (Oxford University Press, 2020).

Kerrigan, Colm, *Teachers and Football: Schoolboy Association Football in England 1885–1915* (Routledge, 2004).

Knight, Brian, *Plymouth Argyle: A Complete Record 1903–1989* (Breedon, 1989).

Lawer, Harley, *Argyle Classics: Memorable Moments in Plymouth Argyle's League and Cup History* (Green Books, 1988).

Murray, Scott, *The Title: The Story of the First Division* (Bloomsbury Sport, 2018).

Olusoga, David, *Black and British: A Forgotten History* (Macmillan, 2016).

Onuora, Emy, *Pitch Black: The Story of Black British Footballers* (Biteback Publishing, 2015).

Riddle, Andy, *Plymouth Argyle: The Modern Era* (Desert Island Books, 2008).

Rule, Fiona, *London's Docklands: A History of the Lost Quarter* (The History Press, 2019).

Russell, Dave, *Football and the English: A Social History of Association Football in England 1863–1995* (Carnegie, 1997).

Sanghera, Sathnam, *Empireland: How Imperialism Has Shaped Modern Britain* (Viking, 2021).

Sharpe, Ivan, *40 Years in Football* (Hutchinson's Library of Sports & Pastimes, 1952).

Sparks, Gordon, *Plymouth Argyle Football Club 1886–1986* (Tempus Publishing, 1998).

Sutcliffe, Charles, Brierley, J. & Howarth, F., *The Story of the Football League* (The Football League, 1939).

Taylor, Matthew, *The Association Game: A History of British Football* (Routledge, 2007).

Taylor, W., *Plymouth Argyle 1929–30: The Team that Won Promotion* (Western Independent, reprint by Plymouth Argyle Heritage Archive).

Tonkin, W.S., *All About Argyle 1903–1963* (Plymouth Argyle FC, 1963).

Twyford, Henry, *Plymouth Argyle Football Club Golden Jubilee 1903–1953* (Plymouth Argyle FC, 1953).

Vasili, Phil, *Colouring Over the White Line: The History of Black Footballers in Britain* (Mainstream Publishing, 2000).

Vasili, Phil, *Walter Tull 1888 to 1918: Footballer and Officer* (London League Publications: Second Edition, 2018).

Wagg, Stephen, *The Football World, A Contemporary Social History* (Harvester Press, 1984).

Walvin, James, *The People's Game: The History of Football Revisited* (Mainstream Publishing, 2000).

Wilson, Jonathan, *Inverting the Pyramid: The History of Football Tactics* (Orion, 2018: new edition).

Woolnough, Brian, *Black Magic: England's Black Footballers* (Pelham Books, 1983).

Archive Collections

Manual of Military Law (1914)

National Football Museum: The Football League and FA Collections

Plymouth Argyle Heritage Archive

1901, 1911, 1921 Census

1939 Register

Newspapers and Periodicals

Athletic News

Athletic News Football Annual

Belfast Telegraph

Birmingham Gazette

Burnley Express and Advertiser

Charles Dickens' Household Words

Chelmsford Chronicle

Coventry Evening Telegraph

Croydon Times

Daily Echo (Northampton)

Daily Express

Daily Herald

Daily Mail

Daily Mirror

Daily News
Daily Record and Mail
Devon and Exeter Gazette
East End News and London Shipping Chronicle
Eastern Counties Times
Edinburgh Evening News
Essex Times
Football Gazette
Football Herald
Gamages Football Annual
The Globe
The Graphic
Grimsby Evening Telegraph
Halifax Daily Courier and Guardian
Halifax Evening Courier
Hampshire Telegraph
Kentish Independent
Lancashire Daily Post
Leeds Mercury
Leicester Chronicle
Liverpool Echo
Liverpool Journal of Commerce
Manchester Guardian
Marvel's Who's Who in Football 1921
Newcastle Evening Chronicle
Northern Whig
Nottingham Journal
The People
Portsmouth Evening News
Reynolds's Illustrated News
The Scotsman
Shields Daily News
Sporting Times
Sports Argus
Sports Budget
The Sportsman
Sunday Dispatch
Sunday Express

Sunday Illustrated
Sunday Independent
Sunday Mirror
The Telegraph
The Times
Western Daily Press
Western Evening Herald
Western Morning News
West Ham and South Essex Echo and Mail
West Middlesex Gazette
Westminster Gazette
Yorkshire Post

Websites
Ancestry
Barking Football Club
Barking History
BFI Player
British History Online
British Newspaper Archive
British Pathé
Centre for the Study of the Legacies of British Slavery
England Football Online
Family Tree of Newham
Find my Past
Football and the First World War
Greens on Screen
Dr Ju Gosling
London's Royal Docks
The Millwall History Files
Old Plymouth
Plymouth Argyle Football Club
Plymouth Argyle Heritage Archive
RSSSF
West Ham United Football Club
The West Ham Years
YouTube

Index